TRIPLE AXIS

Iran's Relations with Russia and China

DINA ESFANDIARY AND ARIANE TABATABAI

TRIPLE AXIS

Iran's Relations with Russia and China

DINA ESFANDIARY AND ARIANE TABATABAI

I.B. TAURIS

LONDON • NEW YORK • OXFORD • NEW DELHI • SYDNEY

I.B. TAURIS
Bloomsbury Publishing Plc
50 Bedford Square, London, WC1B 3DP, UK
1385 Broadway, New York, NY 10018, USA
29 Earlsfort Terrace, Dublin 2, Ireland

BLOOMSBURY, I.B. TAURIS and the I.B. Tauris logo
are trademarks of Bloomsbury Publishing Plc

First published in Great Britain 2018
This paperback edition published 2021

Cover Design: Simon Goggin
Image: Vladimir Putin, Xi Jinping and Hassan Rouhani at the fourth Conference on
Interaction and Confidence Building Measures in Asia (CICA) summit in Shanghai, May 2014.
(ALY SONG/AFP/Getty Images)

A catalogue record for this book is available from the British Library.

A catalog record for this book is available from the Library of Congress.

ISBN: PB: 978-0-7556-4062-1
ePDF: 978-1-8386-0978-8
eBook: 978-1-8386-0977-1

Typeset in Garamond Three by OKS Prepress Services, Chennai, India
Printed and bound in Great Britain

To find out more about our authors and books visit
www.bloomsbury.com and sign up for our newsletters.

CONTENTS

ACKNOWLEDGEMENTS

We benefitted from the support, contribution, and feedback of several friends and colleagues in this process. In particular, we would like to thank Aubrey Kenton Thibaut, Zach Kosbie, Darya Dolzikova, and Henry Boyd, whose assistance and feedback made the book possible. We would also like to thank two anonymous reviewers, whose comments were instrumental in helping us sharpen our argument and improve our work. We would like to express our gratitude to the I.B.Tauris team for their insights, flexibility, and rigorous work. Lastly, both authors would like to thank their families, partners and friends for all their support and help.

The authors are listed alphabetically – they both contributed equally to this project.

INTRODUCTION

After the collapse of its pro-Western monarch with the 1979 Islamic Revolution, Iran became a 'pariah' state. Responding to the Islamic Republic's revolutionary anti-American and anti-Western narrative, US officials routinely describe Tehran using harsh and bombastic rhetoric. Former President George W. Bush placed the Islamic Republic within the 'Axis of Evil';[1] President Donald J. Trump invited all 'nations of conscience' to counter the revolutionary regime;[2] when asked whose enmity she took pride in, former Secretary of State Hillary Clinton noted, 'the Iranians';[3] and Secretary of Defense James Mattis posited that the three gravest threats facing the United States in the Middle East were, 'Iran, Iran, Iran'.[4] Mattis justified his stance using the same sound-bite many US officials and lawmakers have embraced since former Secretary of State Henry Kissinger first coined it – one that Iran's neighbours in the Persian Gulf have also picked up: Iran is not a state, it is 'a revolutionary cause devoted to mayhem'.[5] Countering the Islamic Republic is one of the only issues where both Republicans and Democrats find common ground in an otherwise partisan and polarised Washington.[6] In Europe however, Iran became the source of discord, as some wanted to pursue a harsher line against it, while others were loath to cut off business ties.

Nevertheless, along with the United States, they sought to isolate the Islamic Republic politically and economically. And with the unveiling of two undeclared Iranian nuclear facilities in the early 2000s, one producing enriched uranium and the other capable of producing plutonium – the two pathways to building a nuclear weapon – the international community began to come on board to pressure Tehran to forego its nuclear weapon ambitions. But two key countries were reluctant participants in what became an intricate multilateral and multi-layered effort to bring Tehran back into compliance with its international obligations: Russia and China. Both Beijing and Moscow leveraged Iran's political and economic isolation to penetrate key sectors there. From infrastructure to technology to defence, the two countries created a substantial presence there by the time the United Nations Security Council (UNSC) resolutions successfully targeted Tehran in 2005–10. In turn, the Islamic Republic leveraged its ties with Russia and China, and their interests there, to create a bulwark against Western efforts to isolate Iran again.

Today, Russia and China effectively shelter Iran from complete isolation and provide it with political support, defence assistance, and economic ties that it cannot receive elsewhere. As a result, Beijing and Moscow serve to undermine Western efforts to pressure Tehran. Doing so affords the two powers the ability to poke the West, and the United States especially, in the eye, while providing them access to an important market and granting ties with a critical regional player with access to key resources and theatres. In addition, all three countries share a worldview, one they advance unilaterally and in tandem with one another. They all seek to create or partake in an alternative cluster of international institutions – ones created to balance against those established by the United States in the aftermath of World War II – while also leveraging the existing world order where they can pursue their interests. The three countries seek to assert themselves as regional hegemons and reduce the influence of the West, particularly the United States, in what they view as their own backyards. As we will see, each views the global order through the prism of its own historical experiences. (Ultimately, Beijing, Moscow, and Tehran want the international order to better reflect the interests of 'rising' non-Western states.) But while Russia and China are major powers with permanent seats at the UNSC, field powerful militaries equipped with nuclear weapons, and possess substantial economic resources, Iran is a relatively small power – one that is a potential leader only in its own region, but not beyond. It is impossible to dismiss or isolate Russia or China on the international stage – although Russian interference in US and European electoral processes and aggressive foreign policy led the West to try, with only marginal success on the economic front. But Iran's political, economic, and military prowess is far from consequential and the international community effectively isolated it for years. As a result, while Russia and China see Iran as a convenient partner in stymying the Western order, Iran views the two powers as an instrumental bulwark against Western efforts to isolate it and its own struggle to challenge the world order. Iran's ability to leverage its relations with Russia and China is precisely what we explore in this book.

The challenges to the existing world order unfold as this Western-led international order faces a crisis. America seems to be taking a step back on the world stage, relegating its traditional leadership role on a number of levels. Indeed, as former US President Barack Obama outlined, while America would retain its position as global leader, it would also review its military deployments abroad, including in Afghanistan and Iraq. This trend took on new significance under the administration of President Donald Trump. While Republicans are generally known for their willingness to devote greater time, effort and resources to maintaining America's status as the world's leader, President Trump did the opposite. He disengaged America from various international fora and distanced himself from a number of core traditional security alliances. Meanwhile, the European Union (EU) and some of its member states, France and Germany, in particular, sought to fill the void left by the US withdrawal from the global stage but faced challenges of their own, these challenges include engaging Iran while preserving their alliances with the United States. This, coupled with the serious political changes in the Western world with significant and, at times, surprising elections and decisions in 2016 and 2017 – as epitomised by the 2016 referendum leading the United Kingdom to leave the European Union (known as Brexit) – left an uneasy Western-led world order, which grappled with its future status. The instability of this order opened up further opportunities to those who wish to challenge or change it, including Iran, China, and Russia.

The Roots of Iran's Relations with the Eastern Powers

Iran has grappled with its growing Western-imposed isolation since the revolution. After decades of cooperation with the United States and European countries under the Shah, the new revolutionary government in Tehran – which gained in popularity partially on a platform of anti-Western rhetoric – broke from its former allies. The much-publicised hostage crisis, where Iranian revolutionaries stormed the US embassy in Tehran, taking its personnel hostage for 444 days, followed by some Western countries' support to Iraq's government during the traumatic Iran–Iraq War in the 1980s, confirmed the Islamic Republic's international isolation.[7] Tehran had to adapt and search for new economic, political, and military partners. It is in this context that Russia and China emerged as useful partners to Iran. But tackling isolation is not the only context for Tehran's relationship with Beijing and Moscow.

After its inception, the Islamic Republic made waves in the region through its disruptive foreign policy and its calls for revisionism. Under the leadership of the regime's founder and first Supreme Leader Ayatollah Ruhollah Khomeini, Tehran presented an alternative vision of a government led by the teachings of Islam,[8] which it deemed suitable for countries in the region. The 'export' of the revolution is, to this day, noted as a core tenet of the Islamic Republic and its ideology, albeit increasingly in rhetoric rather than in practice. Though Iran's desires to spread the revolution are tempered today, it continues to see itself and its system as a success story when it comes to developing an alternative to the Western one.

Iran is, however, constrained by its size and capabilities, especially when compared to Russia and China. While it aims to present an alternative world vision, Tehran is aware of its inability to safeguard its interests while challenging the existing world order on its own. As a result, it seeks foreign partners, such ✓ as Russia and China, that will serve its interests and help it gain in prominence in an international system where it is a comparatively small power. Tehran also focuses on regional policy, where it balances between undermining its neighbours' power and influence while ensuring they are not weakened to the point of central authorities collapsing. As a result, and importantly, Iran simply cannot be the threat to the United States or the existing Western world order that it is often portrayed to be. And as we will see, Iranian intentions and capabilities to challenge the Western international order are blown out of proportion.

Russia and China do not face the same constraints Iran does, but they too are not free of restrictions. Similar to Iran, their intent to undermine the international order is often overstated. Neither Moscow nor Beijing has a revolutionary world vision; rather the two powers aim to take advantage of the current world order, undermining it where international law and institutions do not favour them, and operating within them when they do. Russia under President Vladimir Putin developed a more aggressive foreign policy, challenging the Western-led international order and its supporting institutions. Moscow has played an obstructionist role on the international stage since the end of the Cold War, by breaking international consensus and blocking action at the United Nations (UN). Recently for example, Russia criticised the United States for trying to violate Iranian sovereignty when US ambassador to the UN, Nikki Haley, called a UNSC meeting to discuss the wave of protests that broke out in Iran at the end of 2017.[9] At times, Russia has also challenged the cornerstones of contemporary international affairs, sovereignty and territorial integrity, through its actions in Georgia and Ukraine. However, although clearly a cynical move, Moscow is set on justifying its actions through the prism of accepted international norms, as was the case for its intervention in Syria, which it described as supporting the efforts of a sovereign state in crushing terrorists – a talking point both Iran and China often use as well. For its part, China increasingly possesses the most capabilities to challenge the world order but it seems it does not seek to recreate it entirely. Instead, it wants to be the regional hegemon in Asia and to leverage international law and institutions in its own favour. As a result, Beijing plays by the rules when it sees them as promoting its interests, and ignores or undermines them when they do not. For example, the country brought a case against the European Union in the World Trade Organisation (WTO) over its status as a market economy and dumping rules.[10] But it ignored The Hague ruling rejecting the legal basis for Beijing's territorial claims in the South China Sea and calling China's efforts to build them up as illegal.[11]

As a result, while all three aim to present an alternative vision to the US-led Western world order, the intentions to challenge it and ability to do so vary widely. What is consistent, however, is the desire to constrain Western policy-making and presence in each country's respective geographical backyard. The intention is to prevent perceived US-led interference in each region and limit the US' ability to pursue its interests.

In order to achieve their objectives and as a reaction to the US-led order, Iran's bilateral cooperation with China and Russia has increased in recent years. For Tehran, the worldview it shares with Russia and China opens up various avenues for cooperation. Moscow's willingness to support Tehran's policies and narratives drives Iran's relationship with it. In particular, Russia plays an important role in the development of Iran's nuclear industry and supports its regional activities in the Middle East, most notably in the Syrian crisis. Support for Iran's security policies fits in Russia's broader foreign policy, as it seeks to destabilise the current world order by challenging and undermining the very foundations of international law and global institutions, such as sovereignty, territorial integrity, and non-intervention. For its part, as it expanded its presence and visibility in the world, in particular the Middle East, China sought to diversify its energy supplies. In this endeavour, Iran became an important partner. The 'One Belt, One Road' (OBOR) initiative, of which Iran is a critical player,[12] serves as an important vehicle for China's strategic vision, while Chinese economic ambitions provide Iran with an opportunity as it seeks to overcome years of economic sanctions. In fact, both Moscow and Beijing exploited the stringent international sanctions imposed on Iran to expand their foothold and influence in the country. Efforts to create non-Western, non-liberal international institutions such as the Shanghai Cooperation Organisation (SCO), along with deepening security cooperation reflect shared efforts to constrain the spread of Western influence in Eurasia and the Asia–Pacific. Iran is at the centre of these efforts, and involvement in the Middle East region provides Russia and China with a platform to expand their political and economic influence, and project power.

United by a belief that the economic dominance underpinning the West's political hegemony is waning, China, Russia, and Iran are deepening cooperation among themselves, while seeking to reduce their dependence on Western institutions, including the US dollar. The SCO, which Russia and China lead, is perhaps the most significant international institution designed to rival Western cooperative arrangements. China and Russia also advocate for alternative development institutions that reflect their own priorities and lack the conditionality of Western-led bodies, like the International Monetary Fund (IMF). These efforts are in conjunction with individual attempts to wean themselves off Western economic institutions and provide alternative platforms for other similar states to subscribe to. For example, in a move designed to provide an alternative trading platform, China began trading futures-oil contracts using the Yuan in 2018.[13] In addition, economic cooperation among the three states, is expanding. China is one of Russia's top trading partners and an increasingly important source of foreign investment. Russia has exported significant quantities of oil to China since the mid-2000s – becoming China's number one oil supplier ahead of Saudi Arabia in 2016,[14] while a major natural gas sales agreement was signed in May 2014 worth \$400 billion.[15] Key Russian and Chinese interests in the Middle East will determine their foreign policy in the years to come, and Iran is a key component of that. But while scholars and experts have spilled much ink to explain Russian and Chinese foreign policies and the two giants' relations, as well as various aspects of Iran's political, economic, and military affairs, Iran's relationship with Russia and China remains to be assessed.

With its nearly insatiable demand for energy and its growing desire to play a more significant international role, China looks to the Middle East as a major potential area of influence, and Iran is a prime target – one that has become only more attractive with the official removal of international sanctions. Meanwhile Russia was an important lifeline for the Iranian economy under sanctions, and continued to sustain its presence and dominance over certain sectors within Iran, in particular in the fields of defence technology and energy, even as Moscow warily views Tehran as a potential competitor for its lucrative European energy markets. Russia and China penetrated the Iranian market, which Western companies deserted because of the backbreaking sanctions regime. Russia has also been the main player in Iran's efforts to develop nuclear power since Tehran resumed its nuclear programme in the 1980s, after halting it during the 1979 Islamic Revolution. Moscow has been Tehran's main supplier for nuclear technology and fuel, and the two capitals concluded a deal in 2014 for the construction of a number of other nuclear reactors in Iran in the years to come.[16] The understanding came at a significant time, as Tehran and the world powers, including Russia and China, were working towards a comprehensive deal curbing Iran's nuclear programme in exchange for sanctions relief. While Iran has long languished under Western sanctions, Russia, too, found itself facing economic pressure (modelled on the sanctions applied to Iran) following its 2014 intervention in Ukraine. China's importance for the global economy makes it harder to sanction. Beijing has been carefully studying the West's efforts to sanction Iran and Russia, viewing them as a potential harbinger of how the West would handle a conflict with Taiwan or in the South China Sea.[17] Currently, trade tensions between the United States and China - in which President Trump has threatened to levy hundreds of billions of dollars in tariffs on Chinese goods as retaliation for its alleged theft of US intellectual property – have sharpened Beijing's awareness of the potential bite of US-led sanctions and penalties. Moreover, the US government did not hesitate to go after Chinese entities for their links to various parts of Iran's nuclear and missile programmes, as well as Chinese financial entities with connections to North Korea.[18]

All three countries seek to expand their cooperation at the global level, even as regional issues remain a source of tension among them. Russia and Iran are largely on the same side in the fragmented South Caucasus, but as in the Middle East, their cooperation is more a matter of convenience than conviction. Moreover, Russian destabilising activities in Georgia impede on Iran's interests, as Tehran fears volatility in the region and its impact on its own security and economic interests.[19] In the wider Caspian basin, Moscow and Tehran both opposed efforts to bring Central Asian energy west, but have not resolved all of their own disputes. Beijing and Tehran however, do not have any significant flashpoints in their relationship. Minor tensions, such as trade disputes or slow delivery of projects, and China's treatment of its Muslim minority, fostered suspicion, but did not prevent the two countries from boosting their cooperation.

Russia's presence in the Middle East has been important for centuries, while China's has been growing in the past few decades. Iran stands out as a partner for both countries among Middle Eastern states due to several factors. It is a significant state; it is large and resource rich, with a large and relatively youthful, educated population. Iran is one of few countries in the region with the means to pursue its ambitious foreign policy agenda. Indeed, while sanctions and its poor economic situation limit Iran's means abroad, Tehran made up for this with its clear political will to use broad means at its disposal to affect regional crises. The best example of this political will lies in Iranian efforts in Iraq over the past two decades, but more specifically since the rise of the Islamic State in Iraq and Syria – also referred to as ISIS, the Islamic State, and Da'esh – in 2014, as well as in Syria since the start of the civil war in 2011. Tehran demonstrated that limits in means will not affect its will to deploy armed forces – through either its conventional military (known in Persian as, Artesh) or the Islamic Revolutionary Guard Corps (hereafter IRGC, Revolutionary Guards, or simply, the Guards) – or the proxies it works with in the region, chiefly, Hezbollah.

But since the revolution, Iran's poor human rights track record, controversial nuclear programme, support for terrorist groups in the Middle East and beyond, and complicated relations with the West and some of its regional adversaries, like Israel and Saudi Arabia, placed the regime at the forefront of international security discussions. This isolated Tehran from other potential international partners. But Russia and China do not place as much weight on Iran's pariah status as the West does. The presidency of hardliner Mahmoud Ahmadinejad in 2005–13 accelerated the country's political and economic isolation, which began three decades earlier with the advent of the Islamic Republic. Yet, Iran remained an important market with considerable oil and gas resources, leading some European countries to maintain their ties with an increasingly isolated nation for as long as was politically and legally feasible. Despite Ahmadinejad's hardline policies, it was at the end of his tenure that Iran began to explore dialogue with the United States in secret meetings in Oman in 2012. It was only with the election of the more moderate President Hassan Rouhani in 2013 that Tehran could earnestly build on these small exchanges and begin to wholeheartedly re-engage with the United States and work more closely with the EU. But in the time it took for Rouhani to begin re-expanding ties with the West – an endeavour that faced many obstacles, especially after President Trump's election, Russia and China built significant clout in Iran. Both are there to stay, regardless of the slow improvement in West–Iran relations. Notably, though, the development of Russia and China's relations with Iran depend on the extent of the rapprochement between Tehran and the West.

It is precisely because of the uncertain and fragile nature of its relationship with the West, and particularly Europe, that Iran increasingly solidified its ties to and expanded the scope of its cooperation with Russia and China. This is because while Tehran preserved some ties with the EU, and enjoyed decent bilateral ties with many of its member states since the revolution, it firmly believed that Brussels and European capitals would follow the US lead in their interactions with Iran. This impression was further solidified throughout the nuclear crisis as Brussels followed Washington's lead in the imposition of successive rounds of sanctions on Iran. When the nuclear deal's implementation began and European businesses and banks were slow to re-enter the Iranian market because of remaining US sanctions, domestic economic opacity in Iran, and general uncertainty, Tehran's view that it should not wait for the Europeans and should instead capitalise on Russian and Chinese eagerness to work with it was further confirmed. But a number of key events since the nuclear deal have muddied the waters for Iran.

First, Brexit made Tehran nervous that London would follow Washington's lead, rather than that of Brussels, on Iranian affairs, and thus adopt a more hardline approach vis-à-vis the Islamic Republic. Iran's concerns worsened when the 2016 US elections produced an unlikely candidate: Republican Donald Trump. President Trump took a hardline on Iran, and stacked his cabinet with well-known Iran hawks, including several advocates of regime change. The administration immediately toughened its stance on Iran, putting the country 'on notice' within weeks of inauguration.[20] In October 2017, Trump refused to recertify the nuclear agreement, and every successive certification and renewal of the sanctions waiver became a hurdle for all parties involved. Finally, in May 2018, the Trump administration announced America's withdrawal from the Joint Comprehensive Plan of Action (JCPOA) and its intent to reimpose sanctions on and revoke licenses for the sale of aircraft to Iran. And while Iran and the EU and its member states regularly repeated they would continue to implement the deal,[21] Trump's move increased uncertainty surrounding the future of the deal. At the same time, however, difficult relations between Trump and key European leaders, such as German Chancellor Angela Merkel and French President Emmanuel Macron, and the general scepticism of the new administration's intentions and qualifications in Europe, reassured the Iranians to some extent. Meanwhile, High Representative of the European Union for Foreign Affairs and Security Policy Federica Mogherini tried to build on the JCPOA[22] to create new channels of dialogue and strengthen existing ones with Tehran, tackling economic and trade ties, regional security, and human rights.[23] Mogherini also began to serve as a buffer between the Trump administration and Tehran, often stepping in to encourage the Trump team to maintain the JCPOA and regularly re-affirming the EU's commitment to the agreement.[24] However, spring 2018 discussions surrounding the future of the JCPOA between Berlin, London, and Paris served to again renew Iranian anxieties.

Despite warming ties with European countries, Iran viewed it as imperative to build on its existing ties with Russia and China, especially in light of the deepening of conflicts in its neighbourhood. The Syrian conflict and the advent of ISIS and its offshoot in Afghanistan – known as the Islamic State in the Khorasan Province (ISKP) – are two key strategic areas where Iran and Russia in particular share interests. Both Tehran and Moscow supported the Assad regime in Syria and coordinated their efforts to fight ISIS in Iraq. The cooperation broke new ground when Iran granted Russia access to one of its airbases for refuelling in 2016. The episode was exceptional as it was a departure from Iranian policy, and according to some critics, in breach of the Iranian Constitution, which states that the country's territory should not serve as a foreign military base, even temporarily.[25] These efforts reinforced the growing military cooperation between the two countries, and aimed to undermine the Western-led international efforts in the region. While China was not as actively involved in these conflicts, it showed a growing interest in tackling ISIS given the vulnerability of its own Muslim minority the Uyghurs, a Turkic-speaking Sunni ethnic group concentrated in Beijing's far western Xinjiang province. China's interests also lie with Russia and Iran in weakening the West in the region more broadly. More generally, the three countries undertook a number of joint military drills in recent years in key strategic areas. Iran and China conducted joint war games in the Persian Gulf, while Iran and Russia embarked on similar projects in the Caspian basin. Defence cooperation among the three countries is not limited to military drills and operational coordination, and also extends to arms and technology trade. Of particular concern for the West was Russia's role in the development of the Iranian nuclear programme despite the country's failure to fully comply with its international obligations under the Nuclear Non-Proliferation Treaty (NPT), as well as in China's acquisition of modern air defence and anti-access/area denial (A2-AD) systems.

The Iran–Russia and Iran–China relationships are an important piece of the puzzle of contemporary international security with great implications for various regions, including the West, South and Central Asia, and the Middle East. Other nations, which the West seeks to compel or coerce into changing their behaviour, could look to the Iranian model of leveraging the two powers to serve as a bulwark against the West, thus limiting Western ability to influence states. Despite these implications, the relationships have remained a virtual terra incognita. In varying ways, China, Russia, and Iran are the three most significant proponents of an alternative to the post-Cold War liberal global order led by the United States. Powerful states seeking a larger global role, China, Russia, and Iran all chafe against an international order they had no hand in creating and which they believe does not reflect their interests. Individually, and in varying combinations, each rejects the universality of Western liberal principles while pressing for alternative economic, political, and security institutions and arrangements.

***

This book compares and contrasts the key aspects of the China–Iran and Russia–Iran relationships, and their implications for policy-making in a post-JCPOA world. It focuses on the nature of cooperation and competition between Iran and Russia and Iran and China, including foreign policy and strategic interests, economic ties, and defence cooperation. The book omits an in-depth discussion on Russia–China ties, which would be the subject of another lengthy publication.

The book will begin by discussing all three countries' visions of the global order and where they fit into it. All three countries aim to curb post-Cold War US influence and hegemony, and to generally make it difficult for the West to advance its interests, while asserting their own hegemony in what they view as their own backyards. They pragmatically work together in order to achieve these objectives, despite their numerous differences in the many areas they cooperate in, making their respective relations both multi-layered and complicated. The book will then examine political, economic, and defence cooperation between China and Iran and Russia and Iran, comparing and contrasting the depth of the cooperation in each sector. It will then assess prospects for cooperation following the nuclear agreement and the subsequent lifting of sanctions. While Iran was predominantly interested in boosting ties with the West following the nuclear deal, the slow pace and breadth of the promised sanctions relief made it essential for Tehran to maintain its ties with both Russia and China. In fact, Tehran can no longer fully tilt towards the West, as it once aimed to do under reformist President Mohammad Khatami in the late 1990s and early 2000s. This is because while Western presence in Iran has not been consistent, that of Russia and China has and continues to be. As a result, a whole new generation of business owners, engineers, military personnel, diplomats, and other parts of the Iranian population have come of age working with Russian and Chinese businesses, engineers, military personnel, and diplomats and unlike their predecessors, have hardly worked with Westerners. Likewise, since President Trump's election, the JCPOA's rocky implementation process has reinforced Iran's belief that the United States aims to stymie the country's progress and seeks excuses to contain and counter the regime. Hence, today and for the foreseeable future, Iran believes that it must balance its will and ability to work with the West and its inability to break away from Russia and China. Finally, the book will explore recommendations for the United States and Europe, in particular, in dealing with an Iran that can no longer be isolated as effectively as before. These will provide a roadmap for US and European policymakers and scholars to leverage the post-deal environment to the West's advantage, and manage the difficulties posed by the rise of the Iran–China–Russia axis.

CHAPTER 1

IRAN AND THE WORLD ORDER: RUSSIA AND CHINA AS A BULWARK AGAINST THE WEST

Before examining Iran's political, economic and military relations with Russia and China and how they help the country haul itself out of international isolation, it is important to understand Iran's recent history and why the Islamic Republic thinks and functions the way it does. Iran's worldview as well as what drives its foreign policy decisions, and how Russia and China share some of these drivers will provide the context for the examination of Iran's relations with Russia and China.

Iran's Place in the World

The Cold War provided the backdrop for the Shah's worldview and political and security thinking. He saw Communism as the greatest threat faced by Iran. Internationally, he was concerned about the domino effect – whereby states, including his own, could fall one after the other to Communist ideology and rule. Domestically, groups, typically inspired by Maoist or Marxist–Leninist models, sought to undermine or overthrow the monarchy. As a result, the Shah's security apparatus often propped up Shia Islam as a counterweight to Communism. It was only later, when the Islamists emerged as a dominant force, that the Shah's threat perception and attention shifted from Communism to Shia revolutionary ideology. But by then, it was too late. In addition to blending Shia values and Communist ideals, the revolution also incorporated anti-imperialism and anti-Americanism – a response to the Shah's policies and the US and British-backed 1953 coup that overthrew Prime Minister Mohammad Mossadeq. The revolutionaries believed Washington had interfered in their domestic politics, propped up an unjust dictator, and trained and equipped his intelligence services and security apparatus to torture and kill his political opponents. So prominent were the beliefs of America's hands in Iranian affairs that when an earthquake shook the city of Tabas in 1978, a rumour began to spread that it was caused by US underground nuclear weapon tests in Iran.[1] And while many of these rumours had no basis in reality, they spread quickly and shaped people's views of the United States.

The revolution shifted Tehran's strategic outlook, political narrative, and alliances. It replaced the pro-West Shah with the Islamic Republic, whose political narrative was based on several core beliefs. Immediately upon seizing power, Iran's revolutionary leaders advocated for a Muslim awakening and unity among the 'oppressed peoples of the world' to stand up to 'Western imperialism'.[2] The revolutionaries saw the post-World War II order as one created to promote the interests of the West at the expense of those of the rest of the world. The calls were led by the man who emerged as the revolution's key figure and the founder of the Islamic Republic: Ayatollah Ruhollah Khomeini. As a result, Tehran distanced itself from the West, which the Shah had embraced throughout his reign, though not without some tension. As such, Iran developed an anti-imperialist narrative, one denouncing international law and institutions as the West's vehicle for imposing its will on the rest of the world, a narrative further strengthened during the Iran–Iraq War. Indeed, as Iranians saw it, the international order was supporting Saddam Hussein's Iraq, a country that had invaded Iran, and later used chemical weapons against Iranians and its own Kurdish population.[3] Iranian leaders began to denounce the international system and the UN Security Council, in particular, as it stood by and watched these atrocities being committed.[4]

Later, the successive rounds of sanctions the international community imposed on Iran in order to isolate it for its controversial nuclear programme reinforced this view. As a result, along with rejecting Western imperialism, self-reliance became an increasingly important part of the Iranian revolutionary narrative, prompted by its Supreme Leader, Revolutionary Guards, and other power centres. Hence, as we will see later, in response to the isolation resulting from the sanctions, Tehran coined the term, 'resistance economy'.[5] Thanks to this roadmap, Iran aimed to reduce its reliance on oil, boost other areas of its economy and production, become an exporter, rather than an importer, and ultimately build a 'sanctions resistant' economy.[6] In parallel, the Islamic Republic tried to balance this narrative with efforts to present Iran as an upstanding member of the international community. Indeed, despite all its criticism of international institutions, the new regime did not make a decision to quit, forego, or renegotiate its memberships in various fora.[7] Instead, it opted to preserve much of the country's pre-revolution international standing. Nevertheless, despite remaining a part of the international order, the Islamic Republic shaped much of its own political and security narratives around its distrust of the United States and enmity towards Israel. And while Iran remains a member of a number of international institutions, it has failed to comply by its international obligations on multiple occasions, especially those pertaining to nuclear non-proliferation and human rights.

Yet, despite these broad trends, it would be a mistake to characterise the Islamic Republic as a deeply ideological and monolithic entity – as the Western, particularly American, conventional wisdom holds. While the Supreme Leader is the final decision arbiter, he is not the only decision-maker in Tehran. Rather, the regime is composed of multiple power centers and the political elite takes part in lengthy debates on domestic and foreign policy issues. In addition, the regime's general stance towards the international order has not changed much since the revolution and its security narrative remains dominated by the distrust of international law and institutions, anti-imperialism, and anti-Americanism. But each successive government adopted a different approach to foreign policy. Since the early 2000s alone, Iranian foreign priorities have changed drastically in practice, and the accompanying rhetoric has been multi-layered. The following sections assess each recent government's view of the world and its foreign policy attitude.

The government of reformist president Mohammad Khatami (1997–2005) privileged relations with the West, putting forward the idea of the 'dialogue among civilisations'. Under Khatami, Tehran reportedly proposed a 'grand bargain' to Washington, which offered to address some of the United States and its allies' most pressing concerns.[8] But the George W. Bush administration rejected this overture and, as we saw, labelled Iran as a part of the 'Axis of Evil'.[9] The grand bargain failed and the incident only compounded the feeling in Tehran that it could not trust the West because America and its allies were hell bent on toppling the Islamic Republic rather than building relations with it. It also added to the long history of missed opportunities for dialogue between Iran and the United States. Khatami also sought to solve the nuclear crisis, which had emerged during his tenure. Initially, Iran and the so-called EU3 – later named the P5 + 1 or EU 3 + 3 when the European Union, China, Russia, and the United States joined Germany, France, and the United Kingdom – made some progress.

But the process collapsed in 2005, leaving the issue unsolved. Shortly after, hardliner Mahmoud Ahmadinejad was elected president of the Islamic Republic of Iran.

Ahmadinejad's tenure was, in fact, an exception rather than the rule in recent years, in its willingness to antagonise its neighbours and the West, while shifting towards Russia and China, focusing on developing ties with the Non-Aligned Movement (NAM) and establishing an Iranian presence in Latin America and Africa. The Ahmadinejad period saw political and economic upheaval and isolation for the country and the failure to reach a solution over Iran's nuclear file. Interestingly, Tehran is believed to have ceased its consolidated weaponisation efforts in 2003, during the Khatami era, while only pursuing some weapons' related activities under Ahmadinejad, which it ceased altogether in 2009.[10] But it was under Ahmadinejad specifically, that Tehran started to pay the political and economic price for its failure to comply by its international obligations with successive rounds of international sanctions. The negotiations resumed during the last year of Ahmadinejad's tenure in 2012. While this was the first time that Iranian officials met with their US counterparts in secret meetings in Oman, the Iranian side did not seem as forthcoming.[11] But the tone of the talks changed under Ahmadinejad's moderate successor, President Hassan Rouhani.

Rouhani's vision of international affairs, as demonstrated in the negotiations, was in line with his campaign slogan of 'hope and pragmatism'. His worldview entailed 'constructive engagement' with friends and foes alike.[12] Rouhani's first term was largely dominated by the nuclear negotiations, which Iranian officials viewed as a prerequisite to other items on their agenda.[13] In that context, Tehran began to wholeheartedly re-engage with the West, with a particular focus on what it viewed as the P5 + 1's leader, the United States.[14] The talks marked a departure from the previous three decades of lack of diplomatic discussion. The two countries had not directly engaged with one another at the highest levels of their diplomatic corps since the end of the hostage crisis in the early days of the Islamic Republic. This is partly due to Iran's resentment of US presence in its neighbourhood and what it views as American involvement in Iranian affairs before the revolution, symbolised by what many Iranians believe to be a negative role played by the Central Intelligence Agency (CIA) in the overthrow of Mosadeq.[15] The United States, for its part, deeply distrusted Tehran due to the US embassy hostage crisis and the regime's anti-American rhetoric and propaganda, including the famous 'death to America' chants of Iranian Friday prayers. But the taboo of Iranian and US diplomats sitting at the same table was finally broken with the first direct conversation between sitting US and Iranian presidents, when Obama spoke with Rouhani. Following this, Iranian and US nuclear negotiators led by Foreign Minister Javad Zarif and Secretary of State John Kerry began the marathon talks that resulted in the JCPOA. The two countries and the other parties deliberately limited the scope of the talks to the Iranian nuclear programme – though they did touch upon other outstanding points of contention occasionally, particularly regional security, the arrest and detention of dual nationals, and broader human rights, during the informal side-line discussions.[16] For example, the two sides discussed ISIS' takeover of large swathes of territory in Syria and Iraq in summer 2014 on the side-lines of the talks in Vienna.

After Rouhani's election, the United States and Iran created a direct channel between their top diplomats, which subsequently helped resolve a number of diplomatic, political, and military incidents. For example, this channel was significant in the quick release of ten US sailors captured in Iranian territorial waters close to the IRGC base on Farsi Island, in the Persian Gulf. Yet, this semi-détente between the two adversaries did not lead to a great shift towards the West, and away from China and Russia on Iran's part. Upon the election of Donald Trump, the progress made by the two countries during the overlap of Obama and Rouhani was stymied. But the Rouhani government continued to try to pave the way to better relations with the region and the West, especially Europe.

Indeed, despite often taking a backseat during the nuclear talks, the Europeans stood to gain from the JCPOA and were actively pursuing partnerships with Iran. During the talks and in the immediate aftermath of the deal, European officials and business delegations flocked to Iran to explore new opportunities and sign hundreds of MOUs.[17] For their part, Iranian officials and businesses visited European capitals to sell the young and burgeoning market in Iran.[18] But as time went on, it became apparent that initial interest would not translate into a rush back into Iran, and many of the MOUs signed with Iranian counterparts were slow to materialise, if at all. As a result, Iranians did not see a drastic improvement in their living and economic conditions. Rather, sanctions relief was slow and problematic, and did not trickle down to those who needed it the most. Rouhani's government, which had not conducted proper expectation management, and in fact, oversold the possibility for economic recovery, found itself faced with a great deal of criticism over its focus on reaching a nuclear agreement, at the expense of Iran's domestic scene, epitomised by the protests that rocked 80 cities throughout Iran at the end of 2017. It is important to note, however, that the projected rush back into the Iranian market did not materialise, which was partly Iran's own doing. Indeed, Iran's economy is notoriously opaque, devoid of international regulations, permeated by the Revolutionary Guards at every level, and full of barriers to entry for foreign businesses. Eight years of economic mismanagement under Ahmadinejad only served to worsen the situation. While the Rouhani government succeeded in somewhat reducing inflation and boosting growth, it struggled to reduce unemployment and address some of the underlying issues plaguing the Iranian economy, including rampant corruption, inefficiency, and an overstretched banking sector. All of this, along with the continued uncertainty propagated by President

Trump, contributed to the hesitation on the part of foreign businesses looking to invest in or establish a presence in Iran.

As a result, conservatives in Iran once again used the opportunity to criticise the deal, and broader engagement with the United States. Washington and its allies cannot be trusted, they argued, because they seek to impede the Iranian people's progress.[19] According to conservatives, the nuclear issue was the right excuse at the right time for the West to pressure and isolate Iran, and now that it was resolved, the United States and its allies would search for other excuses to continue this trend. As Khamenei put it: America's problem is more fundamental than specific areas of concern US officials and lawmakers point to – including the nuclear issue, human rights, and terrorism. America's problem is the nature of the regime itself and the Islamic Republic as a whole.[20] As a result, far from changing Iran's mindset, the JCPOA's implementation reinforced the idea that Tehran could only rely on itself and expand its ties to non-Western players. In that sense, even though Iran came to the negotiating table wanting to diversify its suppliers, open up competition in its market, and reopen the country to investors, with a particular emphasis on resuming business with the Europeans, it ended up further forging its ties with China and Russia.[21]

Iran's Relations with Russia–China and Revising Ancient Partnerships

Iran has a long history of diplomatic, trade, and military relations with Russia and China.

Chinese officials often refer to their country's relations with Iran as '20 centuries of cooperation'.[22] Starting with the very foundation of Persia during the Achaemenid dynasty (500–330 BC), the groundwork was laid out for what would become the Silk Road connecting China to Europe through the Middle East. The Silk

Road was established around 130 BC, under the Han dynasty. During that period, China and Persia began diplomatic and trade relations, already posting ambassadors to one another's empires. Later, the two worked together to fight a common adversary: Turkic nomadic tribes in Central Asia. When the Arabs invaded Persia in the seventh century, members of the royal family fled to China. In the early days of the Islamic era, Persia, then ruled by the Abbasid Caliphate, and China confronted each other militarily in the Battle of Talas (751 AD) in their first and last war. Throughout and after that era, Sino—Persian scientific and cultural exchanges, trade, and diplomatic relations continued.

Likewise, relations between Persia and Russia also go back centuries. Pre-Islamic Persia already engaged in trade with Russia. But the two countries' close proximity led to a more multifaceted, comprehensive, and more complex relationship. While Persia and China rarely shared borders as their territories changed with wars and transitions of power, Persia and Russia did. As a result, the two empires frequently found themselves at war with one another, but they also had comprehensive diplomatic and trade ties. The cooperation, competition, war, and engagement between the two countries shaped their relationship until the modern era. The Qajar dynasty (1794—1925) resisted colonisation, but Persia did see considerable influence by foreign powers in its domestic politics and backyard,[23] especially by Russia. And while Russia assisted the Qajars in consolidating their military to secure critical roads, the two empires also faced each other in two wars; the Russo—Persian Wars of 1804—13 and 1826—28. They led to devastating Persian defeats and two major treaties: The Treaty of Golestan (1813) and the treaty of Turkmenchay (1828). By the end of these two wars, Persia lost several territories, including in Dagestan, Georgia, Armenia, and Azerbaijan. The Treaty of Turkmenchay was so disastrous that to this day, it continues to symbolise defeat, loss of territorial integrity, and humiliation in Iran. In the twentieth century, the three countries underwent major political changes that would align their interests and deepen their engagement.

Upheavals and Revolutions: How Tehran's Interests Aligned With Those of Beijing and Moscow

Reform and Revolution in Iran

In Persia, the Constitutional Revolution (1905–11) afforded the country its first modern constitution and limited the power of the Shah. A consolidated judiciary – rather than two separate judicial systems, one led by the state and the other by the clergy – was put in place, and the country undertook education reforms. But the constitutionalists' vision was not fully implemented and the central authority was weakened. Ultimately, Reza Shah rose to power, founding the Pahlavi dynasty, the last of over a dozen dynasties to rule over Persia, which at that time became known as Iran. Reza Shah implemented comprehensive reforms and built a modern military for his country, which included an air force and a navy, in addition to the traditional ground forces. He was anxious to make the country more self-reliant, and laid out the foundations for an indigenous military industrial complex. Under Reza Shah, Iran also started to modernise its infrastructure, city planning, transportation, communications, and broader industry. With the start of World War II, the Russians and the British forced Reza Shah, who had developed German-Iranian relations, to abdicate. His son, Mohammad Reza, replaced him and continued his father's reforms. The Shah's modernisation reforms transformed his military into a powerhouse. He also started to invest in the nuclear programme in the 1950s under US president Dwight Eisenhower's Atoms for Peace initiative. In the 1960s, the Shah undertook a series of social reforms, known as the 'White Revolution', which included land reform, enfranchisement of women, formation of a literacy corps, and the institution of profit sharing schemes for workers in industry. In parallel, Tehran began to view Communism as the greatest threat to the state. Left-leaning groups that challenged the monarchy proliferated throughout Iran. They were predominantly divided into two groups: Marxist–Leninists, following the Soviet model, and Maoists, following the Chinese model taking advantage of the leftist groups' lack of cohesion, and capitalizing on popular discontent with the Shah's anti-traditional social and economic policies, the Islamists took on the mantle of the revolution. Led by Ayatollah Khomeini, the revolution toppled the 2,500-year monarchic tradition in the country and installed an Islamic Republic in 1979.

The new regime's ideology was based on Shia Islam. It incorporated elements of Marxism–Communism, anti-imperialism, and anti-Americanism. In the midst of the turmoil in November 1979, the revolutionaries attacked the US embassy in Tehran and took 52 members of the US diplomatic corps and embassy personnel hostage, marking the end of US–Iran diplomatic ties. The Iran–Iraq War started in the midst of the hostage crisis when Saddam Hussein's Iraq attacked Iran. The war further served to reinforce the idea that Tehran was in dire need of relations with other powers to replace the United States, and that it also needed to be self-reliant. It also forged a feeling of isolation and distrust of the international order. At the end of the war, the Islamic Republic started reconstruction efforts, emphasising the economy, which coincided with Iran's efforts to court Russia and China. More than a decade later, in 2002, an Iranian opposition group unveiled the Natanz enrichment facility and the Arak heavy water reactor, opening a new chapter in Iranian history. After a European attempt at finding a diplomatic solution to the nuclear file between 2003–05, Iran became the subject of several UNSC Resolutions and sanctions for its nuclear programme. During that period, Iran, then governed by Ahmadinejad, strengthened its relations with Russia and China. In 2015, Iran concluded the JCPOA with the P5 + 1 after months of marathon talks.

Wars and Revolutions in Russia

In Russia, the turn of the twentieth century was marked by the creation of the Marxist Social Democratic Party in 1897, its split into the Mensheviks and Bolsheviks in 1903, and the Russian expansion into Manchuria, which prompted the Russo–Japanese War (1904–05). In 1905, Russia also underwent a revolution, leading to the establishment of a legislative branch, the Duma, and the Russian constitution. In 1914, World War I broke out and led the country to economic decline, military fragmentation, and political instability. In November 1917, following unrests, the Bolsheviks overthrew the provisional government, which was put in place after Tsar Nicholas was forced to abdicate, and established the 'Dictatorship of the Proletariat' under the leadership of Vladimir Lenin. By the end of the 1920s, the Russian Empire was rebranded the Union of Soviet Socialist Republics (USSR) following a civil war, and Joseph Stalin had replaced Lenin as the political and ideological head of the Soviet government. The Soviet economy became increasingly state-run, while social policy became increasingly rigid. In 1941, Germany broke the Soviet–German Non-Aggression Pact and launched a surprise attack on the Soviet Union. The Soviet Union paid tremendous costs for its victory in 1945. By 1947, the Cold War had begun and by 1949, the Soviet Union had followed in Washington's footsteps, testing its first nuclear device and triggering a decades-long nuclear arms race between the two blocs. By the 1970s, the two superpowers were engaged in a number of proxy wars throughout the world, leading them to seek détente, but this became increasingly elusive after the Soviet occupation of Afghanistan in 1979. In addition, the country under Leonid Brezhnev, suffered from economic stagnation and corruption. The 1980s were marked by Mikhail Gorbachev's vision of economic and political reforms – respectively, perestroika and glasnost – which ultimately led to the collapse of the Soviet Union. After the implosion of the USSR, under Boris Yeltsin, Russia took a number of steps to join the post-World War II, international order shaped by its former adversary, the United States. But by the end of the 1990s, Moscow was once again distancing itself from America. Domestic challenges, including unrest in Chechnya, led to the rise of Prime Minister Vladimir Putin, who assumed the presidency of the Russian Federation in 2000.

Putin consolidated his power in 2004, after winning a second term in office and began to adopt more hawkish policies at home and abroad. In 2008, Russia, then governed by Putin's ally, Dmitry Medvedev, entered a war with Georgia, when Georgian forces attacked Russian-backed separatists in South Ossetia. Russian troops drove Georgian forces from South Ossetia, as well as Abkhazia. The following year, Russia withheld gas supplies to Ukraine over unpaid bills, disrupting the flow of gas into parts of Europe. By the end of Medvedev's term, the Duma had voted to increase the presidential term from four to six years, Meanwhile, despite Russia's increasingly aggressive and expansionist policies abroad, US–Russia relations improved during Medvedev's tenure. In fact, when Republican presidential candidate Mitt Romney brought up Russia as a key threat to the United States, then President Barack Obama, who was running for his second term in office, accused him of living in a Cold War era mind-set, one divorced from the political reality of the two countries' relations. But the warmth was short-lived. Soon, relations between the two states declined once again, when Moscow annexed Crimea in 2014. In autumn 2015, Russia carried out its first airstrikes in Syria, reportedly targeting ISIS. This formalised its involvement in the Syrian conflict on Iran's side, supporting the government of Bashar al-Assad. The Russian refusal to withdraw its forces from Crimea, its presence in Syria, and Russian interference in the 2016 US presidential elections – to undermine the candidacy of the Democrat Hillary Clinton, and in support of Donald Trump – further complicated matters.

Ideology and Pragmatism in China

Inspired by the 1917 Bolshevik Revolution in Russia, Marxist revolutionaries in China, including Li Dazhao and Chen Duxiu, founded the Chinese Communist Party (CCP) in 1921. The CCP was first driven underground at the end of the 1920s, before being pushed to the countryside by the Nationalists in the south in the early 1930s, and finally forced to join the United Front to fight the Japanese in 1936, projecting the party into World War II. At the end of the war, the Chinese Civil War broke out, with the CCP and the Nationalists vying for control of the country. In 1949, the defeated Nationalists retreated to Taiwan and the CCP, led by Mao Zedong, founded the People's Republic of China. In the years following the revolution, internal disagreements over the future of the country surfaced: The extent to which the Soviet model was to be implemented in China, social and foreign policy, and economic development were at the heart of these disputes. A series of disastrous policy initiatives – including the 'Great Leap Forward' from 1958–62, in which over 30 million Chinese died of starvation – intensified the debate and posed challenges to Mao Zedong's grip on power.[24] In that context, Mao implemented the Cultural Revolution in 1966, purging the leadership of challengers, until his death. Many of the founding fathers of the CCP and the People's Republic of China were either effectively side-lined or died, leading to an internal struggle within the CCP on the direction of Post-Mao China. Deng Xiaoping emerged from the debate, left Maoist ideology in the past and set the country on a course of modernisation and economic development; the 'Four Modernisations'. These critical sectors were defence, industry, technology, and agriculture. China also relaxed restrictions on the arts and education. Over the next few decades, China would steadily assert itself as a key political and economic power, as it continued its meteoric economic growth.

In 2012, Xi Jinping assumed the leadership of the CCP and the presidency of China. He coined the term, 'Chinese Dream', based on nationalism and Chinese revival, which encapsulated his vision for China in the twenty-first century.[25] The narrative is based on a historical collective memory known in China as 'national humiliation', which describes China's subjugation by Western powers in the years after the Opium Wars (1842–43) through to the fall of Republican China (1911–49). The importance of this narrative in shaping China's current view of itself on the world stage cannot be overstated. According to this narrative, China was stripped of its rightful place in the world order, had its territory stolen, and its social and political fabric torn apart by a series of unjust treaties imposed by Western powers. The 'China Dream' promises to revive this lost glory – and China's rightful place in the world system – by righting the wrongs imposed on it during its time of oppression. And, as we will see later, Xi codified his vision of China's place in the world, including the China Dream, into the Chinese political fabric during the 19th Party Congress in autumn 2017. China's experience of 'national humiliation' at the hands of the west is an important shadow dynamic that influences Chinese reactions to foreign policy issues on the world stage – such as the South China Sea, and other perceived encroachments on its sovereignty.

Russia and China in Iran's Worldview

As we have seen, historical developments and experiences brought Iran closer to Russia and China, even under previous governments. After all, they all share core values and scepticism of the West and the international order created in America's image. But how do the Russian and Chinese worldviews align with Iran's? And what do the two giants afford Tehran?

Why China?

After the 1979 revolution in Iran, China progressively became a key player in the country, as well as an important mediator in

West–Iran relations. During the nuclear negotiations between the P5 + 1 and Iran, China attempted to facilitate dialogue and allow the parties to reach solutions acceptable to all. But Beijing's role was not always as positive as it sought to demonstrate. It pursued a dual-track policy, exerting its influence 'as both a supporter and a spoiler' in West–Iran relations.[26] Beijing and Tehran's relations have to be assessed in the context of their respective relationships with the West. For China, its political relationship with Iran advances two key goals. First, Beijing sees Tehran as a political partner, blocking two hegemons, Washington and Moscow. Indeed, the Islamic Republic's steadfast belief in independence from foreign influence resonates with Beijing. Second, China sees Iran as an economic asset, with an important market where China has an edge over potential competitors, and a significant source of energy resources.[27] Tehran for its part, sees China as a line of defence when faced with what it views as the often-hostile West, especially in international fora, given its key role as a permanent member of the UN Security Council.[28] Indeed, as we have seen, Iran continues to be part of the international political and legal ecosystem, but one whose compliance track record has at times led to its isolation from other actors within the system, thus pushing it towards similarly minded players. For example, China, along with Russia, was instrumental in watering down and delaying some of the UNSC measures against Iran throughout the nuclear dispute. Yet, Sino–Iranian relations have stopped far short of a formal political and strategic alliance.

The primary driver of Iranian and Chinese policies towards each other lies in their respective strategic goals. Throughout the 1970s, this strategic goal was dominated by their willingness to challenge the Soviet Union. In the 1980s and 1990s, the United States became the key adversary for Iran, which made it seek closer relations to China. Since the beginning of the twenty-first century, the scope of this goal expanded to encompass various sectors, predominantly, energy, economy and trade, and military.[29]

Nevertheless, Sino–Iranian relations are built on a key premise: They would not come at the expense of the two countries' relations with other powers. For instance, during the development of the 'Tehran–Peking axis' under the Shah, Iranian officials were careful to present their relations in a way that would not be perceived as a threat to Soviet–Iran relations.[30] Likewise, since the Islamic Republic's creation, China established itself in Iran, but did so carefully to avoid hurting its relations with the United States and Saudi Arabia. Before the revolution, Iran and China had a limited partnership, but the tensions between China and the Soviet Union facilitated growing relations between Tehran and Beijing.

Following the revolution, Iran faced growing isolation. Tehran needed military, economic, and technological assistance; a void China was well placed to fill.[31] Beijing increasingly positioned itself as an important actor in Iranian security, with joint military drills and arms trades between the two countries. During the Iran–Iraq War, Tehran found itself struggling to protect its territorial integrity having lost the United States as its patron. As the war continued, Iran's military was relying on aging and often obsolete weapons and systems. China stepped in and became Tehran's largest arms supplier by 1986.[32] Economically, too, China became an increasingly important player in Iran. At the end of the war, Iran had to rebuild its infrastructure, which had suffered as a result of months of unrest leading to the revolution, the lack of maintenance during the revolution, and the eight-year long war with its neighbour, so China stepped in. In the 2000s, Western companies left Iran following the tightening of unilateral sanctions by EU states and the United States, as well as six UNSC Resolutions. China remained in Iran and expanded its influence in various sectors. China became Iran's leading foreign investor and trade partner, as well as the biggest consumer of its crude oil.[33] Today, China looks to expand its influence in the Middle East and strengthen Iran as a bulwark against Western influence in the region, while Iran benefits from its ability to turn to China when it cannot rely on other partners.[34]

Chinese presence in Iran does not come without opposition, however. First, Iranian businesses resent Chinese companies' ability to offer cheaper products, which makes them less competitive and hurts them in their own market. Chinese products are so pervasive that even traditional Iranian goods are now often made in and imported from China rather than in the Iranian regions from which they originate. Secondly, Iranian consumers believe Chinese products to be sub-standard. One of the first questions customers ask when purchasing goods is about the origin of the product: 'Was it made in China?'. As a result, they often pick items made in other countries to avoid buying what they see as sub-standard Chinese products. In fact, an important consideration for resuming the nuclear negotiations in 2012 was to break the Chinese and Russian monopoly in Iran and to open up the Iranian market to the West. Indeed, Iranian officials recognised that the products and technology they received from Chinese and Russian companies was inferior to the state of the art products and technology they could receive from the West.[35]

Russia and Iran: A Marriage of Convenience

Like Chinese goods, Iranians also view those items purchased from the Russians as sub-standard. But this is only one facet of the complicated distrust and partnership dominating Russo–Iranian relations. Much like Iran–China relations, Iran–Russia relations have grown since the Islamic Revolution, but continue to be rooted in mistrust. But unlike the more negligeable tensions between Iran and China stemming from the quality of the goods exchanged, delivery timeframes, and prices, Russo-Iranian relations play out against the backdrop of deeply rooted distrust between the two nations. This stems from the two countries' long and complicated history. As we have seen, the Russo–Persian wars of the nineteenth century and the Treaty of Turkmenchay marked the Iranian psyche and are key to understanding the relationship today. To this day,

Iranians consider the Treaty of Turkmenchay a bitter defeat, such that modern failures in foreign policy are often described as a 'modern Turkmenchay'. And as we have seen, Persia lost significant territories to Russia in the two wars and saw the emergence of its modern map. To make matters more complicated, the Russians often interfered in Persia and, later, Iran's internal affairs. On several occasions, they stymied reform movements. As Nasser al-Dinn Shah's First Minister Amir Kabir put it already in the second half of the nineteenth century, he 'wanted a constitution'. But the Russians stood in his way and were his 'great obstacle' to achieving his objective of modernizing his country's governance.[36]

Later, in during the Constitutional Revolution, the Russians would help push back the Constitutionalists in support of absolute monarchy, further strengthening their image as a interfering power among the Iranian populace and elite. Ironically, an American best captured this sentiment during that time. Morgan Schuster briefly served as the head of Persia's Treasury in the 1910s and described what he had witnessed as follows:

> Every utterance and claim has been based on a cynical selfishness that shocks all sense of justice. It is in the pursuit of 'Russian interests' or 'British trade' that innocent people have been slaughtered wholesale. Never a word about the millions of beings whose lives have been jeopardized, whose rights have been trampled under foot and whose property has been confiscated.[37]

In Moscow too, there is distrust of Iran. Historically, the Russian distrust of Persians can be traced back to the Qajar era as well. In 1829, after the Treaty of Turkmenchay sparked anti-Russian sentiment in Persia, crowds gathered at the residence of the Russian envoy, Alexander Sergeyevich Griboyedov, following a religious decree by a cleric against him. Griboyedov purpotedly held captive two Georgian women, and Muslim converts. When a prominent cleric issued a decree calling to defend Muslims against the infidels, the populace gathered at Griboyedov's residence in Tehran and held it under siege before killing Griboyedov and 37 of his companions.[38] In recent years, Russian weariness of Iran increased because Moscow found out about covert Iranian nuclear activities and its undeclared facilities – the enrichment facilities at Natanz and Fordow and the heavy water reactor at Arak – from Western intelligence agencies, rather than from Tehran directly, despite being Iran's key nuclear supplier. As for Iran, it perceived the Russians to be dragging their feet to complete the construction of the Bushehr Nuclear Power Plant and the sale of the S-300 surface-to-air missiles. But despite the Leitmotif of distrust in their dealings, Moscow and Tehran have greatly benefitted from their relationship. During the last decade of the Shah's reign, in the 1970s, the objective of the Iranian–Soviet partnership was to obtain concessions from the United States. Tehran saw the relationship with Moscow as a bargaining chip and a tactical partnership, which it leveraged against its key ally, the United States. But it also used its position as a key US ally, the go-to power in the Middle East, and one of the greatest militaries in the world to set the terms of its relationship with Russia. After the collapse of the Soviet Union, the situation reversed: the main external factor affecting Iranian–Russian relations became the state of Moscow's relationship with Washington.[39]

Today, Iranian–Russian relations are best characterised as a suspicious partnership, rather than a strategic alliance. For both sides, the major motivation behind the relationship is the unipolar world order, in which the United States has asserted its hegemony. The relationship suffers from a number of limitations, which both strengthen and undermine it at once. Limits on the relationship include the lack of any formal common defence and military cooperation in the event of an attack. For example, if the United States and its allies were to attack or otherwise intervene in Iran, Russian assistance would likely amount to little more than calling for mediation. As such, it is difficult to classify the relationship as a formal strategic alliance.[40] But that is precisely what both sides seek. They want to work with one another when their interests align and have the freedom not to do so when they do not.

Iran's relationship with Russia – much like that with China – is influenced by shared security concerns in the region and beyond, bilateral business incentives, political dividends, and potential conflicts of interest. Importantly, limiting the influence of the United States and its allies in the two countries' spheres of influence and backyards remains a mutual security concern. Their partnership also serves as an insurance policy for both parties, by helping to ensure that Iran will not support Islamic agitation in Russia or its neighbouring states, and that Moscow will not get too close to Washington at Tehran's expense. The arms and technology trade between the two is a result of a bilateral business incentive. But the issues surrounding the Caspian Sea and the division of its energy resources are a potential source of discord between the two Caspian powers, as are Russia's intentions in Syria and the potential for improvement in Russia–US relations. What is more, the lack of a substantial trade volume between Iran and Russia remains a point of vulnerability in their relationship. There have been other hurdles too. These include the Russian quasi-monopoly on the Iranian nuclear programme since the late 1980s. This partnership came at a cost for Tehran, which believes that Moscow is not a reliable partner due to its track record of failing to deliver projects on time and its use of energy as a barraging chip. While nuclear relations grew, military ties lessened. In 2000, Iran was the third largest market for Russian arms, but Moscow became disappointed with the profitability of arms sales to Tehran.[41] Moreover, Russian desire to appear responsible on the international stage and to act within the framework of international norms, combined with suspicion of Iranian intentions, limited the two countries' military cooperation and fueled discontent within Iran.

But importantly, Iran and Russia share interests and outlooks on the Middle East region and a vision of themselves in the international order. Ideologically, the two countries oppose perceived American hegemony and unilateralism. Culturally, Russia uses its relationship with Iran to give legitimacy to its claim that it is open to engaging with Islamic nations, despite its repression of its own Muslim minorities. For Tehran, relations with Moscow have served to quiet domestic criticism of Iranian foreign policy and the country's alienation, especially under Ahmadinejad – albeit with limited success. Iranian public opinion is not as inward looking as the government would like it to be and Iranians often criticised their leadership for isolating the country. Following the ups and downs in the Islamic Republic's relations with the West, its leadership has often sought to undermine the country's resultant isolation by highlighting its ties with Russia and China. Similarly, public opinion polls of Russians indicate that despite the cooperation between the two countries, they do not hold a favourable view of Iranians.[42] Russia cannot offer Iran the legitimacy it seeks on the international level, but it has been useful in helping the country bypass the economic pressure and isolation inflicted on it by the West. Before the Joint Plan of Action (JPOA) – or interim deal on the Iranian nuclear programme was concluded in November 2013 – Tehran could not purchase parts for its aging aircraft from the West. For example, the country was also unable to purchase new aircrafts to replace those it was still operating, which dated back to the pre-revolution days. The parts and aircrafts it received from Russia failed a number of times, including a 2009 passenger aircraft crash that left 168 people dead, which displayed just how much Iran's aviation industry had been affected by international sanctions.[43] This strengthened the Iranian perspective that the technology procured from Moscow was inefficient, out-dated, and ultimately dangerous. This was another key incentive for Iran to negotiate with the P5 + 1, as it sought to gain access to companies like the European Airbus and American Boeing, in order to forgo Russian aerospace suppliers.

Despite the mutual distrust between Russia and Iran, the two countries expanded their cooperation in recent years, especially in defence and regional security. From the Middle East to Central and South Asia, Iran and Russia view one another as partners. Their aim is to take regional security issues into their own hands and undermine Western influence. The 2014 Ukraine crisis intensified this trend, as illustrated by the monthly meetings between various levels of governments in Tehran and Moscow. At the highest level, Presidents Putin and Rouhani met four times throughout 2014.[44] This trend accelerated further after Russia, along with its P5 + 1 partners, reached the JCPOA. Since, high-level military and political leaders from Iran and Russia have met several times. Tehran's strategic importance increased for the Russian leadership with the escalation between Russia and the West over Ukraine and the feeling in Moscow that it was losing ground in the Middle East following the Arab Spring. While this feeling was momentarily offset by the victory of Russia's preferred candidate Donald Trump in 2016, the suspicion towards Russia within the US government and the pressure on the Trump administration to be tough on the Russians highlighted that Moscow would have to continue its pragmatic policy of dealing with countries like Iran. At first, the Syrian conflict was another factor bringing both parties closer together. Iran, a key player, feeling alienated from the Western-led efforts to stabilise the country, and Russia, also keen to preserve the status quo with the Assad regime, could join forces. As the conflict progressed however, Syria too became a point of contention in the Russia–Iran relationship. Points of conflict and disagreement emerged, as Moscow and Tehran's goals for and means attributed to helping Damascus diverged. In addition, Iran became increasingly frustrated with its diminishing role and importance in the partnership as the Syrian conflict progressed. But when in Spring 2018, France, the United Kingdom, and the United States hit targets within Syria following new allegations of chemical attacks by the Assad regime, Iran and Russia shifted their focus to their common objectives once again. The Russians however, remained pragmatic. And in May 2018, welcomed Benjamin

Netanyahu, the Israeli leader, to discuss the war in Syria, right before Israel targeted a number of Iranian positions in the country.

Iran, China, and Russia are unified by their resentment of the United States as the dominant global power and their desire for a multipolar system. In the words of Iranian Defence Minister Hossein Dehghan, 'Iran and Russia are able to confront the expansionist intervention and greed of the United States through cooperation, synergy and activating strategic potential capacities ... As two neighbours, Iran and Russia have common viewpoints towards political, regional and global issues.'[45] Sino-Iranian relations also fit this model. All three are looking to leverage the evolving relationship between them to further their own ambitions.[46] And importantly, today, Iran leverages this common objective and their aligned interests to offset Western pressure and ensure it can never find itself in a position to be easily isolated again. This is a key concern for Iranian decision-makers, who saw their country cornered during the Iran–Iraq War and the nuclear episode. While some in Tehran would prefer to establish strategic and all-encompassing ties with other countries, including working with Russia and China on a more ad hoc basis, also allows Iran to minimise foreign influence on its soil and domestic affairs, another key concern for many within the revolutionary elite in Tehran.

As such, China and Russia have remained present in Iran, despite many Iranians preferring to align themselves with the West politically and to do business with Europe and the United States. Both China and Russia are firmly established in Iran, with a clear advantage over other international firms because of their continued experience and knowledge of the Iranian market and political system, especially on defence issues.[47] Iran acquires its missile and nuclear technology from both countries. Likewise, Tehran continues to depend on Moscow and Beijing as its 'allies' in the UN Security Council. Iran also utilises its political, strategic, and military relations with Russia and China to project power, while increasing its actual power too. This is why Tehran has been working on joint military drills and war games with the two powers in the Caspian basin and Persian Gulf. They are a reminder to other regional players and the United States that Iran has a number of tools at its disposal, which it can use, if needed.

Iranian diplomats and businesses have a wide and growing portfolio. Emerging diplomats have carried the tradition of trying to know and understand the West. But Russia has been at the forefront of Iranian diplomatic and political efforts for centuries. Despite Iran–China relations dating back centuries, the two countries have not had the same level of interaction as Iran and the West or Russia, which Tehran has tried to remedy more recently. Today, young Iranians wishing to join the ranks of their diplomatic corps no longer stick to the traditional languages studied by their predecessors. Instead, in addition to English, French, German, and Russian, just to name a few, Chinese has also become a sought-after skill.[48] Yet, Iran's forte remains the West: The Rouhani government includes the largest number of US-educated ministers in any foreign country.[49] Most Iranian diplomats speak English and many have lived and studied in the United States or Europe. And as Western diplomats often like to sarcastically point out, even the most hardline Iranian diplomats, like Ahmadinejad's chief nuclear negotiator, Saeed Jalili, like to showcase their mastery of Western civilisation and culture by quoting the likes of Thomas Aquinas and referring to Georg Wilhelm Friedrich Hegel.[50] Despite this, Iranian officials and diplomats in training continue to express interest in Russia, albeit to a lesser degree than the West. Foreign affairs students and young diplomats are increasingly familiarising themselves with East and South-East Asia, particularly China. But their efforts have yet to match those to understand and engage the West, and to a lesser extent, Russia.

But in the West, many continue to assess and analyse Iranian views and policies based on outdated notions going back to the very early days of the Islamic Revolution.[51] As we will see throughout this book, the Islamic Republic is no longer the ideological revolutionary regime it once was. It evolved and aged along with some of its founding members, becoming more pragmatic, while preserving some aspects of the revolutionary identity of its beginnings. Today, the Islamic Republic is no longer looking to overthrow its neighbours' rulers and to foment revolution in other parts of the Muslim world. This is particularly the case as Iran learned the hard way that fragile and failed states in the region would pose as much of a threat to it as strong states. Instead, Iran is as concerned about a failed state in Iraq as it once was of a strong Baghdad. Nevertheless, the country is also focused on remaining a force to be reckoned with in its backyard, and on diminishing US presence there. In that sense, Iran has followed in the footsteps of two other revolutionary states: China and Russia. Tehran is not alone in viewing the existing Western order with disdain. Russia and China too, harbour alternative visions of the world order. Their visions are shaped by their experiences as modern nation-states, and their interactions with the Western world once they established governments with ideologies that the Western liberal order did not ascribe to.

As the liberal order that spread from the West to the bulk of the world at the end of the Cold War faces a range of challenges, the three countries discussed present an alternative view of the world order in the early twenty-first century. Bilateral cooperation among the three is nevertheless constrained by divergent levels of engagement with the West, political and economic incompatibilities, and competing approaches to security in regions along their respective frontiers. The United States and its allies have been the main guarantors of the post-Cold War status quo. Their ability to ensure the survival and flourishing of an order that respects individual rights, freedom of conscience, non-aggression, the sovereign equality of states, and international law depends in many ways on preventing alternative visions of the world from gaining legitimacy. An alternative vision of the world needs powerful champions to succeed. Despite their differences, the three countries are attempting to advance such an alternative, albeit at diverging levels and efficiency. While Russia and China have a greater presence on the international stage and more levers to work with, Iran by virtue of its size and capability is more of a regional power. If all three countries manage to weather the changes in the international system and respective domestic scepticism to work together closely, they will have considerable impact on the world order as we know it. Understanding their visions of the existing international system, along with the drivers of and obstacles to their cooperation is critical for Western scholars and policymakers committed to adapting existing institutions to meet contemporary challenges. It is also important to understand how Tehran leverages its relationship with Russia and China to circumvent international isolation. This will have a significant impact on policy-making on Iran in a post-JCPOA world, where the country is slowly re-integrating the international order but continues many of its nefarious activities, especially in the Middle East. Moreover, future non-compliant states can and are likely to model their efforts to stymie political pressure and economic sanctions imposed by the West and international community after Iran's and to create a similar bulwark against isolation through cooperation with Russia and China.

Foreign Policy Drivers

Challenging the International Order

Iran, Russia, and China are all driven to varying degrees by their shared objective of challenging what they view as the Western-led international order. Because it lacks the capabilities possessed by China and Russia – two nuclear-armed states with a permanent seat at the UN Security Council – Iran focused its efforts on what it views as its backyard: the Middle East and South and Central Asia. It has, however, consistently questioned international law and its supporting institutions, arguing that they serve the West at the expense of the rest of the world and describing their output as biased. Several key ventures and events are examples of how all three countries have challenged the existing Western-led international order.

First, the three countries have supported and created platforms to compete with and challenge existing international institutions. They have established alternative fora to host dialogue between them, while China has taken the lead on the creation of parallel institutions, supported by Russia. Iran lacks the influence to create or meaningfully support such efforts, but has expressed interest in joining them. These alternative platforms for dialogue are also used to restrain other countries' abilities to operate in Russia, China, and Iran's spheres of influence. For example, Russia and Iran share the goal of pushing the United States and its allies out of the Caspian region, and assert themselves as the key players there. To do so, they began holding the yearly Caspian Summit in 2002. While the summit has so far failed to resolve some of the outstanding issues between the five littoral states of the Caspian (Russia, Kazakhstan, Iran, Azerbaijan, and Turkmenistan) – including delineating offshore waters or the seabed – it has succeeded in bringing these states closer together on a number of other issues. These include boosting trade and infrastructure investments[52] and increasing defence ties.[53] Tehran however, plays a secondary role in the more ambitious international initiatives championed by Beijing and Moscow, but it aspires to have a seat at the table there too. These initiatives include the SCO,[54] created by the two powers in 2001. The body comprises eight countries whose objective is to use the platform for cooperation on military and security, economic, and cultural affairs. Iran has observer status, but it applied for full membership in 2008. While this initial application stalled because of the nuclear crisis, since, Iran applied for full membership again, with China's backing.[55]

Secondly, Iran challenges the international order generally, and the United States' leadership specifically on its own. For example, it rejected the United Nations' resolutions during the Iran–Iraq War, noting that they failed to condemn the Iraqi aggression and use of chemical weapons.[56] Tehran sees Beijing and Moscow's willingness and ability to similarly challenge and undermine US leadership and the international system as an opportunity. While by itself Iran's capabilities are limited, through its cooperation and coordination with Russia and China, it can draw on the two powers' political capital to advance its ambitions and agenda more effectively. Challenging the current world order is not the only shared foreign policy driver between the three countries.

Nationalism and Foreign Policy

Nationalism became a key driver of foreign policy and shapes national security and interests in all three countries. At times, identity-based considerations trump other more practical ones. As a result, observers often perceive the three countries as more ideological than pragmatic.[57] But not surprisingly, nationalism serves as a galvanising force and an important point of tension in the domestic politics of each state, though its role should not be overstated. Nationalism in all three countries is a product of and a driver of their dynamics with the outside world. It is said to be on the rise in all three countries.[58]

In Iran, nationalism was a core tenet of the Shah's vision for the country and its place in the world. The revolutionaries were critical of the Shah's nationalist discourse and policies, some due to their leftist leanings, and others because they believed in a transnational Islamic community. Once the Islamic Republic took power, it initially downplayed the role of nationalism and national identity in its politics and foreign policy, instead highlighting that of religion as the basis for its identity.[59] But with the Iran–Iraq War, the revolutionary establishment quickly recognised the limits of religion as a galvanising factor.[60] After all, Iran houses multiple faiths and minorities, including Sunnis, Baha'is, Zoroastrians, Christians, and Jews. And while religion did not move many Iranians to put their lives on the line, patriotism did. As a result, by the end of the war, nationalism became a vehicle for domestic and foreign policy in Iran again.

No contemporary event illustrates the importance of nationalism in Iranian national security policy better than the nuclear talks. A core driver behind Iran's nuclear decision-making lies in the pursuit of independence and self-sufficiency, concepts as critical to the revolutionary ideology as they are to Iranian nationalism. The programme became a major point of contention between Tehran and the international community in 2002, when a dissident group exposed two nuclear facilities – the Arak heavy water reactor and the Natanz enrichment complex – that had not yet been declared to the International Atomic Energy Agency (IAEA).[61] Following this, the EU3 began talks with Iran to curb its nuclear activities. But a key sticking point emerged, and impeded the European powers' ability to move towards a settlement: Zero enrichment. Iran refused to give up what it interpreted as its 'inalienable right to enrich' under the NPT[62] – a right it associated with sovereignty and nationalism.[63] The West disagreed with this interpretation, instead highlighting Iranian noncompliance due to its failure to declare its facilities in a 'timely manner' to the IAEA, as per its commitments under international law.[64]

The Islamic Republic began to politicise enrichment as an issue of nationalism and national pride during the 2003–05 round of talks. At the time, as the Europeans were pushing back on Iranian enrichment, Tehran started to build an intricate narrative justifying its nuclear ambitions and enrichment, and garnering support for them.[65] Iran tied the issue of enrichment to national sovereignty and the powers' insistence on stopping enrichment on Iranian soil as yet another example of the West trying to stymie the nation's progress.[66] Likewise, it suggested that enrichment was a component of Iranian scientific and technological progress, and just the latest manifestation of a great history of scientific endeavours.[67] The popular support for domestic enrichment helped strengthen the Iranian position that zero enrichment was simply out of the question.

When the talks resumed, seven years later, they progressed once the P5 + 1 negotiators conceded that zero enrichment was not an attainable goal.[68] This implicit recognition of the link between enrichment and Iranian nationalism changed the framing of the nuclear issue. The main objective of the subsequent talks became to limit Iranian enrichment, rather than stop it altogether. Having managed to maintain its key redline, Iran accepted to limit its enrichment capacity, although at times, it prioritised preserving symbolic elements of it, such as centrifuges operating without enriching uranium in the Fordow facility, over actual enrichment capacity.[69] This was designed to help the negotiators sell the deal at home, given the politicised nature of and the visibility of the enrichment issue and its connection to nationalism.

In China and Russia, key issues also serve to highlight the role of nationalism in the national psyche. This brings the two states closer to Tehran, which can find a sympathetic ear in those capitals as it faces continued pressure from the West. China and Russia too, feel the West challenges their national rights.

In China, no other foreign policy issue is as unifying for the population as Taiwan. While the government built a certain narrative and propaganda around what it calls the 'Taiwanese question', and used it to rally the population around the flag, today the issue has taken on a life of its own. In other words, just as enrichment has become an important national subject in Iran, with buy-in from the regime's base and the broader population – including parts of the opposition to the Islamic Republic,[70] Taiwan also transcends political leanings in China.[71] The official narrative surrounding the Taiwan issue is based on the 'nationalist principle' that the island has been part of China 'since ancient times'.[72] The narrative of national humiliation also plays a powerful role in nationalist sentiment over Taiwan, and over the South China Sea more generally. The sense of injury from its

'100 years of humiliation' makes US meddling in cross-strait affairs that much more of a flashpoint – in China's view, it is an example of a Western power seeking to subjugate it once again and deny Chinese access to its rightful territory.

Beyond the issue of Taiwan and more broadly, Chinese nationalism really began to enter rural China's psyche in the 1930s.[73] Mao Zedong leveraged it to build a strong state. He did so by 'shifting loyalties away from peripheral and parochial identities and towards the central organs of a new state. In other words, the successful harnessing of state power would depend on completing a programme of nation-building.'[74] Nevertheless, more recent scholarship on China has challenged the conventional wisdom that Chinese nationalism is on the rise, particularly as it pertains to the country's youths.[75]

In Russia, since the end of the Cold War, nationalism has replaced Communist ideology as a driver of foreign policy and policy towards the West. In fact, 'ethnic nationalism' has been on the rise in Russia since the collapse of the Soviet Union and the end of the Cold War.[76] But, because it poses a threat to Russian unity given the country's diversity, nationalism in Russia is framed by the state as what Emil Pain calls, 'imperial nationalism', which allows it to portray the country as a great state, representing 'a Europe different from the one supposedly dominated by American-led liberalism.'[77] And nowhere is this clearer than the intervention in Crimea, which epitomises Putin's view of Russian nationalism. As it is framed in Russia, Moscow's intervention in Crimea is 'a protection of "ours" – and "ours" are Russian, no matter where they live.'[78] In other words, a key driver behind Russian actions in Crimea lies in the notions of co-ethnicity that, Russia argues, bring together its own population and the ethnic Russians in Crimea.[79] And as we will see later, this nationalism is not separate from anti-Western sentiments growing in the country. But this does not mean that Russians look to undertake an expansionist agenda, instead, many oppose further expansionism by their country.[80] Moscow, and Putin himself, do not have an interest in recreating the Soviet Union – a Soviet Union 2.0,[81] as some have called it. This would generate criticism by ethnic nationalists, while adding to the state's burden to provide for and secure new territories as it already struggles with parts of its territory today.[82]

Nationalism is an important opposition and galvanising force in Iran, as it is in Russian and Chinese politics and, as a result, serves as an important driver of foreign policy. It is tied to inherently political ideas, such as sovereignty and territorial integrity, as it is to history, culture, and language.[83] It is also tied to these countries' view that because of their long and rich histories, they are, and must remain, forces to be reckoned with. As a result, prestige as an element of nationalism plays a key role in shaping the three countries' views of themselves and their places in the world. Nevertheless, it is fundamental to understand the limits of nationalism as a driver of foreign policy and not to overstate its role in shaping Iranian, Chinese, and Russian thinking and worldviews.[84]

Forces to be Reckoned With: The Quest for Prestige

Iran, Russia, and China see themselves as consequential powers. They see their rich histories as part of their national identities and prestige, and believe that they must project power to maintain this prestige. As a result, they strive to be taken seriously and treated with dignity, as Iranian officials often put it.[85] For example, some proponents of the nuclear talks in Iran saw their country's nuclear file as what afforded Tehran a seat at the table to negotiate with the world powers. According to their worldview, thanks to its nuclear programme, Iran was deemed important enough for the six world powers to devote critical resources, time, and their highest levels of government to the task.[86] The negotiating team did not share this view and did not see the talks as a source of pride, but rather as a national security and interest issue to settle.[87] In other words, merely sitting at the table across the P5 + 1 was not an achievement but they saw the deal they were negotiating as one – as they strived to uphold the country's national redlines and preserve its sovereignty and dignity.[88] Opponents of the deal, for their part, saw the agreement as undermining national prestige: Why should Iran bow to the powers and limit its nuclear activities? After all, the country had a revolution precisely to stop foreign powers from interfering in its affairs. They criticised specific provisions within the deal – such as the procurement channel created by the JCPOA – as undermining the country's sovereignty.[89]

China and Russia also share Iran's belief that they must be taken seriously and treated with dignity. They assert themselves as forces to be reckoned with in their respective geographical backyard and spheres of influence, and beyond, as in the case of Russia and the defence of its interests in the Middle East. For example, while the West views Chinese actions in the South China Sea as 'aggressive', the Chinese view them as defensive: Beijing is merely asserting its sovereignty on its 'rightful' territory. It further views them in the context of 'national humiliation': Today's China is a powerhouse and will not bow down as it did a century ago.[90] The same can be said of Russia's intervention in Crimea, partly the result of Putin's inability to accept his country's loss of prestige.[91] The notion of prestige plays an important role in shaping another driver of foreign policy in the three countries: Domestic politics.

Domestic Politics and Bargaining Games

Despite typically being viewed as a monolith, lacking serious domestic politics and internal debate,[92] Iranian domestic politics play an important role in the country's foreign policies, as they do in Russia and China. In fact, the policy outputs of each country are a direct result of their politicking, internal bargaining, and bureaucratic push-pull dynamics. Often, a course of action is chosen over another due to domestic pressure. Each country has several important power centres, which shape the domestic foreign policy discourse, process, and policy outcomes.

In Iran, the main power centres lie in the office of the Supreme Leader, the IRGC,[93] the government, and the opposition bloc. While the Supreme Leader is the final arbiter, he is not the only decision-maker in Iran.[94] And Iranian foreign policy decision-making is not a top-down exercise by the Supreme Leader as Western pundits often assert.[95] Rather politics are fluid and policy result from bargaining and debate. Domestic politics largely shaped the nuclear talks and resulting agreement. When hardliners put too much pressure on the negotiators, Khamenei stepped in to shield the negotiators and allow the talks to continue. Likewise, IRGC commanders also helped manage expectations and steer critics in the way warranted by their commander in chief.[96] As a result, Rouhani and the negotiating team had to explain themselves in media outlets and in parliament. Likewise, as the Syrian conflict became increasingly unpopular in Iran, Khamenei and his advisers had to focus greater efforts on selling Iranian presence there to maintain domestic support.[97] They framed Tehran's involvement in Syria as part of their counterterrorism strategy, noting that if they did not fight ISIS there, they would have to fight it on the streets of Tehran and other Iranian cities.[98] It is clear that domestic politics determine the nature and scope of Tehran's policy output and involvement in international affairs.

Yet, in Western analysis of Iran, the role of domestic politics in the country is often underplayed, while that of ideology is overstated.[99] To be sure, with the 1979 revolution, ideology emerged as a driver shaping Tehran's foreign policy and narrative. But in practical terms, the Islamic Republic has not focused as much on exporting the revolution since its early days and has, in fact, privileged interests and pragmatism over ideology in most areas.[100] For example, the country negotiated and worked with America where the two countries' interests overlapped, particularly on the nuclear issue, in Afghanistan, and Iraq, even as hardliners chanted 'death to America'.[101] In its neighbourhood too, Iran has often pursued pragmatic policies despite an ideological narrative. In the South Caucasus for example, Tehran sees Yerevan as its top partner, even as Christian Armenia is in a frozen conflict with Shia Azerbaijan.[102] Only in a few issues has Tehran remained mostly ideological, in particular as it pertains to Israel. Nevertheless, the Islamic Republic's ideology continues to shape its rhetoric, which in turn affects its foreign policy.

In Russia, the key power centres are the Kremlin and Russia's oligarchs — or businessmen who made their wealth after the collapse of the Soviet Union. Both have gained considerably more power in the Putin era. In China, foreign policy is the output of a trinity of power centres: the Chinese Communist Party, government, and military.[103] But while the CCP has a 'high concentration of political power', specific individuals have a tighter grip on power. Foreign policy and military affairs are the most 'sensitive area, demanding an even concentration of decision-making power.'[104] This means that the leader and his immediate circle of just one or two individuals - including allies such as the recently named Vice President Wang Qishan and top economic advisor Liu He, among others - have the final say on foreign policy decisions that the Politburo or Standing Committee puts forth.[105]

Regional Superiority and Defence

Ultimately, while each country's policies have global implications, each sees its primary objective as being its own region's hegemon, asserting itself and projecting power in that area. This can be achieved either individually, or by joining forces to project power and undermine Western presence. Iran sees Iraq, Syria, and Afghanistan as key areas of influence and believes it has the upper hand in the Persian Gulf. It also believes it is a major force to be reckoned with in the Middle East. Iran and Russia have joined forces to assert themselves as an axis in the Caspian region, conducting joint drills and military exercises in the Caspian,

Sea while banning foreign navies from the area.[106] For its part, Russia sees Eastern Europe and the former Soviet Union as its own sphere of influence, and views itself as the natural hegemon there. Likewise, China sees itself as the rightful hegemon in Asia, and believes it should be the centre of the Asian order and the dominant force in the South China Sea.

Joint military cooperation between Iran and Russia, on the one hand, and Iran and China, on the other, serves not only to project power and to counter Western and NATO presence in their backyards, but also serves to boost defences, which is a central goal for all three states. In particular, Iran's defence has been largely undercut since 1979, when it lost both its powerful ally and defence system and weapons provider, the United States. Since then, the country's defence establishment has undergone major changes, including by the creation of redundant intelligence and military institutions, such as the IRGC, to help break the monopoly on security in the country. Decades of sanctions have impeded the country's ability to procure weapons and other equipment,[107] and pushed Iran to seek greater self-sufficiency in matters of defence. But this has come at a cost, as its conventional forces have suffered. As a result, in recent years, Iran has conducted a number of military drills to visibly boost its defence ties, at times these drills have included participation from Kazakhstan and Oman, in addition to Russia and China.

In fact, while Iran's Gulf Arab neighbours and the West see its activities in the region as 'expansionist',[108] Tehran sees much of it through the lens of defence and security. In Iraq, Iran wants to stabilise a country with which it shares a porous border, ethnic and religious, and economic interests,[109] and one that was ruled by an adversarial actor for decades, leading to an eight-year devastating war. Iran's objective is to balance between wanting to preserve Iraqi unity and territorial integrity, by helping the central government and its armed forces fill the power vacuum in the country, while at the same time preserving a degree of influence there and making sure it is not strong enough to challenge it again. In neighbouring Syria, Iran also has defence objectives, along with broader national and regime interest ones. Tehran sees its presence in Syria as a critical component of its 'campfire strategy',[110] an important part of its counterterrorism toolkit. It believes that by fighting ISIS there, it will avoid having to fight its operatives on its own streets.[111]

Russia and China, too, see defence as a key driver of their foreign policy. Both countries, like Iran, hold ceremonies where they display their weapon systems and troops to reassure their domestic constituency and deter their adversaries. And while Russia suffers from conventional inferiority vis-à-vis the United States,[112] it maintains the world's largest stockpile of nuclear weapons along with America.[113] Russia and China have also conducted military drills with one another, including in the South China Sea.[114] Their aim is to send a message and to deny the US power projection in what they consider to be their respective backyards.

Economic Considerations

The economy is another key consideration for all three countries. For the Islamic Republic, this began with the end of the Iran–Iraq War where reconstruction became a major driver of their outreach to potential partners in and outside their immediate region. Following successive waves of international sanctions, Iran's growing isolation and subsequent inability to feed its economy meant that countries like China and Russia became increasingly important to it. For China, the economy is the single most important driver of foreign policy. Beijing aims to challenge US economic might and build economic power, which will grant it significant influence. The country continues to grow above 6 per cent, albeit at a slowing rate, and continues to expand both the number of countries it trades with and the volumes of trade per country.[115] As China becomes an increasingly important trade partner for countries in the world, it also expands its ability to influence others. As a result, some US friends and allies will undoubtedly increasingly find themselves in a difficult position where they will not be able to steadfastly support American policies and presence, especially if this conflicts with their main trading partner: China. For example, in Australia, a stout US ally in a region traditionally outside Chinese influence, some voices increasingly call for accommodating China. For them, Beijing's position as their country's number one trading partner makes Sino-Australian trade ties critical to its economic well-being.[116]

Beijing and Moscow were partly driven by economic interests when they took part in the nuclear negotiations with Iran. Indeed, both understood that, while they had better access to the Iranian market than others, international sanctions and Iran's pariah status made it difficult to exploit the promising market fully.

Sanctions: A Catalyst

Along with more general economic interests, the multi-layered sanctions regime on Iran was a fundamental driver of its foreign policy for more than a decade, and still is today. It was also a key catalyst for its relations with Russia and China. After the revolution, Iran's isolation was only further entrenched by the Iran–Iraq War and Western support for Saddam Hussein, as well as developments in Iran's nuclear programme, which prompted an ever-increasing spiral of economic measures against it. As one Iran analyst put it,

> Not the product of a single policy, the sanctions regime has mutated over three decades, been imposed by a variety of actors and aimed at a wide range of objectives. The end result is an impressive set of unilateral and multilateral punitive steps targeting virtually every important sector of Iran's economy, in principle tethered to multiple policy objectives (nonproliferation; anti-terrorism; human rights) yet, in the main, aimed at confronting the Islamic Republic with a straightforward choice: either comply with international

demands on the nuclear file, or suffer the harsh economic consequences.[117]

In 2006, unable to verify Iranian compliance with its international nuclear obligations, the IAEA referred Iran to the UN Security Council, leading to the adoption of resolution 1737 in December 2006; the first of the UN-led international sanctions against Iran.[118] But prior to this international effort, the United States had already begun to isolate Iran for a range of other outstanding issues, beginning with the hostage crisis and the Iran–Iraq War.[119] In 1984, America prohibited weapons sales and all US assistance to Iran, under the Iran Sanctions Act (ISA) and designated Iran a state sponsor of terror, which deprived it of any financial defence assistance, in the middle of its war effort.[120] Washington later extended the ISA after the war to prevent Tehran from rebuilding its conventional military capability.[121] President Bill Clinton's administration significantly ramped up sanctions against the Islamic Republic in response to its sponsorship of violent non-state actors in the region and efforts to expand its nuclear programme.[122] By doing so, it targeted investments in the Iranian oil and gas sector in particular and barred US firms from trading with and investing in Iran.[123] In August 1996, the US administration imposed extraterritorial sanctions for the first time, discouraging firms from third-party countries to invest in the Iranian energy sector, to Europe's great frustration.[124] With the Iran Sanctions, Account-ability and Divestment Act (CISADA) in 2010, President Obama further expanded sanctions, and banned petroleum sales to Iran.[125] He also further isolated the Iranian financial sector by cutting foreign financial organisations doing business with Iran from the US market.[126] Two years later, the Iran Freedom and Counter-Proliferation Act designated Iran's entire energy and shipping industries as a proliferation concern. It targeted the provision of insurance to Iran, the country's ability to pay for transactions in gold, and the state-run media.[127]

The United States was not the only country to impose extensive unilateral sanctions on Iran. Others, such as Australia, Canada, and Japan also followed suit.[128] Most notably, after the failure of the negotiations with the three European powers, the EU also turned to sanctions to punish Iran and to coerce it to return to the table. The EU's measures were two-pronged: First, they were modelled after UN sanctions, which were implemented following EU legislation that implemented UN resolutions. Second, EU measures mirrored more extensive US sanctions, beginning with a 2007 EU Council decision.[129] EU unilateral measures imposed restrictions on trade with Iran, in the financial sector, and in transportation.[130] But the EU generally agreed to and implemented its sanctions with a slight lag. Indeed, these sanctions were multi-layered and complicated, and the product of extensive consensus building among the member states.[131] Perhaps the most significant of the EU measures was the January 2012 ban on imports of oil from Iran, implemented in the summer of 2012, because of the importance of oil to the Iranian economy.[132]

In Iran, decades of stringent sanctions and eight years of economic mismanagement under Ahmadinejad, caused record high inflation, unemployment, and a generally poor economic state.[133] The international isolation led Iran to turn to Russia and China to offset the effect of sanctions as much as it could. The deepening of Iran's ties with its eastern partners coincided with the ratcheting up of sanctions on Russia's government after its annexation of Crimea by the United States, the EU, and others, giving Moscow a renewed desire to work with Tehran. Under US Executive Order 13660, America authorised sanctions on those responsible for violating the sovereignty and territorial integrity of Ukraine, including travel restrictions and the seizing of assets.[134] These measures were subsequently expanded as the crisis continued. The EU, for its part, also agreed to extensive sanctions against Moscow and Russian nationals involved in the annexation in March 2014, which it has since renewed.[135] In 2017, despite

President Trump's efforts to ease tensions with Russia, the US Congress approved a series of sanctions following Russia's efforts to meddle in the country's presidential elections in 2016.[136] After the initial 2014 measures against it for its annexation of Crimea, Russia too looked for partners to offset their effect.

Meanwhile, after Rouhani's election in 2013, improving the state of the economy became a first order priority. This partly explained Iran's return to the negotiating table to close its nuclear file once and for all. But after the JCPOA, as the promised economic recovery was slow to materialise, the public and ruling elite became more suspicious of the JCPOA's benefits. This was exacerbated by the high expectations promoted by the Rouhani administration, which sought to effectively sell the deal both before and after it was sealed. This culminated in mounting discontent, which broke out at the end of 2017 with a wave of protests in over 80 cities in Iran over the state of the economy. As a result, much-needed economic development is likely to over-shadow other foreign policy drivers in the foreseeable future.

As established, Iran's desire to maintain, if not expand, its ties with Russia and China is the result of the Islamic Republic's systemic suspicion of the West coupled with the slow sanctions relief, that did not result in the touted economic gains. But it was also the result of Tehran's alternative vision for the existing US-led world order. Moscow and Beijing also share Tehran's desire to re-shape the world order, with their own visions in mind. While Moscow and Beijing have greater ambitions and means at their disposal, Iran is more regionally focused. Nevertheless, the desire to counter a US-led order has brought Iran closer to Russia and China on multiple fronts, including political, economic and military.

Conclusion

Iran, China, and Russia are often seen as revisionist powers in the West. Yet, closer examination of their intentions and capabilities show them under a different light. To be sure, all three countries seek to undermine and minimise US and Western influence at their borders and in their neighbourhoods. They all want to assert themselves and project power in their respective backyards, which they perceive as their rightful spheres of influence. As a result, all three harbour regional ambitions, more so than global ones. Nevertheless, while both China and Russia have the capabilities to disrupt the international order, Iran does not. Iran is limited by its capabilities and as a result, its intentions match those capabilities. In contrast, Russia has the most ambitious revisionist agenda, as it has shown time and again that it will not hesitate to disrupt the world order by violating international laws and norms. For its part, China has considerable resources thanks to its large economy. But while Beijing has championed alternative institutions to those created by the West in the aftermath of World War II, it has chosen to leverage its considerable influence in both the existing and alternative world orders. As we will see throughout this book, the three countries' main drivers of foreign policy and the catalyst for their relationship are not revisionism, but political, economic, and military considerations. Having examined the contours of Iran's worldview and where Russia and China fit into it, in the following chapters, we will discuss how Iran's worldview and shared beliefs and interests with Russia and China shape its political, economic, and defence relations with them.

CHAPTER 2

IRANIAN POLITICAL RELATIONS WITH THE TWO POWERS

Previously, we saw how Iran sees itself and the international system and argued that Russia and China fit in this worldview by serving as a bulwark against the West. We outlined the origins of Iran's relations with the two giants, as well as their shared beliefs and interests. In this chapter, we will build on this discussion to assess Iran's contemporary political relations with the two powers.

The Shah and the Communists

Under Reza Shah, Iran began a programme of comprehensive reforms intended to make the country more modern and self-reliant. After his forced abdication, his son and successor continued the programme. Interestingly, Reza Shah relied on the United States and Germany to make Iran less reliant on other foreign powers, namely the British and the Russians, both heavily involved in Persia for decades. Under Mohammad Reza Shah, Iran formed a close partnership with America. And as the Cold War progressed, the Shah, who also viewed Communism as the greatest threat to the state, became closer to and relied more on the United States. With America's help, Iran developed nuclear power and built a military powerhouse.[1] Importantly, the Shah believed that his government was safe from domestic and foreign threats at a time of turbulence, because he had the backing of one of two major powers. As a result, Iran neglected relations with countries like China and Russia.

Imperial Iran and Soviet Russia

In the early days of the Pahlavi dynasty under Reza Shah, Russia continued to play a multi-faceted role in Iran, as it had for decades. But as time went by and the Shah's suspicion of Communism grew, Tehran began to balance Moscow's presence in the country against continued alliance and collaboration with Washington. However, the Shah, like his father, wanted to make his country more self-reliant, especially towards the end of his reign. He was also cognisant of the fact that all his eggs were in the US basket, and when America dragged its feet in its defence relations with Iran, the Shah began to contemplate détente with the Soviet Union.[2] As such, Iran began to manoeuvre between its ally, the United States and Soviet Russia, with whom it wanted to build ties and, this, despite Soviet ideological leanings.

Iran's efforts to engage its northern neighbour prompted a visit to the Soviet Union by the Shah in the summer of 1956. The overthrow of the Iraqi monarchy in 1958, made the Shah uneasy. He therefore continued dialogue with the Soviets, with a view to establishing a non-aggression pact, which would allow Iran to reduce its reliance on America. But the negotiations collapsed in 1959 under Western pressure, prompting an aggressive Soviet propaganda campaign against the Shah's government, which Moscow accused of trying to dupe the Soviets into a pact that the Shah would then leverage to gain greater benefits from his relationship with the United States.[3] The collapse of the talks also ended Soviet leader Nikita Khrushchev's willingness to deal with the Iranians, unless they took a step back from their alliance with America and showed the Soviet Union some goodwill.[4]

These developments unfolded against the backdrop of US–Soviet tensions in the early 1960s. In May 1960, the Russians shot down a US U-2 plane conducting reconnaissance flights over their southern borders.[5] The incident prompted Khrushchev to request a pledge from Iran to deny US and British access to its airspace for intelligence gathering purposes. In September, the Shah reassured the Russians that Iran would not grant foreign countries the right to set up military bases, which could be used to attack Soviet territories.[6] This served as the basis for further dialogue with the Soviet leadership, including over possible economic and technical cooperation, especially in infrastructure development, effectively setting the scene for further collaboration in the future.

In 1966, the Shah announced the establishment of a 'national independent foreign policy',[7] paving the way for further engagement of Soviet Russia. But the two neighbours were still unable to cooperate extensively until Iran and the Soviet Union established official diplomatic relations in August 1971, opening the door to further dialogue and cooperation, which led to a long list of joint economic and technical cooperation projects until the revolution in Iran.[8]

Imperial Iran and Communist China

The Shah's opinion of China followed the US line of hostility towards the Communist government there. When Tehran joined the 1955 anti-Communist Baghdad Pact, it established ties with Taipei, earning it a rebuke from Beijing.[9] Despite this, the Shah encouraged China's admission to the UN and authorised trade between the two countries in 1966.[10] The Shah's rush to establish ties with China was partly the result of the Soviet Union's efforts to build ties to other regional powers, particularly India and Iraq in the 1960s. The Shah did not want Iran to be left behind.

But China began to encroach on what the Shah saw as his own backyard, when it undertook efforts to expand its foothold in the Persian Gulf following the British retreat in 1968. These efforts collided with Iran's objective of keeping the Persian Gulf area free of foreign intervention, allowing Iran to gain what it viewed as its rightful hegemonic place in the region. Nevertheless, in the early 1970s, Peking invited the Shah's sister to visit the country.[11] And once US President Nixon visited China in July 1971, it became possible for the two countries to establish diplomatic ties.[12] Although Iran and China initiated diplomatic ties in August that year, it was hardly smooth sailing after that. Indeed, Tehran still had to balance any relationship with Peking with its interest in preserving and strengthening its alliance with Washington.

Nevertheless, in the last decade of the Shah's rule, the number of high-profile exchanges increased steadily. The Shah looked to China to appease a growing Communist opposition in his country. In order to appeal to that faction and to assert his authority domestically and on the world stage by receiving the endorsement of a powerful world leader, the Shah worked to foster increasing exchanges between their two countries. This engagement included a September 1972 delegation visit by Empress Farah Pahlavi and Premier Amir Abbas Hoveyda to China, followed by a June 1973 trip by the Chinese minister of foreign affairs, Ji Peng-fei and, later in 1975, Deputy Premier Li Xian-nin to Iran.[13] During these visits, officials discussed areas of convergence in their foreign policy, including on security in the Persian Gulf area and the Indian Ocean.[14] When Premier Zhou Enlai and Chairman Mao Zedong died in 1976, a delegation of Chinese officials was dispatched to Iran to reassure the Shah's government of the continuity in China's foreign policy. The foreign visits continued despite the domestic upheavals that were shaping Iran's political landscape. The Chinese visited Iran on the eve of the Islamic Revolution, when the Shah invited the Chairman of the Communist Party of China, Hua Guofeng, to Tehran in August 1978.[15] This visit was the first by a

Chinese leader to a non-Communist country.[16] It also marked one of the last visits of a world leader to the Imperial State of Iran before the Islamic Republic replaced it. The trip led to the signing of a cultural agreement in August 1978. By the time the revolutionaries successfully deposed the Shah a few months later, despite their differences, Iran and China had established a cordial relationship.

As established, the revolution shifted Tehran's strategic outlook, political narrative, and alliances. The transition of power and ideological changes resulting from it afforded the two Communist states with an opportunity to build stronger ties with and influence the new regime and assert their power in a key region. As a result, after the Islamic Revolution, Hua apologised for visiting Iran during the Shah's reign and expressed his country's desire to grow ties with the Islamic Republic. Ayatollah Ruhollah Khomeini, then Supreme Leader, accepted the apology, stating that Iran should have friendly relations with Muslim and non-Muslim nations.[17] The two countries found some components of their respective ideologies aligned, in particular their anti-imperialist and anti-hegemonic rhetoric.[18] Initially, during the political upheavals that ultimately led to the overthrow of the Shah, Beijing and Moscow welcomed the rise of leftist parties in Iran.[19] They assumed the revolution would provide the space for the Communist Tudeh Party and other leftist groups in Iran to gain traction. The Islamic Republic gradually found itself isolated from the rest of the international community. But Russia and China were less uncompromising in their dealings with the new regime. And when it became clear that the Islamists were the winners of the power struggle that followed the revolution, officials in the two countries still preferred to engage their new counterparts in Tehran rather than isolate the nascent government. Both states also appreciated the Islamic Republic's anti-West stance. But the Chinese and Soviets were surprised to find that the new government in Tehran rejected all foreign influence,[20] focusing instead on itself and calling for 'neither West, nor East', but instead, a 'third way'.[21]

The 1979 Revolution: Continuity or Change?

Bumpy Relations with Russia

Despite the change in government in Iran, the Soviet Union remained interested in Iran for strategic reasons. Indeed, Iran and the USSR shared a long border, and Iran remained a large country with oil and regional clout.[22] Immediately after the revolution, Moscow made it clear that its intention was to establish neighbourly relations with Tehran, and it became the first country to send its ambassador to meet with Ayatollah Khomeini.[23] For Russia, the Islamic Revolution was a win, since it kicked out the overly pro-US Shah, making it imperative to maintain this advantage over America in a significant region. But for a time, it seemed cordial relations were not to be, after all, as the ideology of the Islamic Republic was fundamentally opposed to that of the atheist Communist state.

By the end of its first decade in power, the revolutionary regime had purged the leftist elements that had joined forces with the Islamists to topple the Shah. And in its early days, led by an ideological divide, combined with the historical distrust of Russia, the new leadership took a number of antagonistic steps towards the USSR. Rhetorically, the Islamic Republic adopted an anti-Soviet stance and Ayatollah Khomeini referred to the USSR as the 'lesser Satan'.[24] Practically, Tehran appealed to the UN to denounce parts of the Russo-Persian Treaty of Friendship of 1921, which replaced the humiliating Treaty of Turkmenchay, and raised the price of gas sent to the USSR, before cutting it off completely in February 1980.[25] A number of Soviet policies served to further taint the relationship. The Soviet Union's invasion of Afghanistan in 1979, combined with its support for Saddam Hussein's Baathist regime during the devastating Iran-Iraq War, only emphasised that the Russians could not be trusted in the mind of the Iranians. Nevertheless, as the effects of the war became too much to ignore, pragmatism won over in Tehran. Some officials began to call for greater economic ties with countries like the USSR, in order to help overcome the boycott of Iran's economy and the country's own structural shortcomings, as well as the growing perception of the threat posed by America in Iran's backyard.[26]

As a result, Iran began to take a number of steps to show its determination to establish relations with the USSR, including by toning down its anti-Soviet rhetoric.[27] In 1987, Soviet Deputy Foreign Minister Yuli M. Vorontsov visited Tehran to deliver a proposal for peace talks between Iraq and Iran in Moscow, which Iran rejected. However, the proposal formed the basis for further exchanges and discussions.[28] The visit was followed by an Iranian trip to Moscow led by then Deputy Foreign Minister Mohammad Javad Larijani, which resulted in an agreement on economic and political cooperation, complicating the USSR's relations with neighbouring Iraq.[29] But ties between the two countries remained limited until the collapse of the Soviet Union. According to a declassified CIA assessment of the relationship, the USSR tried to foster ties with different minorities and the remaining leftist elements in Iran in order to secure its influence in the country in the event of the Islamic Republic's collapse. By doing so, the Soviets tried to ensure that America would not regain a foothold in Iran.[30]

The end of the Iran–Iraq War combined with the Soviet retreat from Afghanistan and the rapid demise of Communism in Eastern Europe by the end of the decade helped usher in a new era in Russo–Iranian relations. Despite his misgivings about Communism and suspicions of the Soviet Union, Ayatollah Khomeini called for friendly, neighbourly relations between his country and its neighbour shortly before his death in 1989. He did so addressing President Mikhail Gorbachev, whose government took this overture as a sign that ideological differences would no longer constitute a barrier to relations.[31] The address was followed by the first Soviet visit to Tehran since the 1979 revolution led by Foreign Minister Eduard Shevardnadze. After Ayatollah Khomeini's passing – which prompted then President Khamenei to succeed him as the new Supreme Leader, leaving the presidency open – the new president, Ali-Akbar Hashemi Rafsanjani visited the USSR, and signed an agreement on economic, scientific, and technological cooperation until the year 2000. This constituted a Russian pledge to help Iran develop its defensive capabilities, as well as a declaration on 'respect for national sovereignty, and territorial integrity, non-aggression, non-interference in each other's internal affairs, and non-use of force'.[32] At the end of the 1980s, the US intelligence community judged that the relationship would likely continue, despite the multiplicity of potential spoilers, such as Iran–Russia rivalry in Afghanistan and the Islamic Republic's ideology.[33]

And continue it did. Russia and Iranian ties grew throughout the 1990s, as they renewed and increased energy ties, undertook joint infrastructure development projects, and explored the expansion of military cooperation. But a number of sticking points continued to exist. With the collapse of the Soviet Union, a number of new countries were established in what was now Russia and Iran's backyard. Importantly, the two states were no longer the only two countries bordering the strategic Caspian Sea. And with new stakeholders and more interests at odds, new disagreements between the littoral states over the division of the sea and the resources it harbours emerged. By the end of the 1990s, Tehran and Moscow sought to implement a new regime of equal rights. But these disagreements paled in comparison to Iran's dismay over the secret US–Russian Gore–Chernomyrdin agreement, signed in 1995, whereby Russia agreed to limit the sharing of nuclear know-how and cease the sale of conventional weapons to Iran by 1999, after it fulfilled existing contracts.[34] In practice however, Russia continued its sales to Iran. Russian willingness to ignore American complaints and concerns and continue supplying Iran with nuclear technology and conventional arms indicated that, in a sign of the times to come, relations between Moscow and Tehran would continue as long as it suited both capitals. As a result, despite a number of disagreements, political relations grew as both countries began working together to address joint areas of interest.

The newly independent Soviet Republics also presented new opportunities for Tehran to expand its influence and provided both areas of cooperation and tension with Moscow. In Tajikistan, the growth of a Muslim opposition could only engender Iranian sympathies, but Tehran was careful to establish links with all parties taking part in the elections for the new government. And when pro-Russian Rahmon Nabiev won the elections, Iran was quick to pursue cordial ties. Nevertheless, Tehran was also careful to prioritise Moscow in its interactions with Dushanbe. In an interview designed to reassure Russia, then Iranian Foreign Minister Ali Akbar Velayati elaborated on why his country had not recognised the new government in Tajikistan:

> Our [Iran's] position is clear. We went to these republics through the Moscow gate. The Islamic Republic does not intend to take advantage of the existing sensitive circumstances in the Soviet Union. We, as a neighbour of the Soviet Union, wish to see that their situations return to normal as soon as possible. We respect whatever the people of that country as a whole desire, and the republics [of Central Asia] in particular.[35]

In 1992, the ethnic Muslim opposition rose up against the government of Nabiyev, beginning five years of civil war. While the opposition was mainly Muslim, it followed Wahhabism – the ultra-conservative Sunni brand of Islam represented by the Al Saud leadership in Riyadh, which Iranians view as a source of extremism. It is unclear how much Iran involved itself in the conflict,[36] but to Moscow's relief, the leadership in Tehran worked with Russia to reach a favourable peace accord in 1997.

But Tajikistan was not the only area where Russia and Iran worked together. The Iranians did not side with the Muslims in the first Chechen war of 1994–96, to Moscow's delight.[37] As in the case of Tajikistan, Iranian leaders showed, and continue to

69

show, that their ideology can and does take a backseat when it comes to national interests. Indeed, despite advocating for the freedom of 'the oppressed peoples', especially Muslims, Iran never became an active advocate for the Chechens, a group whose rights have been routinely violated by the Russians.[38]

In Afghanistan, Iranian and Russian interests aligned when the Al-Qaeda-backed Taliban overthrew the government of President Burhanuddin Rabbani, took over Kabul, and proceeded to consolidate their power in 1996.[39] This effectively brought Tehran and Moscow together to work against the Taliban, which they both considered a terrorist government. To do so, they backed the Northern Alliance led by General Ahmed Shah Masood. The alliance brought together some 15,000 troops, made up of various ethnicities, mainly Tajiks and Uzbeks, fighting the Taliban from its stronghold of Badakhshan in the north-eastern part of the country.[40] The fight went on for five years with Iran and Russia, along with Tajikistan, supporting the Northern Alliance. But in 2001, the United States and its NATO allies invaded Afghanistan in response to the 11 September 2001 attacks on America. As former US envoy to Afghanistan Ambassador James Dobbins put it,

[M]any believe that in the wake of Sept. 11, the United States formed an international coalition and toppled the Taliban. It would be more accurate to say that the United States joined a coalition that had been battling the Taliban for nearly a decade. The coalition – made up of Iran, India, Russia, and the Northern Alliance, and aided by massive American airpower – drove the Taliban from power.[41]

The ebbs and flows, and the pragmatism, in the relationship continued after the rise of President Putin. Russia was suspicious of Iranian reformist President Mohammad Khatami and his 'Dialogue of Civilisations' proposal, fearing that it would lead to a rapprochement with the Americans at Russia's expense.[42]

Nevertheless, in October 2000, in a measure the Iranians appreciated, Putin publicly repudiated the Gore-Chernomyrdin agreement and announced further arms sales to and cooperation with Iran. But this coincided with stalemate over the delimitation of the Caspian Sea and the Iranian perception that Russia was acting unilaterally to secure its interests, at Iran's expense. It slowly became apparent that one of the characteristics, and strengths, of the growing relationship between Russia and Iran was their ability to separate and compartmentalise the areas of agreement and disagreement. This allowed the two countries to shelter overlapping and common interests from their divergences and work with each other on certain areas even as they disagreed or stalled on others. As a result, and as a symbol of the pragmatism that characterises their relationship, Russia and Iran continued to cooperate in the energy sector, and on developing joint policies to fight terror, drugs and arms trafficking, which they reiterated in the Tehran summit declaration in October 2007. The pragmatism that characterised Russo–Iranian relations also became a feature of Sino–Iranian relations.

China and the Islamic Republic

Practical considerations (or 'calculations of power') drove Tehran and Beijing towards each other after the fall of the Shah. China stepped in to fill the void left by Europe and the United States after the Islamic Revolution, and throughout subsequent years of war and economic sanctions on several levels. Politically, Tehran had to turn towards a great power for support after it lost Washington following the fall of the Shah. Indeed, despite its revolutionary narrative based on the idea of independence and self-sufficiency,[43] the Islamic Republic recognised the inevitability of a certain level of dependence and reliance on other nations, and consequently tried to balance its ideals with the reality of lack of capacity and globalisation. Beijing was well positioned to fulfil this role for Tehran because of its shared 'anti-imperialist' and 'anti-hegemonic' ideology.[44]

China was quick to recognise the new Islamic government in Iran on 14 February 1979 so that it could maintain good relations with the country. But Iranians were wary of the Chinese, as they were of the Russians and other powers. The beginning of the Iran–Iraq War, however, served to accelerate the mending of ties between the two countries. Moscow's support for Baghdad during the war, including through the provision of arms, compounded the increasingly warming relationship between Tehran and Beijing. Yet, the relationship did not come without some tensions and challenges. At first, China found itself in a difficult position because it had to balance Iran and Iraq, since it had hoped to preserve good relations with both. But Iran's 'neither East, nor West' policy actually fit in with China's worldview, including anti-imperialism and solidarity between developing countries. This, especially as America became increasingly hostile towards Iran. No longer a US ally after the revolution, Iran needed a benefactor in the UNSC. In July 1980, the UNSC voted to condemn the Iranian revolutionaries taking over the US embassy in Tehran. China abstained. Throughout the hostage crisis, China was careful not to upset either side. The country could sympathise with the Islamic Republic's chosen course, as the hostage crisis was similar to the Communist Party of China's seizure of the US Consulate in Mukden 32 years prior, in 1948.[45] China also abstained from subsequent resolutions imposing economic sanctions on Iran.[46]

After that, official visits picked up in pace, and the two countries expanded economic, cultural, technological, and scientific cooperation, including student exchanges, research programmes, and joint training programmes in a number of fields, all facilitated by mutual visa exemptions put in place in 1989.[47] For Iran, dealing with China became easier after Beijing abandoned 'socialist' economics and revolutionary Communism under Deng Xiaoping in the 1980s. As the war dragged on, China continued its defence of Iran by not heeding calls to help protect Kuwaiti ships against Iranian gunboat attacks and condemning the US downing of the civilian Iran Air Flight 655 on 3 July 1988, which killed all 290 passengers on board.[48] In May 1989, in a first since the revolution, then Iranian President Khamenei visited China, and highlighted that Iran 'seeks cooperation with countries that had left no unpleasant memories on the Iranian mind during the war', and as such, his country had 'chosen friendship and cooperation with China'.[49] Tehran declared support for Beijing's crackdown in Tiananmen Square in 1989, describing it as a legitimate effort to maintain law and order.

The end of the Cold War presented a renewed opportunity for Iran and China to come closer together still. The emergence of a new world order, led by the United States, left both countries feeling the need to stand up to America and claim equal rights for all in the international community.[50] China would be useful to Iran thanks to its international standing, as well as its permanent membership to the UN Security Council – particularly helpful from Iran's perspective after the imposition of international sanctions in the mid-2000s. In what would become an important milestone in the relationship, then Foreign Minister Ali Akbar Velayati and President Hashemi Rafsanjani visited Beijing in April and September 1992 respectively. The two countries agreed on a number of joint projects, including in the military and nuclear fields.[51] They also discussed cooperation in the region to address growing fears of an increase in Turkish influence – encouraged by the United States – in Central Asia, and to end the civil war in Tajikistan.[52] Interestingly, Iran was intent on portraying the visits as the coming together of two great powers against rising American hegemony.

But Tehran wanted to go a step further: Iranian officials hoped to create an anti-American axis, which would include their country, as well as China, Russia, India, and Pakistan. They floated the idea during Rafsanjani's visit to China.[53] But the Chinese were not prepared to become involved in such an initiative. They did, however, agree to conduct research and open discussions on how this could eventually be achieved. But it was following the intensification of US efforts to isolate and contain Iran – as outlined in President Bill Clinton's policy of 'dual containment' in 1993 targeting Iran and Iraq – that Sino–Iranian relations gained a new momentum.[54] Indeed, China saw US measures to sanction and isolate Iran as interfering in a country's internal affairs, and a clear demonstration of what it had long seen as brash American hegemony, which needed to be contained. And Iran saw in China a way out of international isolation. As a result, growing US pressure on Iran served as a driver behind increased Sino-Iranian cooperation.

The following sections will assess the critical points of alignment and divergence between Iran and China on the one hand and Iran and Russia on the other.

Sanctions: Looking East

Much of the relationship between Iran and Russia, on the one hand, and Iran and China, on the other, was determined by each country's relationship with the United States. While the Americans had begun sanctioning Iran during the war, President Clinton's policy of 'dual containment' laid out the foundations for what would become the international sanctions regime targeting the Islamic Republic's sponsorship of terrorism and nuclear activities. In March 1995, Clinton banned US firms from Iran's oil sector. By doing so, he stopped the first US firm since the revolution, Conoco, from investing in the oil and gas sector in Iran.[55] Two months later, Washington extended the ban to a full trade embargo before imposing unprecedented extraterritorial sanctions on foreign companies interested in doing business with Iran in 1996. The gradual tightening of the noose forced Tehran to well and truly look east in order to make up for the slowing of business with the West.

In March 1995, as America was creating the basis for international sanctions, Velayati embarked on an East Asia tour, which included a stop in China, followed by Vietnam, Thailand, and Malaysia. In meetings with his Chinese counterpart, Foreign Minister Qian, Velayati reiterated the importance of the China–Iran axis in countering the imposition of Western values – a clear nod to the Chinese disdain for the US-led order. For their part, Chinese officials agreed that security in the Middle East could only be secured by regional states.[56] Iran welcomed China's political support in an increasingly hostile international arena and the Iranian media was full of praise for China's friendship and its reliability[57] – a far cry from increasingly isolated Iran, it provided the regime with another overture to push for its anti-West bloc composed of itself, China, Russia, Pakistan, and India. But China remained reticent to take such a definitive stance and instead continued to denounce US measures against Iran.[58] To Tehran, while limited in effect, Beijing's political support served to legitimise its position and demonstrate that the country was not alone. As a result, Iran did its utmost to nurture the relationship with both China and Russia.

But from Tehran's perspective, the relationship did not always go as planned for reasons that were beyond its control. Indeed, at the end of the 1990s, China re-evaluated its Iran policy because of pressure from the United States. Indeed, just as with Russia, the ties between Iran and China were often marked by their interactions with the West in general, and with America in particular. Coinciding with the rise to power of Khatami in 1997, Beijing decided to adopt a more conciliatory position vis-à-vis Washington and, as a result, agreed to end the sale of some military equipment and nuclear cooperation with Tehran.[59] And fewer official visits took place. China's decision to cease military sales and nuclear cooperation made Tehran re-examine its appraisal of Beijing as a reliable partner and affected China's reputation and influence in Iran. Much like with Russia, Iran and Iranians perception of China as an unreliable partner characterised the two states' ties for years to come. Nevertheless, pragmatic considerations meant that China continued to cooperate with Iran in a number of fields, including by supporting the Middle Eastern nation at the UN Security Council and through trade.

By the end of the decade, and after a sharp downturn in US–China ties, Tehran and Beijing resumed cordial relations. After discussions, in 2000, the two countries set up regular vice foreign ministerial exchanges as a way to maintain political dialogue. In June 2000, the first visit by an Iranian president to China since 1989 took place and spearheaded cooperation on a wide range of issues. It was during this period that energy ties between the two states expanded significantly. Indeed, as China's energy needs grew, its oil imports from Iran increased by over 80 per cent from the previous year in 2000, and then by another 55 per cent in 2001.[60] However, the agreements did not refer to a Sino–Iranian 'partnership' – considered a step too far for Beijing. Instead, it emphasised that Sino–Iranian ties would not become a formal alliance; rather remain a mutually beneficial relationship. Nevertheless, both countries continued to highlight the value of the relationship in the face of the unipolar system and a hegemonic America.

As we saw, during his time, President Khatami spearheaded a diplomatic initiative focused on dialogue and an improvement of relations with the West – an initiative dubbed the 'dialogue among civilisations'. Despite the potential effect this could have on Iran's relations with China – namely a potential shift in focus and attention away from it – Beijing offered its support to Tehran in this initiative. Russia, however, was suspicious of this endeavour, loathing the impact of a US–Iran rapprochement on Iran–Russia relations and on the federation's anti-American stance. Khatami's initiative was fruitful in some political and security areas. For example, it paved the way for US–Iranian cooperation in Afghanistan in 2001, including efforts to establish a stable Afghan central government following the toppling of the Taliban.[61] But the Bush administration's 'Axis of Evil speech' spearheaded a more assertive foreign policy stance towards the

Islamic Republic. The same was true of Beijing and Moscow. The United States reversed long-standing policies such as ambiguity over the defence of Taiwan through an intensification of military links between America and the contested island, prompting concerns from China and Russia.[62] In Russia, US assertiveness and Putin's leadership, made Russia's foreign policy increasingly nationalistic and anti-American. And Putin developed closer ties with Iran. As a result, high-level exchanges between Russia and Iran picked up in pace and culminated in President Khatami's visit to Moscow in March 2001. The unveiling of two undeclared Iranian nuclear facilities in 2002 prompted renewed efforts by President Bush to target the Islamic Republic. His administration expanded US sanctions and included new designations of Iranian organisations and individuals involved in Iran's missile and nuclear programmes.[63] In response, Russia joined Iran in highlighting that Iran was party to the NPT and in compliance with its obligations, prior to declaring greater collaboration between the two countries on the development of the Iranian civil nuclear programme.[64] The growing Russo–Iranian ties were worrisome to the United States, which sought to isolate the Islamic Republic. Nevertheless, the United States did not change course and, in 2002, Bush included Iran in his famous 'Axis of Evil' speech – despite Iran's efforts to lessen tensions and cooperation with America in Afghanistan – prompting China to criticise the statement. As the Chinese put it, 'We disapprove of the use of such words in international relations'.[65] Then Chinese President Jiang Zemin conducted a high-profile visit to Tehran only three months after the speech, further highlighting Chinese disapproval of the US administration's policy on Iran.

In the context of the US-led war on terror, Jiang undertook a five-nation tour. The tour aimed to foster a 'better common understanding of the international community on condemning terrorism and maintaining the global strategic balance' rather than succumbing to the American way of combatting terror.[66]

After the meeting between the Iranian and Chinese leaderships, the Iranians highlighted the two countries' joint opposition to the US-led unipolar world.[67]

Russia–Iran relations in the aftermath of the launch of the 'War on Terror' did not advance as smoothly, largely because of enhanced US–Russia ties. Indeed, having felt the brunt of a growth in fear of Islamist terrorism, Moscow showed sympathy with President Bush's counterterrorism and war efforts, leading to an improvement in US–Russia relations. Consequently, Russian focus on Iran lessened. But soon, the tides turned again when the US administration embarked on a path to topple Saddam Hussein's regime in Iraq in 2003. Iran, Russia, and China opposed the war and attempted to avert it through dialogue, to no avail. When the United States succeeded in ousting Saddam Hussein, Iranians increasingly feared that their country would be next on the Bush administration's target list.[68] This, coupled with the failure of the EU3 negotiation process on Iran's nuclear programme, and the resultant increase in US sanctions on Iran, highlighted the importance of relations with China and Russia for Iran.

Reluctantly Imposing Sanctions

Initially, it was unclear whether the United States would succeed in getting Russia and China on board to pressure Iran into halting elements of its nuclear programme. Both countries were loath to accept the imposition of international sanctions on Iran, preferring a diplomatic solution to a show of strength. Each successive UN Security Council Resolution on Tehran could only be passed after the proposed provisions were watered down to suit Moscow and Beijing because both countries kept threatening to use their veto power.[69] Russia and China initially steadfastly stood their ground when faced with pressure from Washington to divest from Tehran in order to better isolate it. After the revelation of the Fordow enrichment plant in 2009, as the United States and its European allies were pushing for additional multilateral measures against

Iran, China signed a $5 billion deal to develop the South Pars natural gas field and a $3 billion deal to expand two of Iran's oil refineries.[70] But despite this, both China and Russia were steadfast in their belief that Iran should not be allowed to develop a nuclear weapon. In fact, to Iran's great dismay, in September 2008, the Russians drafted a resolution, which passed unanimously, urging Iran to comply with its obligations and past UNSC resolutions. Moscow was at pains to highlight to Tehran that the resolution did not impose any new sanctions. But this was to no avail. The Iranians were outraged, Majles speaker Ali Larijani stated that, 'the countries of the Iran Six are applying a policy of double standards to Tehran.'[71] This incident further served as a reminder to Tehran that Moscow and Beijing were not reliable political partners.

As international pressure against the country increased, the Iranian public and factions within the regime grew more critical of Ahmadinejad. During the contested 2009 presidential elections, reformist candidate Mehdi Karroubi attacked Ahmadinejad for isolating Iran. Ahmadinejad famously countered by saying that his country had made a number of friends, including Venezuela and Bolivia. But to the Iranian public and much of the elite, Venezuela and Bolivia were not adequate partners and did not do much for the country's international or regional standing. Instead, they wanted to have political and economic ties to more 'relevant' countries. Later, in 2013, Rouhani repeated much of the same criticism vocalised by Karroubi four years prior: Ahmadinejad's belligerent rhetoric and actions had isolated the country. Rouhani promised to bring Iran back into the international community and normalise its economic and political standing.[72] But while Rouhani, like Khatami, looked West, he also sought to resume closer ties to Russia and China.

In 2010, UN Security Council Resolution 1929 imposed the most extensive international sanctions on Iran's nuclear and missile programmes. The negotiations were difficult for Washington and its allies. Up until then, China and Russia had consistently opposed the imposition of wide-ranging sanctions on Iran.[73] And when UN Security Council resolutions targeting Tehran's programme were passed, Chinese and Russian efforts served to water them down. Once again, to secure their consent, the text of the resolution had to be softened. According to Thomas Christensen, former US Deputy Assistant Secretary of State for East Asian and Pacific Affairs, Beijing agreed to Resolution 1929 'only after watering [it] down to protect China's economic interests and to reduce damage to Iran's overall economy.'[74]

For both capitals, dealing with Iran's nuclear programme was complicated. On the one hand, they wanted to protect their partner against US-led efforts to isolate a lesser non-Western-aligned power, perceived as hegemonic and overbearing. Both also wanted to maintain good relations with Iran, including for economic reasons. But on the other hand, both Beijing and Moscow sought to be seen as responsible international actors, and neither wanted a new member of the nuclear club – especially a member with clout in the strategic Middle Eastern region and with the ability to close the vital Strait of Hormuz. As a result, their diplomacy on the nuclear issue seemed bipolar. Nevertheless, Russian and Chinese acquiescence was a significant victory for the United States and its European allies because the sanctions regime could only be effective if implemented universally, blocking off the path to circumvention.[75] Indeed, until Russia and China came on board, Iran continued to offset the impact of sanctions by turning to both powerhouses to boost its trade. But with Beijing and Moscow on board with the push for additional sanctions on Iran, Tehran was effectively isolated politically and economically.

The Thorn in Russia–Iran Relations: The Caspian

Going back to the 1930s and 1940s, Iran and the Soviet Union sought to remove 'foreign interference' from the Caspian region. For example, in a 1935 treaty, the two countries declared the

Caspian as 'regarded by the two Governments as a Soviet and Iranian sea.' Later, in 1940, they reiterated this idea: 'the parties hold the Caspian to belong to Iran and to the Soviet Union.' In other words, 'no third state had any rights in the sea, including the right of navigation.'[76] Decades later, Iran and Russia took this language and content of these treaties to the Caspian Summits of the 2000s, which sought to bring the three new countries of the basin on board.

In 2010, the five countries of the Caspian region held a summit in Baku. There, then President Dmitry Medvedev posited, 'If at any moment we relax in our mutual cooperation, there is no doubt that other states will want to interfere with our concerns – states that lack a know-how of or a relationship with the Caspian but whose interest stems from economic interests and political goals.'[77] The statement set the tone for the Caspian Summit process. Russia and Iran both see the summits as a platform to push against what they view as 'foreign interference', namely by the West, in the affairs of the Caspian – and by extension, their own. The summit resulted in a security cooperation agreement, but it was less successful in addressing the elephant in the room: the Caspian's legal status and the delineation of its waters. Indeed, depending on the legal denomination of the Caspian, the distribution of its oil and gas resources would change: If labelled a sea, the five countries would have to divide the Caspian into national sectors, with access to their sector's oil and gas resources only, if deemed a lake, however, the body of water and its resources would be divided equally between the countries.[78]

But the 2010 meeting was not the first time the five countries had met to discuss the legal status and delineation of the Caspian. After the collapse of the Soviet Union, Russia, Kazakhstan, and Azerbaijan signed bilateral agreements dividing up the body of water. And despite Iran not recognising the deals, the three countries began to build on them by developing oil and gas resources in the northern areas of the basin. Prior to that, Iran and the USSR held equal shares of the basin's resources.[79] Later, in 2007, they met in Iran to settle the issue without producing an agreement. There too, the host and Russia pushed back against foreign interference in the region.[80] As Ahmadinejad stated then, 'all Caspian nations agree on the main issue – that all aspects related to this sea must be settled exclusively by littoral nations [. . .] the Caspian Sea is an inland sea and it only belongs to the Caspian states; therefore only they are entitled to have their ships and military forces here.'[81]

The fourth Caspian Summit was held in Astrakhan, Russia in 2014. There, the five littoral states agreed to the Russian–Iranian proposal to ban the presence of foreign powers in the waters of the Caspian.[82] This proposal came in the context of the crisis in Ukraine, the nuclear negotiations between the P5 + 1 and Iran, and, perhaps most importantly, as the United States helped Azerbaijan, Kazakhstan, and Turkmenistan bolster their military defences. Indeed, America was helping the three countries develop their own navies as part of a general trend of greater cooperation between the Caspian states and the West. In the aftermath of the Ukraine crisis, NATO also courted some of Russia's neighbours, such as Azerbaijan, to boost ties.[83] Discussions with Kazakhstan even included the possible establishment of a military base in Aktau port to help the United States and NATO boost and facilitate their efforts in Afghanistan.[84] The agreement to lock out foreign powers placed obstacles on the West's way to secure such a presence. Despite this victory for Russia and Iran, the other littoral states of the Caspian did not give up the idea of becoming significant players in the region's security.

In 2015, Kazakhstan and Azerbaijan signed a defence cooperation agreement to boost ties and conduct joint drills.[85] Azerbaijan not only hosted the leadership of the US and South Korean navies in November 2016, but also participated in a host of US Coast Guard-led training programmes. Kazakhstan, for its part, sought to avoid the purchase of Russian military equipment and to diversify its suppliers. As a result, it concluded a joint venture agreement with France's Sagem for the development of drones in 2010.[86] Aside from boosting their status as regional military powers, this type of activity was intended to allow these countries to present a stronger front when faced with Russia and Iran and their interests in the Caspian.

Relations with the West are also critical to the littoral states of the Caspian due to the sea basin containing 48 billion barrels of oil and up to 292 trillion cubic meters of natural gas in 2012.[87] And the Trans–Caspian natural gas pipeline route would further supply Europe with natural gas by bypassing Russia. This is a source of tension between Moscow and Tehran, as Russia has worked to obstruct the construction of the pipeline. Iran has been pushing for an equal share of the territorial boundaries of the Caspian. This would provide Tehran with a 7 per cent increase in its share of the waters, from its current 13 per cent, to 20 per cent ownership of the sea border for all littoral states, in order to benefit from the off-shore oil stockpiles.[88] Nevertheless, the attempt from the smaller states in the region to guarantee their own security and court Western involvement in their military growth has continued to push Iran and Russia to further boost cooperation. This increase is particularly visible in the military realm, where the two states have intensified the extent and number of their joint drills and their efforts to guarantee the security of the Caspian Sea for the foreseeable future.

The Last Round of Nuclear Negotiations

Contrary to popular belief, it was under President Obama that US and international sanctions against Iran really increased. This ramping up coincided with significant EU and UN sanctions on Iran, including UN Security Council resolution 1929, which involved Russia and China, and the EU oil embargo in 2012.[89] These were the most damaging measures against the Iranian economy.[90]

The successive rounds of sanctions left Iran in a difficult position, worsening the already mismanaged economy. And while Russia and China were helpful in offsetting part of the isolating effect of these measures to begin with, increasingly, both countries succumbed to pressure from America and drew down some of their interactions with Iran. In addition, specific measures, such as the UN ban on the sale of conventional weapons, meant that even if they wanted to, Moscow and Beijing could not sell weapons and military gear to Tehran. As a result, international sanctions and political isolation, combined with a number of significant domestic issues stemming from Ahmadinejad's tenure, the Iranian political elite began to explore the option of renewed negotiations with the West in order to find a solution to the long-running nuclear crisis.

Prior to the election of President Hassan Rouhani in 2013, under the auspices of Sultan Qaboos bin Said al Said, Oman brokered an initial meeting between the US State Department and Iranian officials to resume the negotiations over Iran's contested nuclear programme.[91] The Obama administration had made it clear it wanted to resolve this long-lasting problem. And the Supreme Leader in Iran seemed to favour exploring solutions through talks with the international community. With the election of former chief nuclear negotiator, regime insider, and moderate Hassan Rouhani, a diplomatic solution became possible. Surrounded by a savvy and technocratic team, and afforded a mandate by Khamenei, Rouhani was able to begin nuclear negotiations in good faith. On the opposing side, the show of unity within the P5 + 1 was notable during the final round of negotiations, which began in 2013.[92]

Initially, it was unclear whether Russia and China would work alongside the rest of the P5 + 1 to advance the same position. After all, they had an interest in maintaining their privileged and well-established access to the Iranian market, unfettered by Western interest and companies. Moreover, the two powers had stymied Western efforts to isolate Tehran and bring it to the table for seven years. And the nuclear talks were not taking place in a vacuum. The negotiators were meeting against the backdrop of ongoing international incidents and events, such as the Russian invasion of Crimea and the Syrian civil war. In addition, Moscow refused to work with Washington on other shared interests. For example, the Russians refused to attend the final Nuclear Security Summit held in Washington, DC during President Obama's last year in office, despite sharing the administration's goal to secure fissile material and prevent nuclear terrorism.[93]

As a result, it came as a positive surprise to the Europeans and Americans that the Russians continued to 'play ball' when it came to the nuclear talks.[94] Russian and Chinese objectives aligned largely with those harboured by the West. The P5 + 1 was united in its goal of preventing the proliferation of nuclear weapons in the Middle East. For Moscow and Beijing, as for the Europeans, the anticipation of facilitated business with Tehran also presented a tremendous incentive. These objectives ensured the Russians isolated the nuclear negotiations from other problem areas in their relationship with the Americans and their European allies. For their part, the Chinese were driven by another consideration: They wanted to gain political capital from the talks and the emerging deal. Indeed, throughout the talks, Chinese negotiators sought to portray their country as a facilitator, who could mediate between different parties and help create diplomatic solutions to difficult international challenges.

After long and arduous talks, multiple misunderstandings and changes in perspectives, the P5 + 1 and Iran agreed to the JPOA on 23 November 2013. The JPOA was an interim deal designed to buy the negotiators time by limiting and suspending some of Iran's sensitive nuclear activities in exchange for limited and reversible sanctions relief. The interim deal was extended twice before finally leading to the signing of the JCPOA on 14 July 2015. This final agreement rolled back and suspended parts of

Iran's nuclear programme, while subjecting it to the most intrusive negotiated verification measures to-date.[95] In exchange, Iran obtained comprehensive relief from the unilateral and multilateral sanctions stemming from its nuclear programme. But one critical exception remained: US sanctions.

Facing opposition in Congress, the Obama administration opted to lift unilateral US sanctions through Executive Waiver; merely suspending sanctions implementation, rather than 'terminating' them through the legislative process.[96] Only upon IAEA confirmation of the purely civilian nature of Iran's programme would Washington terminate these sanctions. Initially, this obstacle did not seem as truly impeding the process to Tehran. Indeed, when the UN, EU, and unilateral state sanctions were lifted on Implementation Day in January 2016, the international business interest in the Iranian market was already significant. In a matter of weeks after the signing of the JCPOA, high-level German and French officials went to Tehran with significant business delegations to explore avenues for trade.[97] The United Kingdom, Austria, Spain, Poland, and Sweden swiftly followed suit before the end of 2015. By January 2016, after President Rouhani's European tour, Iran had signed nearly 40 billion Euros worth of deals with a wide range of European businesses, including but not limited to, Total, Peugeot, Airbus, and Vinci.[98]

But this initial rush by European firms to conclude MOUs was slow to lead to actual contracts and payments for Iran because of the remaining obstacles and risk of doing business in the country. Financial institutions, in particular, were fearful of processing payments for new contracts. By the two-year anniversary of the agreement, Iranian officials had become frustrated with the slow pace of relief and resumption of business, calling on European officials in particular, to help their country benefit from the deal so that its implementation could continue without any hiccups.[99] Meanwhile, Russia and China concluded a number of contracts with Iran, only serving to highlight their value to the country.

Russia and Iran in Syria

Iran entered the Syrian theatre in the early days of the conflict. By the time the civil war entered into its third year, in 2014, Tehran had reportedly sent hundreds of operatives and over 50 IRGC commanders to help President Bashar al Assad.[100] One year later, in 2015, Russia followed suit. The Russian involvement in Syria was critical, as it provided Assad with an ally with veto power in the UN Security Council, which Moscow used to block a number of UNSC Resolutions.[101]

As the conflict progressed, the dynamics of the Russia–Iran relationship shifted, from one where Tehran felt it was calling the shots in Syria to a Russian-led joint effort. The perceived reversal of the dynamics of the relationship was problematic to Iran. After all, Moscow was key to Tehran's efforts to appear as an unavoidable and key powerbroker in the Middle East. But Iran would have to share the credit for preserving Assad's grip on power with Russia if it took a backseat and allowed the power to take the lead in the campaign there. Earlier in the conflict it seemed impossible to come to a resolution of the Syrian crisis without Iran present at the negotiating table – to the great dismay of Gulf Arab states and conservatives in the West. But as the conflict progressed it became clear that it was Moscow, not Tehran, whose buy-in was indispensable to negotiations and to a resolution of the conflict. Indeed, Tehran's influence over Assad seemed to be waning and shaky at best. But Tehran's woes were not limited to the reversal of the dynamics of the relationship. They continued to view the Russians with suspicion, and a number of events during the course of the Syrian conflict worsened this. For example, the Russians publicised their use of an Iranian military base in August 2016 even though it had been agreed that both countries would keep it quiet.[102] Finally, the very presence of Russia in the Syrian conflict presented Iran with a real conundrum. One of the core beliefs of the Islamic Republic is that the security of the Middle East region should be left to the countries in the region. As a result, publicly Tehran is against any foreign intervention in its region, which it deems counterproductive.[103] As such, Russia's involvement in Syria is problematic, but Iran cannot turn away from it either. Tehran knows that without Russia, Assad and his men would not have made the gains they have in the past few years. Some Iranian officials and experts have begun to accept that the Middle East can no longer be left to itself and that some degree of foreign involvement in the region is inevitable.[104]

Iran needs Russia to maintain its influence and continue to make gains in favour of the Assad regime, but also to ensure that it has a 'big brother' with skin in the game present. Russian airstrikes and air cover for the Syrian army's movements have been vital in ensuring their advances. The presence of the Russian giant gives Iran international political and diplomatic clout as well as a seat at the table, which it acquired more easily with backing from Russia. In addition, as the Assad regime became increasingly toxic – due to the significant increases in civilian deaths and its gross disregard for international non-proliferation norms and the laws of war, including the repeated use of chemical weapons – it became increasingly important for Russia and Iran to work together so they are not perceived as isolated in their support for such a dictator.

Conclusion

Political relations between Iran and the two powers have had their ups and downs but they have remained fairly pragmatically driven. For all three countries, safeguarding their interests comes ahead of political or ideological leanings. For the Islamic Republic, this has been a godsend. Indeed, the Islamic government's ideology and its activities, including human rights violations and support for terrorist groups, posed a problem to Western countries. As a result, Iran's relations with Russia and

China gradually became instrumental in allowing the revolutionary regime to escape isolation. Moscow and Beijing were powerful partners, with seats at the table in key fora, particularly, the UN Security Council, where they had veto power. Importantly, the two countries were willing to use this power to stand up to what they perceived as the hegemonic Western order, led by the United States. Both countries used this to help Iran, most notably when it came to imposing evermore stringent international sanctions on the Middle Eastern nation. And the two powers also served to amplify the Islamic Republic's voice and support its narrative of independence, rooted in the notion that it must stand up to foreign powers, which seek to determine its fate. For the Islamic Republic, having two such powerhouses side with it carried significant political capital and weight. Chiefly, these political relations became the basis for economic and military ties, which expanded significantly in the past 30 years, despite increased pressure from the United States and its allies to divest and turn away from Iran. The following chapters will outline how Iran built economic and military ties with Russia and China.

CHAPTER 3

IT'S THE ECONOMY, STUPID

Until 1979, Iran's economic priorities mirrored its political alignments: Its eyes were on the United States first and Europe second. But, as we have seen, Iran's growing isolation after the revolution made other partners, especially Russia and China, more attractive. Iran's economic focus on the two countries came in two waves. The first started in the aftermath of the Islamic Revolution and continued throughout the 1980s and early 1990s, when it became clear to Tehran that many Western firms would not uphold their contracts and deals with their Iranian counterparts because of the new regime's rhetoric and policies. Business with the United States became impossible following President Carter's Executive Order 12170, imposing the US trade embargo on Iran.[1] The second wave began in a patchy manner at the end of the 1990s, and more earnestly, in the early 2000s, continuing until today. This second wave started as the international community tightened sanctions on Iran due to its controversial nuclear programme, and continued after the 2015 nuclear deal, as Iranians perceived the benefits of sanctions relief as slow and limited. The successive waves of sanctions, followed by the limited trickle down effect of the sanctions relief, forced Tehran to turn to Moscow and Beijing, which were less supportive of the sanctions to begin with.[2]

While both were more than happy to develop their economic endeavours in Iran, they were somewhat constrained by the more stringent international sanctions on the Islamic Republic, especially with UNSC Resolution 1929 in 2010.[3]

Nevertheless, Iran's energy sector was a prime area of interest for both countries. Beijing's desire to diversify its energy basket drove its interest in Iran. Moscow's interest centred mainly on the Iranian nuclear sector. For its part, Tehran was eager to attract significant investments in infrastructure development in the 1990s from both Russia and China, as it reemerged after a decade of revolution and war. Tehran also solicited Chinese and Russian help in technology exchanges in sectors such as the aerospace industry, where it could no longer rely on Western parts and components. But economic relations between Iran and Russia, on the one hand, and Iran and China, on the other, differed. While Iran saw Russia as a partner in specific areas, such as nuclear technology, it viewed China as offering economic benefits across the board. Following nearly four decades of growing economic cooperation, today, Iran's business community is used to the Russian and Chinese presence in its market. The two countries and their business communities also have a better understanding of the inner workings of the Iranian economy and political scene – a significant advantage over Western firms looking to engage with the Iranian market.

The Shah's Economics: Russia and China on the Backburner

Under the Shah, Iran developed extensive economic ties with the United States and with European states. As we saw, the Cold War context shaped the Shah's worldview. He saw Russia's Communist ideology as a grave threat to his country's security, and nurtured ties with the United States and its European allies. The Pahlavi dynasty's economic objective was to modernise the Iranian economy, infrastructure, and broader industry. Reza Shah created the basis for modern Iran's economy, trade, and industry, during his decade-and-half-long reign. Among his key achievements were the establishment of modern transportation systems and networks, including an expansive railroad system,[4] telecommunications (postal service and telegraph), and financial and industrial infrastructure.[5] It was during that time that the monarchy established Bank-e Melli – the first modern state-owned bank, serving as the country's central bank until the creation of the Central Bank of Iran in the 1960s.[6]

Following in his father and predecessor's footsteps, the Shah undertook a series of social and economic reforms in the 1960s, known as the 'White Revolution'. The White Revolution was meant to build on Reza Shah's work and further propel Iran into modernity, both socially and economically. It included land reform, enfranchisement of women, formation of a literacy corps, and institution of profit sharing schemes for workers in industry.[7] To do this, the Shah intensified ties with America and European countries. In the 1950s, the Shah laid out the groundwork for his country's nuclear programme, a task facilitated by US President Eisenhower's 'Atoms for Peace' initiative.[8] At first, Iran's main source of revenue was through the export of fossil fuels to the West.[9] But later, the country became an attractive tourist destination for foreigners, particularly Western Europeans and Americans.[10] Iran's cultural heritage spanning several civilisations and its natural riches were inviting enough, but the Impress Farrah Pahlavi, the Shah's wife, was keen on creating other attractions for Western tourists to visit the country. The Shiraz Art Festival and the creation of museums with Persian artifacts and contemporary Western art were part of this attempt. By the end of his reign, the Shah was able to extend loans to international institutions such as the IMF, as well as Western countries.[11] The Shah's plan was to invest for the long-run: He exported fossil fuels and invested part of the revenue to create a nuclear energy programme with the help of the United States, Germany, and France.[12] This would help diversify the country's energy sources.[13] At the same time, the Shah worked with Japan to build a desalination plant to tackle his country's water scarcity challenges.[14] Similarly, he imported other civilian goods, including aircraft, cars, electronics, and home appliances from Europe and the United States. But the Shah invested in his security and defence sectors too. He wanted the option to weaponise his nuclear programme if he needed,[15] while beefing up his conventional forces by procuring weapons from the West, and the United States in particular.[16]

The Shah's economic ties with the West came at the expense of relations with Russia and China. The Shah was highly suspicious of the Communist regimes in both countries and, with the United States as a key ally and economic partner, he did not see the need to concern himself with Moscow and Beijing. Despite this, pragmatism marked relations between Iran and Russia. Leonid Brezhnev, the head of the Soviet Union's Communist party, visited Iran in 1962, paving the way for the first economic and technical cooperation agreement with Iran a year later in 1963.[17] The deal covered the joint development of infrastructure and construction of sites of importance to both countries, including hydro-technical facilities on the river Aras, which housed a dam, a water reservoir, and two electric power stations. The agreement also laid out the basis for Soviet credits to Iran, which amounted to $750 million until 1983.[18] The two countries built on the 1963 deal to sign the Soviet–Iranian Agreement of Cooperation in 1966, whereby Soviet organisations would participate in Iranian infrastructure development through design and technical assistance and the supply of equipment, including the development of a gas pipeline and the export of gas to the USSR from 1979–85. For this, the USSR extended a credit of $289 million to Iran.[19] A 1967 declassified CIA memorandum discussed economic and energy relations between the USSR and Iran: It highlighted key setbacks in the implementation of the aforementioned and subsequent agreements, calling communiqués between high-level trade delegations from both countries 'deliberately vague and confusing'. The document also emphasised the inconsistencies between the goals of the two parties, as well as their capacity to fulfil them.[20] Nevertheless, the memorandum recognised that the agreements would form the basis for longer-term trade relations. The infrastructure constructed as a result of the agreement would require 'maintenance and replacement parts', and the credit accumulated from gas sales to the USSR would make Iran a 'captive market for Soviet exports'.[21]

Meanwhile, as we have seen, the Shah refused to recognise the People's Republic of China, accept its accession to the UN, or authorise trade relations with China until the late 1960s.[22] This was despite China's desire to build trade ties with Tehran. Eventually, Tehran ramped up efforts to build relations with China, but only once two facts became clear. First, it became clear to Tehran that Moscow was not just focusing on Soviet–Iran relations, but rather building ties with Baghdad and Delhi as well. As a result, the Shah wanted to be sure Iran too, could diversify its partners. Secondly, relations between the Soviet Union and China were deteriorating. This made it easier for Tehran to position itself as a potential partner for China, especially since the Shah considered it too influential to ignore. After the establishment of diplomatic relations between Peking and Tehran in August 1971, official visits to both countries increased, as did trade delegation visits.[23] A trade credit agreement, signed in April 1973, helped boost trade between the two countries.[24] Iran exported mostly industrial goods like minibuses, trucks, refrigerators, television parts, chemical fertilisers, and agricultural machinery, while China exported paper and stationary items, sporting goods, food, tea, machinery, and steel products. After further state and delegation visits, in 1977, the two countries signed an agreement allowing for $30 million of exports from Iran to China, including 300,000 tons of oil.[25] While the volume of trade between the two countries grew rapidly between 1971, when Iran recognised the People's Republic of China and the end of the Pahlavi dynasty, it was still a small percentage of the general level of foreign trade for both countries.[26]

Revolutionary Economics and the Communist Powers

When the revolutionaries came to power in Iran in 1979, Tehran faced growing isolation as its former international partners steadily cut off ties with a regime they deemed unstable and dangerous. This, combined with its isolation during the Iran–Iraq War, led the new revolutionary leadership to embark on a path to achieve self-reliance. But the new leadership understood its country's shortcomings and inability to become fully self-reliant rapidly and without foreign help. As a result, it developed ties to states willing to establish or re-establish ties with Iran. And, once again, it turned to China initially, and later Russia, to fill this gap. But while Beijing immediately supplied Tehran with weapons and support, Moscow provided arms to Baghdad. Tehran saw broader economic engagement with Beijing as increasingly significant as the war unfolded, and later during reconstruction efforts. After a preliminary Iranian economic delegation visit to China in 1982, a Chinese economic delegation travelled to Tehran in March 1985. The exchange resulted in a MOU on economic, trade, and technical cooperation and was expanded to a trade agreement in August 1987, allowing trade between the two states to expand to $500 million per year.[27]

Iran's International Isolation and its Effects

As discussed in earlier chapters, the United States started to isolate the Islamic Republic through economic measures starting in the early days of the new regime's reign and ramped them up significantly in the mid-1990s through its extra-territorial sanctions. But it was only when the IAEA Board of Governors referred the Iranian nuclear file to the UN Security Council for noncompliance that the international community also adopted sanctions in December 2006.[28] But the pressures on the Iranian economy did not just stem from the international community joining America in isolating the country. By the time Rouhani was elected in 2013,

Iran had undergone eight years of economic mismanagement under Ahmadinejad. While Ahmadinejad attempted to improve the economic lives of lower income families, his policies resulted in record double-digit inflation, rising unemployment, a plummeting currency, and rising corruption.[29] The population's growing grievances and the leadership's concern that they may translate into popular unrest – similar to those of 2009 – shaped the 2013 presidential elections. As a result, Rouhani focused much of his first campaign on much-needed economic improvement and growth.

The poor state of the economy combined with the successive waves of international sanctions on Iran forced Tehran into the arms of those still willing to trade with it, mainly Moscow and Beijing. Both were at times subject to US pressure to draw down their relations with Iran. But, in the end, despite some ups and downs, they continued to embark on economic and business ventures with Iran, albeit within the limits set by sanctions. Nevertheless, four main areas for cooperation between Iran and Russia, on the one hand, and Iran and China, on the other, emerged: Infrastructure, energy, technology, and trade.

It's All About Energy

Iran's fossil fuel resources have been a source of as much tension and controversy in the country, as they have been of wealth. Under Reza Shah, the sector invited foreign presence to help exploit oil and gas, which the country lacked the capacity to do on its own. The development of the Iranian energy sector would not have been possible without foreign players, and the British in particular. Two key drivers shaped Iran's approach to its energy sector after World War II: First, Iran was reliant on foreign powers to develop its own oil[30] and gas and unable to maximise profits from the sector. This reliance on foreign powers fed into the narrative of the Shah's opponents, and ultimately contributed to the Islamic Revolution. Secondly, as we saw previously, the Shah believed that his country could not rely on oil and gas as sources of revenue and energy resources down the line.[31] Both of these challenges continue to plague Iranian energy policy today.

Fossil Fuels

Iran's hydrocarbon resources are one of the country's greatest assets and rank among the world's largest. Hydrocarbon resource stockpiles sit between Saudi Arabia and Russia – and, in fact, are almost equal to those of the former: with barrels of oil and gas reserves at 302.5 for Saudi Arabia, 301.7 for Iran, and 198.3 for Russia.[32] What makes the Iranian energy sector particularly interesting, however, is the fact that unlike other major fossil fuel producers, its extraction rate has remained relatively low.[33] Several factors stemming from the country's political and economic isolation contributed to this, including its limited access to foreign investors and customers, inadequate technology, and aging and incomplete energy infrastructure. As a result, Iran continues to retain substantial reserves both on its territory, and in oil and gas fields shared with neighbouring countries in the Caspian and Persian Gulf, including South Pars, the world's largest gas fields, which the country shares with Qatar.[34] All this makes the Iranian hydrocarbon industry a lucrative one. But the sector also suffers from deep and structural challenges. As Iran's oil minister, Bijan Zangeneh put it; 'the problem we are facing now in the petroleum industry is not finance, but management.'[35] Iran's energy sector has created both competition and cooperation with Russia and partnership with China – its greatest oil and gas customer.

China emerged as the world's fastest growing energy consumer during the first decade of the twenty-first century.[36] First, the country became more energy dependent because of its economic-liberalisation policies and resulting development. Secondly, in the late 2000s, it undertook efforts to reduce its reliance on coal due to pollution.[37] As a result, by 1994, the country had become a net oil importer and, by 2011, the biggest energy consumer worldwide.[38]

It became imperative for Beijing to diversify its energy imports. Enter the Iranian energy sector, which had potential. And as Western firms left or refused to enter Iran because of international sanctions and the country's pariah status, China emerged as a natural partner in the energy trade. Iran's lack of refining capabilities further benefitted China.[39] Beijing seized this opportunity to invest in the Iranian energy sector, positioning itself to eventually become its primary beneficiary. China's 1997 agreement with Iran on cooperation in oil and gas exploration in Iran set the scene for the increase in energy relations.

In the following years, China increasingly asserted itself in Iran's oil sector. After exporting oil exploration machines to Iran in 2000, the China Petroleum and Chemical Corporation (Sinopec) helped the country renovate aging oil refineries and took part in drilling and exploration.[40] In 2002, Tehran and Beijing signed 10-year oil agreements.[41] At the same time, however, Khatami was looking to the West and Western-aligned nations for oil and gas joint ventures and deals. As discussed previously, Khatami was eager to turn his country towards the West and the oil and gas ventures served this broader objective. For example, upon the discovery of the Azadegan oil field – containing roughly 26 billion barrels of oil – Iran offered to grant exploration rights to a Japanese firm in 2000.[42] But the revelations of Natanz and Arak kick-started the nuclear crisis and drove a wedge between Iran and potential energy partners. At first, the Japanese missed the deadline to sign a conclusive deal for Azadegan. But with the E3 talks underway, they finally reached an agreement with the Iranians in 2004.[43] Ultimately, however, Japan withdrew from the process due to US pressure.

At the same time, Khatami had signed a $20 billion balancing deal with the Chinese to reassure them. The deal – the largest such agreement on natural gas – provided for the sale by Iran of 2.5 million metric tons of liquefied natural gas for 25 years starting in 2008.[44] In 2004, Iran also granted China's CNPC exploitation rights to its oil and gas fields.[45] Following this, the two countries signed another agreement, worth $70–100 billion granting China purchasing rights to 250 million tons of liquefied natural gas (LNG) for the following 30 years. That year, the total volume of trade between the two countries reached $22 billion, of which 65 per cent was oil.[46] A year later, Iran and CNPC signed a contract worth $4.7 billion, which granted the firm the right to exploit South Pars, a deal that Iran initially intended to sign with France's Total.[47]

Iran stood to gain from China's growing involvement in its energy sector, especially China's help and investment to develop the Iranian energy infrastructure. For example, in June 2006, the North Drilling Company (NDC) of Iran and China Oilfield Services Ltd (COSL) signed an exploration agreement for the management, repair, and maintenance of the Alborz semi-floating platform. This agreement allowed Iran to drill deeper for oil in the Caspian Sea – a difficult task without Chinese assistance and equipment.[48] As international sanctions were beginning to roll out, China's involvement with Iran's energy sector became fivefold: oil, LNG, upstream and downstream development, upgrading refineries and improving oil recovery, and building new oil and gas pipelines. Importantly, these areas of cooperation with Iran were not prohibited under UN sanctions.[49] Iran quickly became China's third largest source of crude imports, behind Saudi Arabia and Angola until 2012, when Russia surpassed it in 2012.[50]

As we saw, Beijing maintained economic and trade ties with Tehran during the period of mounting international sanctions on the Islamic Republic. In fact, China's energy ties to Iran even benefitted from the sanctions, as it was able to gain privileged access to the Iranian market. Sanctions limited Iran's ability to look elsewhere for business partners, leading the country to work with whoever was willing to maintain ties with a pariah state. According to a European diplomat cited by the *New York Times* in early 2016 after Xi and Rouhani met, 'Where we had to stand on the sidelines, the Chinese have been filling the void (. . .). They are way ahead of us'.[51] Exports (largely of crude oil) from Iran to China grew by 24 per cent and imports from China by 25 per cent, between the final round of UNSC sanctions in June 2010 and the JCPOA's signing in July 2015 – by far the largest growth for Iran.[52] Bilateral trade between Iran and China reportedly stood above $33.8 billion in 2015, after peaking at approximately $52 billion in 2014.[53]

But the sanctions still affected the two countries' ability to trade. Following US pressure to isolate Iran, China dragged its feet on a number of joint-projects. It also reduced its investment in Iran, which dropped down in the Chinese foreign direct investment flow ranking from 12th to 22nd between 2011 and 2014.[54] Beijing also sharply decreased its purchase of Iranian crude oil in order to comply with UN sanctions and, following diplomatic pressure from the United States and Europe, looked elsewhere to fill the void – including increasingly towards Iran's Gulf Arab neighbours. Yet China remained Iran's largest oil export market. As a result, Iran constituted 8 per cent of China's crude oil imports in 2012 and 2013, compared to 11 per cent in 2011.[55] At the end of 2013, with the interim deal secured, Chinese buyers raised Iranian imports back to pre-sanctions levels. But the damage was done, although the JCPOA lifted sanctions targeting Iran's energy sector, China continued to diversify import sources to reduce geopolitical risks and oil supply uncertainties, even as it increased its involvement in Iran's energy sector. Moreover, while in many of Iran's oil fields, China took over after other foreign firms were pushed out following the tightening of sanctions, in others, they too, were pushed out. This time, Iranian firms were pushing back against Chinese ones, as they grew tired of the slow pace of Chinese investment and development, the poor quality of their technology, and their disregard for local cultures and wildlife.

After European oil firms, such as Royal Dutch Shell or British Petroleum, did not re-enter the Iranian market as rapidly as anticipated,[56] the Iranian oil ministry under technocrat Bijan

Zangeneh began to once again discuss more favourable terms with the Chinese to incentivise their return. As such, the Iranians offered such favourable terms in financing, exploitation and development of oil and gas fields, like Azadegan and Yadaravan oil fields, as well as the significant South Pars gas fields. The Iranian and Chinese energy sectors were discussing these new terms against the backdrop of their respective experiences dealing with each other at the height of sanctions.

Indeed, as we saw, the China National Petroleum Corporation International (CNPCI) took over the North and South Azadegan oil fields located in Southwestern Iran in 2010 after further sanctions on the country forced other foreign investors, such as Inpex Corp. of Japan to leave. But delays blamed on US pressure to discourage business with Iran, coupled with the reported poor treatment of local wildlife, led Iran's oil minister to ask the Chinese to leave.[57] It was only when Iraq began to rapidly develop its portion of the field under a deal with the technologically superior Shell Oil Company that Iran realised it was better off with China's out-dated technology than no technological advantage at all. In addition, that the Chinese were largely still in place meant that pumping barrels could begin almost immediately, and afford the Iranians the ability to offset the advantage gained by Iraq thanks to a deal concluded with Shell, a technologically superior firm. These experiences complicated Iran–China energy ties in the wake of the JCPOA, but, eager to see quick benefits from the deal, both parties moved fast to re-establish joint ventures in the sector.

Unlike Sino–Iranian relations, where energy served as an important catalyst, the hydrocarbon sector is arguably one of the most complicated aspects of Russo–Iranian ties. While supply and demand dynamics characterise the nuclear cooperation between Tehran and Moscow, the two countries are potential competitors in fossil fuels. The JCPOA's signature and implementation served as a potential overture for Iranian natural gas to replace Russian supplies to Europe. This was particularly attractive to Europeans, as tensions between Moscow and Brussels on the one hand and Moscow and individual member states on the other have been on the rise since 2014. This is not to say that there is no cooperation in that sector between the two countries. For example, the National Iranian Oil Company (NIOC) signed a number of agreements with Russia's Gazprom to develop South Pars in 1997.[58] In the 2000s, exploration, production, and distribution deals were concluded between Tehran and Gazprom and other Russian firms. In that same period, the two countries also pursued joint ventures in oil and gas refining and export services. At the same time, they also worked with Qatar to extract reserves in the Caspian Sea. In 2008, the two parties signed an agreement to trade natural gas to increase export efficiency and profits.[59] And Russia also offered to help Iran exploit its oil and gas fields. In 2009, the two sides signed cooperation deals at their eighth joint economic commission meeting, which included the creation of a joint investment company to facilitate their energy partnership.[60] During the nuclear talks, the two sides also concluded exploration and production and infrastructure development deals.[61] The deals were concluded despite Western opposition and US pressure to stop the Russians from working with the Iranians. As a result, despite its potential to become a rival for Russia in the long-term, Iran's underdeveloped hydrocarbon industry and energy infrastructure makes it a short- to medium-term opportunity for cooperation. Russia has technology and expertise that Iran lacks and seeks, especially in the post-JCPOA years as it works to attract investors and businesses once again.[62]

Following the JCPOA, Tehran desperately tried to update its energy infrastructure and attract investors and firms to the sector. The country's oil and gas resources have the virtue of remaining relatively untapped, a factor separating it from other big players in the global energy market. At the same time, the Iranian leadership continues to work towards diversifying its energy sources including exploring the nuclear option, an endeavour started by the Shah in the 1950s.

Nuclear Energy for All

As established, the Shah was eager to build his country's energy infrastructure and diversify its energy resources. At the time, more than today, nuclear energy was considered a sign of progress, wealth, and modernity. And the Shah aspired to paint an image of his country as a modern, Westernised state, and a force to be reckoned with in the world economy. He also wanted to make sure that once fossil fuel reserves began to wane, his country would still have essential energy resources and capabilities.[63] Thanks to its many applications, ranging from medical research and treatment to power generation, nuclear technology was an ideal sector for investment.[64] In particular, the Shah laid out the groundwork for a nuclear energy industry.[65] This, as he saw it, would allow Iran to invest in a long-term project that would enable it to become more self-sufficient. But the nuclear programme would also pave the path to a military nuclear programme, should the country ever need it – a hedging strategy adopted by the Shah,[66] and the Islamic Republic after him.[67]

The Islamic Republic shared the goal of making its country's fossil fuel sector less dependent on foreign powers. But it also believed that a country with such tremendous sources of energy did not need to invest in nuclear energy, a technology it saw as futile. As the revolutionaries saw it, Iran's nuclear programme was a product of the Shah's ignorance and willingness to pay for superfluous technology sold by the West to fill its own pockets.[68] In 1980, the Minister of Energy, the Under Secretary at the Ministry of Energy and head of Atomic Energy Organisation of Iran (AEOI), and the first President of the Islamic Republic, Abolhassan Bani-Sadr, halted the programme, positing that, 'The construction of these reactors, started by the former regime on the basis of colonialist and imposed treaties, was harmful for the country from the economic, political and technical points of view, and was a cause of greater dependence on imperialist countries.'[69] But by the mid-1980s, the government revisited the decision.

The Islamic Republic resumed the Iranian nuclear programme, only to discover that Iran no longer had suppliers. Prior to 1979, the United States and Germany were the country's main suppliers. The former provided Iran with the Tehran Research Reactor (TRR), the first such reactor in the country, and highly enriched uranium to fuel it. The latter started to build what would eventually become the Middle East's first nuclear power plant in Bushehr. And the Japanese were working on a desalination plant next to and feeding from Bushehr.[70] At the same time, the Shah invested in a joint European venture, which sought to provide the consortium partners with the enriched uranium needed to fuel their plants, while allowing them to remain compliant with the NPT's provisions. As such, France – whose NPT nuclear weapon state status made it a safe bet from a nonproliferation perspective – would host an enrichment facility, built by the consortium members, and sell them the enriched uranium.[71] The venture was called Eurodif and Iran was one of six countries to invest in it. But with the Shah's collapse, the Americans, Germans, and Japanese left the country and its nuclear sector. For its part, Eurodif suspended Iran's participation and was no longer willing to provide it with fuel. It took a decade for Tehran to receive the money it had invested back, and shaped the way Iranian officials viewed collaboration with foreign states on its nuclear programme.[72] At the same time, Iran informed the IAEA of its plans to build a reactor powered by indigenous uranium. After inspections, the Agency accepted to help Iran under its Technical Assistance Programme before pulling out following US pressure.[73]

Without those suppliers, Iran had to find new ones to complete its nuclear programme. It quickly turned to three main players: Pakistan's Abdul Qadeer Khan, China, and Russia. AQ Khan helped the country develop covert elements of its programme, especially the uranium enrichment component.[74] But Tehran also needed to resume work on its nuclear infrastructure, including completing Bushehr and building other reactors. For these activities, Iran turned to China and Russia. Beijing showed interest in developing this relationship with Tehran, helping it develop its uranium resources. It drew up plans to supply two nuclear power plants to Iran in 1992.[75] But following pressure from America, China, too, suspended these plans. With the Chinese ejecting themselves from the Iranian nuclear market, the Russians found an open field. Russia signed an agreement with Iran and began to construct the Voda Voda Energo Reactor (VVER) 1000WMe light water reactor in Bushehr, which had been left incomplete and was bombed several times by the Iraqi Air Force during the war.[76] In the following two decades, the Russians developed a quasi-monopoly on the legal and declared components of the Iranian nuclear programme, providing the country with technology few were both willing and able to supply to the isolated, non-compliant state. While the Iranians were weary of the Russians and their reliability as suppliers, the Russians distrusted the Iranians because of Tehran's covert nuclear activities, including work on the Natanz and Fordow enrichment plants. Indeed, despite Russia being a nuclear supplier to Iran, Tehran failed to disclose its nuclear plans to Russia. Instead, Moscow found out about Tehran's covert activities once the facilities were unveiled by a dissident group in the case of Natanz and Washington, Paris, and London in that of Fordow.[77]

The JCPOA broke this monopoly by bringing in another critical player, China. This was a critical step for Iran and a key driver behind its decision to return to the table and negotiate the JCPOA. Tehran wanted to diversify its suppliers to gain additional levers on Moscow to avoid it from 'dragging its feet' on delivering projects, as it believed the Russians had done during the completion of Bushehr.[78] Moreover, Iran also wanted to expand and update its nuclear energy infrastructure and did not believe Russia to be up to the task. As a result, during the nuclear talks, AEOI and Foreign Ministry officials held multiple meetings with various suppliers, including European and Chinese firms, to discuss possible future collaboration. Lastly, the Russians' history of using energy as a bargaining chip, as it did when it suspended or threatened to suspect gas transfer to its neighbours, such as Ukraine,[79] make the Iranians uneasy.

Beyond Energy: Trade and Infrastructure

By the early 1990s, Iran was in dire need of infrastructure development. Indeed, a revolution followed by an eight-year devastating war left many of the country's cities worse for wear and its economy in a shabby state. The war of cities − a series of air raids, missile attacks, and artillery shelling into major Iranian cities by Saddam's Air Force intended to erode Iranian morale − left the country's infrastructure in dire need of rebuilding. But Iran's internal economic and legal structure, combined with growing international isolation, made it difficult for Tehran to acquire much of the materials and funding it needed to rebuild its aging and crumbling infrastructure. As a result, as part of its reconstruction plans, Iran undertook reforms to facilitate foreign investment in the country.

A growing China, eager to expand into energy-rich regions, met Iran's need for rehabilitation and reconstruction. As a result, after the war, trade and infrastructure cooperation between Tehran and Beijing developed rapidly. Chinese financing and processing of payments for projects with Iran were instrumental to this fairly fast-paced development. When former Chinese President Yang Shangkun visited Tehran in autumn 1991, Rafsanjani invited China to bid for the Tehran metro project.[80] Five years later, China's International Trust and Investment Corporation (CITIC) Group and the Tehran Urban and Suburban Railway completed negotiations for the development of the capital's metro. The first line was completed in 2001, after a number of hiccups stemming from the size of the project, the difficulty of coordinating between different partners and providers, and Tehran's complicated topography – which includes desert and mountainous terrain in a large and ever-expansive city.[81] For Iran, the project was a test case of whether it could work with and rely on China. In the end, Tehran was satisfied, although the city's residents complained about the slow pace of progress on several metro lines. Nevertheless, China continued its investment in the Iranian rail sector with, for example, the completion of the Tehran Sadeghieh subway station for $250 million in 2006, and plans for expansion of the country's rail network.[82]

China also became involved in other parts of Iran's infrastructure, including electricity, dams, cement plants, steel mills, shipbuilding, motorways, and airports.[83] Indeed, China's main shipbuilding firms won contracts to build tankers for Iran in the early 2000s, financed by China's Eximbank.[84] Meanwhile Chinese and Iranian firms jointly built and financed the Taleqan reservoir dam south of the Alborz Mountains. The China Machinery Equipment Import and Export Company (CMEIC) and Shanghai Electric Group received funding from Eximbank to build an electric power plant in the Azerbaijan province in December 2000.[85] But with the imposition of successive rounds of sanctions, many of these infrastructure projects stalled.

During that same period, Iranian–Russian infrastructure cooperation was more limited than that of Iran and China. In the 1990s, existing infrastructure development schemes in the Middle East and Central Asia excluded Iran and/or Russia. Iran was victim to its growing international isolation, while Russia still felt the aftermath of the Cold War as Eastern European states sought to align themselves with the West and the EU in order to protect themselves from their giant neighbour. Indeed, in 1993, the 12 member states of the EU were joined by the 14 member states of the Eastern European, Caucasian, and Central Asian regions and, specifically excluding Russia and Iran, formed the Transport Corridor Europe-Caucasus-Asia (TRACECA).[86] The organisation was intended to support the political and economic independence of the former Soviet Union states through assistance in transport infrastructure development. As a result, Moscow and Tehran began working together at the end of the 1990s to re-develop port and rail infrastructure and ties between them to mirror Soviet-era cooperation and transport links. This decision resulted in an agreement between Russia, Iran, and India in 2000, which outlined plans for a new North–South Transport Corridor.[87] The corridor would connect Russia to India via Central Asia and Iran by ship, rail, and road in order to reduce the costs of trading among them and increase delivery speed. The plan also involved routes to Europe. This ambitious plan included building a road and railway link between Qazvin–Rasht–Astara, developing Iran's Chabahar port, and building a railway link between Kazakhstan–Turkmenistan–Iran. Construction on most of the parts of the plan began in the second half of the 2000s.[88] But political ups-and-downs in the Russia–Iran relationship made the initial implementation phase difficult. The project picked up in the mid-2010s, as Iran also began to trade with China and Russia in a number of other areas.

Trade between Iran and China rapidly grew in a wide-range of fields, beyond energy and infrastructure. These areas included health, sugarcane, silk and textiles, electrical goods, pharmaceuticals, and ceramics.[89] Initially, there remained an Iranian deficit in their trade until 1999 – Iran was importing more from China than it was selling to it.[90] And although some of this deficit was overcome by the rapid growth in Chinese petroleum product imports, it remained a source of discontent in Tehran, as it did not provide for diversification in Iranian exports to China.[91] As a result, China pledged to import some non-oil commodities from Iran as well. By 2007, China was Iran's main trading partner and, by 2008, bilateral trade had reached $27 billion – a 35 per cent increase from the previous year.[92] At the height of sanctions and until after the interim deal in 2013, the trade deficit switched with a gap in favour of Iran. By 2014, China imported

$27.5 billion worth of goods from Iran, whereas its exports to Iran were at $24.3 billion.[93] China's share of investments in the Iranian economy also grew from 1 per cent in 2009 to 6.5 per cent in 2015.[94] This increase prompted Tehran to open its first overseas commerce centre in Beijing in 2009, intended to streamline joint projects in a variety of sectors in both countries, and to organise an Iran–China trade cooperation conference in Tehran in May that same year.[95] These joint projects and increased trade ties occurred as sanctions were steadily increasing. For example, as European car makers began to leave Iran, Chinese brands like Chery, Lifan, and Changan, flooded the market.[96] By then, China's extensive knowledge of the Iranian market and the different influential actors and organisations afforded it an edge. And Iran's undervalued currency and cash-starved companies made it an attractive market for the Chinese.[97]

Nevertheless, there have been some points of contention in the two countries' trade relations. Their grievances include the slow pace of investment projects and delivery. For example, in 2014, Tehran cancelled the $2.5 billion contract it had previously signed with CNPC to develop South Azadegan due to recurring delays.[98] In addition to the delays, the Iranians aired their grievances with the quality of Chinese goods. As the chairman of the Iran–China Chamber of Commerce Asadollah Asgarowladi put it in 2015, 'We believe that the quality of Chinese goods exported to Iran must be improved and the ground be paved for an increase in investments by both countries in each other and by their joint companies.'[99]

Iran's trade and infrastructure cooperation with Russia lagged behind that undertaken with China in that period. During the 2000s, Iran's trade and cooperation with Russia grew to encompass a number of other areas, albeit to a smaller degree. The two countries reached a major telecommunications contract in 2008, followed by one on agriculture in 2009. That year, Russia's third largest mobile phone operator, Megafon, stated it would invest $4.5 billion to expand coverage in Iran.[100]

Iranians have found that trading with Russia and China has been beneficial for a number of reasons. First, unlike Western firms, neither country made economic relations conditional on 'acceptable' political processes or behaviour. Neither Russia nor China was as concerned about the potential risks of transferring dual-use items to Iran or their end-use. For example, Iran required magnetic resonance imaging technology (MRI) for its medical sector and for research purposes. But the technology's potential alternative use to examine missile castings and the structure of solid missile propellants made it difficult to procure from the West – at least not without agreeing to extensive and regular inspections. China, however, did not have the same qualms about selling the technology to Iran.[101] The same could be said for Russia's involvement in Iran's nuclear industry, despite the dual-use risks. While Russia was careful to ensure it respected all international agreements, in order to maintain its reputation as a reliable and respectable nuclear provider, it did not ask any questions or make its involvement conditional on changes in Iranian behaviour. This was a significant benefit for the Islamic Republic, who saw Western divestment from Iran because of the political changes, differences in ideology and behaviour the West deemed unacceptable. In addition, according to Iranians, both Russia and China were more willing to transfer entire processes to Iran, enabling it to take steps towards its ultimate goal of becoming self-sufficient in a number of sectors, rather than having to continuously rely on foreign providers. Western firms are often concerned about ensuring that jobs remain in their markets or for their populations, whereas Chinese firms, for example, are interested in selling entire production processes. Likewise, while the West is concerned about providing adversarial or unstable states with the full infrastructure and know-how to replicate the technology it possesses – not the least since that would make countries less dependent and, therefore more difficult to sanction and isolate – the Russians and the Chinese do not have such concerns.

This is evident today in a number of deals, such as the sale of the Russian Sukhoi Superjet, which involves the transfer of production facilities to Iran.[102] In addition, neither Beijing nor Moscow is as concerned about how its technologies or systems are used after sale, unlike with most Western firms.

But by the end of the first decade of the twenty-first century, a number of obstacles made it difficult for both countries to exploit their full trading potential with Iran. Both lacked joint customs agreements and legal arbitration boards. Likewise, their import-export regulations were not coordinated. Lastly, financial and banking obstacles – which had already formed a barrier to exchanges in the past – were about to worsen.

Technology and Aerospace

As we saw previously, a key driver behind Iranian economic decision-making lies in the country's quest for self-reliance in technology. During the Iran–Iraq War, the country started or resumed a number of key programmes, some of which were inherently dual-use or were later expanded from purely military to encompassing both military and civilian applications. For example, the country started what has become one of the oldest drone programmes in the world during the war.[103] At the time, Tehran was mainly concerned with the military applications of the programme. But it has since expanded it for uses in other arenas, such as environmental monitoring.[104] Throughout the 2000s, especially, Iranians laid out the foundations for a number of high-tech programmes, leading to what has become a booming sector in the country's economy.[105]

Today, the country is home to a growing technological sector, dynamic startup community, and a number of entrepreneurs. Partly thanks to the sanctions in place and their inability to access major products and platforms, such as Uber, AirBnB, and Amazon, to name a few, Iranian startups have developed similar services indigenously.[106] And with international sanctions in place, these companies developed without much foreign competition. Some of these startups are located in the Pardis Technology Park, just outside Tehran, which has gained a reputation outside of Iran's borders as the country's own 'Silicon Valley'.[107] Planning for the park started in 2000 and by the time the nuclear talks started, the venture had already attracted a number of businesses. In that same period, Iran also made considerable progress in fields such as nanotechnology. By the time of the JCPOA's implementation, Iran ranked fifth in the world in nanotechnology research publication output.[108] The country also invested in advancing technology for use in agriculture, medicine, and space. All in all, Iranians see their country as one of the most active scientific and innovative hubs in the world and believe that they have to carry on that tradition. To that end, the country hopes to create a diverse and comprehensive science and technology landscape, which encompasses both military and civil components. The dynamic and fast-paced Iranian scientific and technological scene is a matter of prestige and nationalism, as much as it is a practical one. Iranian officials often paint the picture of an independent country with a resilient and innovative science and technology sector that has become more diverse and robust over the years in their statements, especially when discussing the impact of sanctions. As Khamenei put it,

From the womb of all sorts of sanctions, which have been forced upon the country for many years, all of a sudden a satellite of Hope [paronomasia on the name of the Omid – hope, in Persian – satellite] comes out and is projected into space. From the womb of all the concentrated efforts [the West] has made, all of a sudden the ability to enrich uranium – which is limited and in the monopoly of the great powers and, which [they believe] should not [be provided to any country] without their authorisation – grows in this

country and comes to life and shows itself. This is proof that
the enemy has not succeeded, its sanctions are not effective, its
threat is also ineffective. Why? Because this nation has kept
its firm determination, which is based on its deep faith, and
moves on and goes forward and they cannot [stop it].[109]

Nevertheless, the country and its dynamic science and technology
sectors crave exchange with the outside world. And although
many Iranian students, researchers, and entrepreneurs hope to
enter the United States and Western Europe to continue their
studies, complete training programmes, or work in their fields,
they too, are increasingly looking to non-Western countries, and
China in particular. This is because while many young Iranians
leave their country to go and study abroad, particularly in the
United States and Europe, and some end up staying in their host
countries, exchange with America especially remains fairly
limited – a matter further complicated by the Trump
administration's controversial 2017 'Travel Ban', which stopped
or significantly delayed the entry of Iranian nationals (and other
mostly majority Muslim states' citizens) into the United States,
even for small-scale conferences or educational exchanges.
Educational exchanges with Europe were also limited, despite
efforts by the civil society to boost them. These additional
difficulties did not exist with Russia and China. Iran also looked to
Russia and China to help them develop parts of its technology
sector that the West deserted. For example, in 2010, China
and Iran signed a $130.6 million telecommunications deal for
networking equipment. As part of this deal, in 2012, Iran received
a surveillance system that would allow it to monitor domestic
telecommunications.[110]

However, both Russia and China have a poor reputation in Iran
when it comes to the technology sector, in particular. The Iranian
population and leadership view the technology and products they
provide with suspicion, and with reason. For example, as we saw

previously, China was exporting its vehicles to Iran at the peak of sanctions. Western vehicles had become too pricy for many Iranians who needed to tighten their belts due to sanctions, inflation, and price hikes. Geelran, a Chinese company, produced its 'low-range vehicles on Iranian assembly lines', including 'old platforms' for sale in that market. At the time, China also supplied Iran with cheap, low quality products in exchange for oil.[111] Iranians have a similar distrust of Russian technology, including its aerospace industry.

After Western companies refused to sell Iran aerospace technology, Iran started to work with Russia to populate and maintain its fleet. Indeed, Iran's once striving aerospace sector, symbolised by the country's flagship carrier Iran Air, crumbled under sanctions. And the fate of the Iranian aerospace industry came to represent the impact of the country's isolation on the daily lives of the Iranian people in their own eyes. During the 1990s and 2000s, Iran was unable to purchase spare parts for its aging fleet. As a result, the safety of Iranian civil aviation took a blow. In the decade following the collapse of the first round of the nuclear talks, Iran counted 16 airliner incidents and nearly 600 deaths.[112] And Iranians expressed their frustration by pointing the finger at two critical players. First, they blamed US sanctions, which they believed unjustly targeted not their leadership but the broader public. Secondly, they criticised the subpar Russian technology their country was acquiring. The Tupolevs and Ilyushins gained a poor reputation because of these incidents and their names became synonymous with danger.[113]

Nevertheless, after a series of accidents during summer 2009, Iran and Russia signed an agreement for Iran to purchase five Tu-204 passenger jets, while the Iranians indicated their willingness to procure another 100 such aircraft.[114] A noteworthy element of this deal was that major components of these aircraft would be produced in Iran under licence – which would satisfy both the short- and medium-term goal of updating the Iranian fleet, while allowing the country to work towards its long-term goal of becoming more self-sufficient. Nevertheless, the Iranians again expressed their disenchantment with the Russians on this front. In the words of the Managing Director of Iran's Air Tour Company, Mehdi Sediqi, 'on many occasions, the Russian companies are reluctant to fulfill their undertakings despite their preliminary pledges.'[115] It is for this reason that Iranian officials saw updating their country's civilian fleet as a top priority during the talks and wanted the JCPOA to provide for it clearly and concretely.[116]

Under sanctions, Russo-Iranian cooperation also grew to other areas. For example, by the time the nuclear talks started, Russia was working with Iran to develop its drone programme, a cooperation that only deepened once the two countries began to work together in Syria.[117] Likewise, the cooperation extended to helicopter supply, where the Russian helicopter manufacturer Verthalutirussia entered a contract with Iran to sell civilian helicopters through Fanavaran Aseman Giti in 2009.[118]

Conclusion

Despite their ideological differences, Iran had already established economic ties with both Russia and China under the Shah. After the Revolution, these relations were momentarily interrupted, but during and in the immediate aftermath of the Iran–Iraq War, Tehran pragmatically turned to its new eastern partners to help its reconstruction efforts and boost trade. Interestingly, the nature and scope of Russia–Iran and Sino–Iran economic relations differed. China and Iran cooperated on a wide-range of economic issues, from infrastructure investments, to energy, to finance; whereas with Russia, economic relations were initially focused on a few key issues, including, but not limited to, nuclear cooperation. As the West and the international community tightened sanctions, Russia and China became increasingly important to Iran economically. And initially, both Moscow and Beijing were only too happy to oblige, increasing economic cooperation with Tehran as much as was possible. But following pressure from the United States and Europe, both were forced to draw down some of their activities in Iran, especially following evermore stringent UN sanctions.

With the international sanctions, Iran's business community developed in much the same way as the country's diplomatic corps and military personnel. A generation ago, businesses and business leaders in Iran knew how to work with Americans and Europeans. Iran's new generation of businessmen and women today has little or no experience working with those players because of the US trade boycott established after the revolution and the extensive sanctions regime enacted in response to Iran's human rights violations, support for terrorism, and missile and nuclear activities. But Russia and China's presence in the country meant that Iranian business institutions and their leadership had to reorient their expertise towards better understanding those who were active in their market, as possible partners, and often, as competitors too. Today, these changes endure in the Iranian system and also mean that Western businesses have a harder time understanding the Iranian market compared to those who had been present throughout the years Iran was under sanctions.

CHAPTER 4

DEFENCE AND SECURITY COOPERATION

A constant tension characterises modern Iranian defence policy: On the one hand, the country strives to be a self-sufficient and an independent power – a core aspiration of the revolutionaries and the Islamic Republic. On the other hand, the country's ambitions are stymied by its practical short-term requirement for advanced military capabilities that require some form of dependence on at least one outside power – especially as the country has become involved in a number of theatres in its neighbourhood, which are a strain on resources. Both the successive imperial governments and the Islamic Republic seem to have historically mishandled this balancing act. Iran's relationship with Russia and China in the defence sector today is a continuation of this problem.

Already in the mid-twentieth century, the Shah aimed to modernise Iran's security apparatus and military industrial complex. To do so, he needed foreign assistance. As a result, he built extensive security ties with the United States, which sparked criticism from the religious establishment and parts of the population. When the revolution began to brew, its leaders denounced the Shah's intelligence apparatus and military establishment as American agents. They hoped to shift Iran's political and economic ties, aiming to disassociate the country from the West and make it self-sufficient. But once the revolution toppled the Shah, and Iran found itself embroiled in a long war with Iraq, the revolutionaries understood that their ideal of complete independence from foreign powers was not viable in the real world. They could not provide for their country's security without some level of support from the outside world. As a result, Tehran began to look earnestly towards China and, later, Russia, to fill the void. As time passed, Beijing and Moscow deepened their security ties with Tehran and further penetrated into the country's defence sector, as they did in other realms discussed so far. Today, the two countries account for most of Iran's military exchange.[1] A key strength of the Russian and Chinese defence industries, militaries, and governments lies in their extensive ties with all quarters of Iran's defence establishment, ranging from Artesh to IRGC. This is particularly important given that the Revolutionary Guards run much of Iran's military industrial complex.[2]

Iran's Defence and Security Relationships Before 1979

Before the Islamic Revolution, Iranian security matters and defence followed two general trends. First, Reza Shah, the founder of the Pahlavi dynasty, attempted to make the country more self-sufficient by developing the country's indigenous defence capabilities. Reza Shah modernised the Iranian military and created the Navy and Air Force, to make the Artesh operational in all three domains: Land, sea, and air.[3] During that time, Reza Shah invested in a military industrial complex, which would allow the country to ultimately become self-reliant in defence and undercut the role and influence of foreign powers, especially the British and the Russians in Iran.[4] The Russians had played a key role in shaping up Persia's military and law enforcement until then.[5] This was despite the two countries' already deeply rooted distrust of one another and the two bloody wars they fought in the nineteenth century. By the time Reza Shah came to power, the Russians were deeply embedded in Persia's security fabric.

After Reza Shah's abdication, without indigenous capabilities allowing him to modernise his country's security apparatus and defence sector, the Shah turned to the Americans, who became Iran's main defence and arms supplier, in addition to its main ally. As a result, after the overthrow of Prime Minister Mossadeq in 1953, Washington was heavily involved in the Iranian defence sector. The Shah accepted $829 million in military assistance, in addition to $1.3 billion worth of new weapons systems, from America between 1950 and 1963.[6] And this trend only increased with time.[7]

The ever-increasing sale of US weapons to Iran was not the subject of consensus in Washington, with many in Congress and the national security establishment objecting to it as the wrong course of action.[8] But the Shah played on Washington's fear of the spread of Communism and Arab nationalism in the region to ensure the flow of weapons to Iran, becoming the most important importer of military hardware in the Middle East by 1969.[9] Then between 1972 and 1974, US weapons sales to Iran more than tripled.[10] In May 1975, then Secretary of State Henry Kissinger described how US arms shipments to Iran increased under President Nixon and Washington's view of this relationship as follows: 'we adopted a policy which provides, in effect, that we will accede to any of the Shah's requests for arms purchases from us (other than some sophisticated advanced technology armaments and with the very important exception, of course, of any nuclear weapons capability).'[11] These sales also included technical assistance on the deployment of some of the systems, as well as capacity-building, including military advice from top US military personnel.[12] At the same time, the Americans helped set up Iran's first intelligence agency, known as SAVAK. The United States also provided training and advised the Iranian security apparatus. With American backing and a modern and powerful military, Iran was able to assert itself and take the security of the Persian Gulf into its own hands.[13] As a result, the Shah's security thinking involved a degree of outsourcing, but his ultimate goal was to follow his father's footsteps and achieve self-reliance.

Iran's Defence and Security Relations After the Revolution

The notion of self-sufficiency and independence from foreign powers also drove the revolutionaries, who believed that their country had become too reliant on foreign powers and America in particular. As a result, as was the case in other fields, Iran turned away from the United States, a matter that was sealed for decades to come with the hostage crisis. But while the country aimed to become self-sufficient and meet its own defence and security needs, it also recognised that the vacuum left by its previous allies and suppliers, chiefly the United States and other Western powers, needed to be filled. During the Iran–Iraq War, Iran started to work on several key defence and dual-use programmes, including the previously dormant nuclear programme, ballistic missiles, drones, and started a space programme. But it also first turned to China before turning to Russia for its defence needs.

Two years into the war, US officials believed China and North Korea accounted for more than 40 per cent of Tehran's arms supplies.[14] During the war, some countries only supported one side, while a number of them supported both sides. China was in the second latter category in what 'is a testament to Chinese diplomatic skill that, in spite of the fact that China also served as a major arms supplier for Iraq, Beijing was able to parley its arms sales to Iran into the beginnings of renewed partnership.'[15] For China, this relationship served several purposes. First, and at face value, the arms trade with Iran opened an important market for the Chinese defence sector. Secondly, this was a geostrategic win for Beijing, which saw partnership with Tehran as a viable way to assert itself in an important region, traditionally under US influence. Lastly, this cooperation was important as China was eyeing Iran as an energy supplier.[16] And, for Iran, China was an attractive supplier, which provided it with technology other powers would not, without 'strings attached', in that Beijing neither posed a threat to Iranian sovereignty, nor was it interested in meddling in Iranian affairs. It also did not use arms sales as a bargaining chip or an instrument of pressure to make Tehran change its behaviour domestically or internationally.[17] As a result, Tehran came out of the war believing that China could be a viable partner – this at a time where the Islamic Republic was generally sceptical of foreign assistance because of the way countries had sided with Iraq, the invading power, in the war. This stems from Chinese punctuality in fulfilling its contracts, as well as its willingness to 'help Iran solve its problems as defined by the Iranian government'.[18] After the end of the war, China became a key defence partner for Iran.

Contrary to China, Russia is viewed as untrustworthy, unreliable, and often dragging its feet to complete sales and honour its contracts. Already during the Iran–Iraq War, though neutral on paper, the Soviet Union supported Baghdad.[19] After the war, followed shortly after by the collapse of the Soviet Union, Russia became Iran's main nuclear supplier and expanded its presence in other sectors of the Iranian security sector. This is because while Iranians viewed China more positively than Russia, Beijing was a 'fair-weather' friend to Iran, especially once the nuclear-related sanctions began to kick in starting in 2005 and the UN imposed its arms embargo on Iran in 2010.[20]

Today, as the Islamic Republic enters its fourth decade, it continues to balance its two objectives of self-sufficiency and meeting its immediate needs and does so by working with Moscow and Beijing.

The Islamic Republic's Security Needs and Military Industrial Complex

With the revolution, Iran lost its conventional strength and its beneficial alliance with America. Subsequently, the country shifted its military doctrine and adopted asymmetric approaches to make up for its conventional inferiority – a doctrine that remains in place today. As a result, Tehran worked predominantly through various militias and non-state actors in key strategic areas, which provided it the influence it coveted without having to stretch its own resources thin or put boots on the ground. The doctrine also afforded it plausible deniability. Since the revolution, the IRGC has become the country's main security organisation, with considerable say and influence over Iranian intelligence and counterintelligence, special operations, terrorism and counter-terrorism, weapons and defence system acquisition, and military operations. This means that any country wanting to work with Iran in any of these areas must accept that it will inevitably cross paths with the Guards. And while the West sees the IRGC as an illegitimate force, responsible for much of Tehran's nefarious activities at home and abroad, Iran sees it as an integral part of its security apparatus. And without saying so publicly, so do Russia and China.

Iran hopes to acquire the ability to provide for the security of its borders, population, and interests. And while observers in the West often see Iranian activities in the region as the Islamic Republic expanding its influence,[21] the Iranian establishment sees much of its own security policy through a purely defensive lens.[22] The truth can be found somewhere in the middle. Iran sees itself as entitled to considerable influence given its history, size, resources, and position in the region. For example, when the Americans criticise Iranian activities in the Persian Gulf, Iranian officials are quick to point out that, the Persian Gulf is their backyard, and it is the United States that has no business operating there.[23]

Iranian political and military officials, and lawmakers, sometimes boast about their country's influence in the region. This was the case of Ali Reza Zakani, a hardline member of the Majles, when he claimed that Tehran controlled four Arab capitals; Baghdad, Beirut, Damascus, and Sana'a.[24] Such claims do nothing but fuel Tehran's neighbours' concerns. Since then, Gulf Arabs, Israelis, and Americans have picked up this sound-bite and posited that Tehran was on its way to acquire a fifth Arab capital, presumably, Manama.[25] This is despite domestic criticism of these comments. For example, as Foreign Minister Zarif put it,

> [...] in some places, despite our positive policies, the other party has a flawed perception of [Iran]. Some off-the-cuff and irresponsible views communicated, none of which have been expressed by our officials, such as the views about the control of Arab capitals, which was both incorrect and incompatible with reality, as well as against the policies of the Islamic Republic of Iran, had a very destructive impact on the psyche of Arab societies.[26]

In addition, some Iranian activities in the region, including its involvement with the Houthis in Yemen, are not a vital security issue in Iran,[27] and are instead, undertaken to poke the Saudis in the eye.

Iran's involvement in the region is not just intended to project power. Like most countries, it also hopes to deter states and non-state actors from attacking its territory, population, and interests. Indeed, state and non-state actors have targeted Iran on a number of occasions since the revolution. Examples of such threats include the Iran–Iraq War, as well as terrorist operations by such groups as Jundullah in its Southeastern province of Sistan-Balochestan and active in the border areas with Afghanistan and Pakistan, or ISIS, which views Shia Islam as blasphemy. This threat perception drives much of Iran's desire for power projection and deterrence, which it achieves through ties to non-state actors, military drills, and defence systems testing. Another result of this threat perception is that Iran aims to balance its neighbours' capabilities: It neither wants central authorities so strong that they can challenge it substantially, as Iraq once did, nor does it wish to see states so weak that they collapse or fail and provide the breeding ground for terrorist groups, as was the case in Iraq in 2014. Iran works with designated terrorist groups where it can, not just for offensive purposes, but also for defensive ones: If it works with them, it can deter them more easily and effectively.[28]

Given its experience with foreign powers, Iran also aims to be self-reliant in the production of defence systems and weapons. As Iranian officials are quick to point out, unlike their Gulf Arab neighbours, who outsource their security and derive it from outside sources, namely the United States, Iran can stand on its own two feet. In May 2017, Rouhani highlighted this in reaction to Trump's visit to Riyadh: 'we produce our own weapons'.[29] Tehran also aims to be self-sufficient in a wide range of areas and in all three traditional operational domains, as well as space and cyber realms. And its drone programme, as we have seen, has also expanded since it was established during the Iran–Iraq War.

Following two noteworthy events, Iran invested considerably to beef up its cyber-capabilities. The first was the domestic upheavals of the post-2009 presidential elections, which led the IRGC to increase its presence in the intelligence and counterintelligence spheres, undermining the civilian-led Ministry of Intelligence and Security. The second was a 2010 foreign attack on the country's enrichment programme, known as Stuxnet. The computer worm reportedly decreased the plant's enrichment efficiency, with officials recording up to 900–1,000 centrifuges being decommissioned, although it is unclear exactly how many of these were due to the worm – as opposed to standard breakage, which routinely plagued Iran's first-generation centrifuges, in particular.[30] Nevertheless, the malware set Iran's nuclear aspirations back by approximately two years.[31]

Following this attack, and now painfully aware of their adversaries' ability to strike at critical infrastructure, Iranian decision-makers invested significantly in defensive and offensive cyber-capabilities. The Stuxnet incident also further involved the IRGC in the cyber realm. Since then, the Guards developed one of the world's most comprehensive and advanced cyber programmes.[32] The programme affords Tehran control, deniability, distance, and asymmetry. And, as we have seen, this fits in Iran's broader modus operandi and doctrine. Helped by the critical mass of an educated, internet savvy population, the country has made considerable progress in a short period. It has become one of the top five countries in cyber-capabilities, alongside Russia, China, and the United States.[33]

Today, Iran's defence sector is comprised of organisations that are active in all these areas. Several key organisations make up Iran's military industrial complex. They are all subsidiaries of the Ministry of Defence.[34] First, Iran Electronics Industries (SA Iran, as it is known) specialises in electronics, IT, and communications technology, including satellites.[35] Secondly, the Defence Industries Organisation (DIO) produces a number of vehicles and delivery vehicles, operating on land, sea, and air. These include tanks, armoured vehicles and personnel carriers, missiles, fighter planes, and submarines.[36] Thirdly, the Iran Aviation Industries Organisation (IAIO) solely operates in aerospace. It produces aircraft (in cooperation with the Russians), jet engines, and other parts.[37] Lastly, the Iranian Space Agency (ISA) is in charge of Iran's dual-use space programme, including rocket launchers and satellites.[38] Due to its dual-use nature, the ISA is not a subsidiary of the Ministry of Defence, instead operating under the jurisdiction of the Ministry of Communications and Information Technology.

To address all of the country's defence needs in these areas, Iranian lawmakers passed a bill in 2016 requiring the Iranian government to spend 5 per cent of its annual state public budget on defence, significantly boosting defence spending for the foreseeable future.[39] Tehran's priorities in defence spending and acquisition lay in three critical areas: Modernising its air force and air defence, beefing up its cyber capabilities, and developing its counterterrorism apparatus.[40]

In the short term, Iran aims to meet its military and security objectives, by arming and equipping itself and the militias and national security forces it supports in the region, including in Syria, Iraq, and Lebanon. In the long run, Iran hopes to become a defence supplier in its own right. To do so, the country is working to boost its domestic defence capabilities. In fact, much of its defence needs are currently met by its own domestic production.[41]

But Iran is also aware of its shortcomings and understands that in order to build up its own military industrial complex, it must acquire defence systems and weapons it cannot produce indigenously. Given the restrictions it faced under international sanctions and until its nuclear programme is deemed to be purely civilian, China and Russia continue to be Iran's best bet. They have the technology Iran seeks, the willingness and ability to work with its armed forces and security apparatus, including the IRGC, and the flexibility to involve the country in the production process, allowing it to build its knowledge base.

Building an Army and Overcoming the Arms Embargo

Russia and China's willingness to work with Iran is important because of the arms embargo and sanctions that limit Tehran's arms procurement and defence cooperation. Following the failure of the first round of negotiations between Tehran and the Europeans on Iran's nuclear programme, the UN Security Council adopted resolution 1737 in December 2006. The resolution outlined an embargo on the export to and import from Iran of certain items and technology potentially related to nuclear weapons.[42] While the resolution does not refer directly to conventional weapons, it includes missiles and other technologies that can be used for both conventional and military applications. When subsequent rounds of talks failed to produce an outcome, a 2010 UNSC Resolution expanded on the arms embargo outlined in UNSC Resolution 1737 and adopted conventional arms and ballistic missile embargoes against Iran in paragraphs 8 and 9 of the resolution.[43] The resolution also provided that the embargoes would be lifted if Iran agreed to implement all measures related to previous Security Council resolutions and negotiate on its nuclear programme. As a result, the conventional and ballistic missile embargoes should have been lifted when Iran agreed to the Interim Agreement on its nuclear programme in 2013. Instead, they were maintained throughout the end of the negotiations and most importantly, in a significant concession by Iran, for another five years for the embargo on conventional weapons and eight years for the ballistic missile embargo – once the IAEA certifies that the country's nuclear programme is purely peaceful in nature.

As a result, until 2020 at the earliest, Iran's ability to purchase armaments and military gear will be subject to Security Council approval, which gives the permanent members of the Council veto power over such deals.[44] While having to present the potential military sales to the Council is a nuisance, it was enough of a loophole for Russia and China to once again explore the sale of military hardware to Iran, which Tehran cannot get from any other serious providers because of its status as a pariah state. US and other unilateral sanctions on the purchase of weapons and ballistic missile parts will likely remain unless individual states decide otherwise. But once the stated five and eight years for conventional weapons and ballistic missiles respectively elapse, Iran will be free to purchase whatever military and missile kit it wants from the international market. This will likely provide a significant boost to Russian and Chinese sales of military arsenal to Iran, given their history of collaboration in this field and the existing links between their military industrial complexes, most notably with Russia.

Moreover, while other states may still refrain from providing the Islamic Republic with weapons and military equipment, Russia and China have no qualms doing so. In fact, the post-JCPOA fanfare surrounding military cooperation between Iran and China, on the one hand, and Iran and Russia, on the other, suggest as much.

Iran–China Defence Cooperation

Just two weeks after the JCPOA's implementation began in January 2016, Xi Jinping visited Tehran. This was the first such visit by a Chinese head of state in years.[45] It included meetings with the highest echelons of the Islamic Republic, including with Khamenei and Rouhani. Following the visit, Beijing upgraded Sino–Iran relations to the status of 'comprehensive strategic partnership', making Tehran one of its priorities.[46] Despite the upgrade and the positive tone of the discussions, the visit did not result in a more formal military alliance or security guarantees for a number of reasons.

First, China believes it must balance its willingness to sell equipment and weapons – especially as the arms embargo is lifted after eight years of JCPOA implementation – and work with Iran on other military ventures, with its other relationships. Indeed, China does not see the utility of picking a partner over another, preferring instead to pragmatically work with anyone that serves its interests. For example, China wants to avoid creating unnecessary tensions with the United States as a result of its military assistance to Iran. In addition, China has 'comprehensive strategic partnerships' with other countries, notably Saudi Arabia, Iran's most significant regional rival. Riyadh is 'by far the largest importer of arms in the Persian Gulf' and the numbers may be even more significant than the official data suggests.[47] As a result, Beijing remains vigilant, and balances its relationship with Tehran, on the one hand, and the Middle Eastern state's adversaries, like Washington and Riyadh, on the other. And so far, this balancing act has revealed itself to be successful for the Asian power.[48] For China, its relationship with Iran is valuable because it sees the Islamic Republic as a bulwark against US influence in the Middle East.[49] But while strengthened military and security ties between China and Iran are inevitable,[50] it is important for China to ensure that these ties do not encroach on its ability to foster relationships with countries that do not view Iran positively.

Secondly, China's view of and approach to its foreign relations and relationships with other countries is different to states, such as the United States. Indeed, America has a set cluster of established allies that are key to its national security and interests. In most cases, Washington's relationship with its allies are very much set, even if the allies do not always serve Washington's interests or values. For example, Washington has steadfastly stood by Riyadh as it continues its involvement in Yemen, despite the Saudi-led coalition's operations there causing a humanitarian crisis and promoting instability.[51] Beijing however, approaches its relationship strictly based on its interests. In other words, China adopts a pragmatic approach that is not set in stone and where allies are not necessarily viewed as a long-term investment. This allows Beijing to ensure that its relationships always serve its interests and revisit them when needed. As a result, China is able to work with various countries when its interests dictate it and can manage expectations among its partners. For example, while the Saudis and their Gulf allies have traditionally harboured a set of expectations, which, they believe, the United States should fulfil – creating tensions when they are perceived as unfulfilled, as they were under Obama – Iran does not have any such expectations from China. This kind of arrangement, and resultant lack of a formal alliance, works for Beijing. But it also works for Tehran, which has made the rejection of foreign power and influence in its domestic affairs a pillar of its ideology.

Defence Equipment and Arms Sales

Iran's defence procurement from China ranges from small arms to surface-to-air missiles, to anti-ship mines, to tanks and fighter jets.[52] As established, Iran also seeks to be involved in at least a part of the production process. This allows Tehran to procure better equipment immediately, while building domestic capacity for the long run. And China provides Tehran with the flexibility, affordability, and tools to pursue these two objectives in its defence contracts.

Until 2005, China was instrumental in the controversial Iranian ballistic missile programme. In fact, 'Chinese-entity ballistic missile-related assistance helped Iran move towards its goal of becoming self-sufficient in the production of ballistic missiles'.[53] In the early 2000s, China reportedly helped Iran develop surface-to-surface ballistic missiles, while the China North Industries Group (Norinco) allegedly supplied it with missile technology.[54] In addition to missile technology, China has also been suspected of involvement in the transfer of WMD-related technology to Iran. As a result, the United States sanctioned eight Chinese entities for the sale of advanced and conventional weapons, as well as chemical and biological weapons components to Iran.[55] In 2005, following the Islamic Republic's growing isolation stemming from its nuclear file, China decreased its defence cooperation with Iran. Yet, in 2008, Beijing surpassed Moscow as Tehran's chief weapons supplier, with the latter procuring anti-ship and anti-aircraft missiles from it.[56] By 2010, the two countries were expanding their cooperation, as Iran opened a Chinese-built plant to produce radar-guided anti-ship missiles and Beijing helped Tehran develop an upgraded version of its own anti-ship cruise missile, the C-802.[57] Iran–China defence ties truly picked up once the nuclear talks resumed, extending to several areas.

In fact, in the aftermath of the JCPOA, Iran joined Pakistan as one of the two top importers of Chinese weapons.[58] Indeed, rumours that Iran was interested in acquiring Chinese fighter jets resurfaced (the purchase was initially discussed right after the agreement was signed).[59] Today, Iran is also reportedly interested in airborne radar and unmanned aerial technologies that China has developed, to feed into its own research and development in this sector. Just weeks after the JCPOA, in October 2015, one of the aforementioned defence firms, SA Iran, signed an agreement with the Chinese to use their BeiDou-2 satellite navigation system for military purposes.[60] This navigational system is more accurate than commercially available GPS services, which could be used to improve Iran's missiles, drones, and other hardware. Iran has also demonstrated an interest in Chinese air and naval military technologies, sending Iranian generals to China to visit aircraft factories and air bases, and discuss future possible purchases, both immediately before and after the JCPOA.[61] China is also an attractive cyber supplier for Iran.[62] This is partly because Beijing is a powerhouse in cyber security. But it also has similar needs and objectives as Tehran in the cyber realm.

China's involvement in Iran's security sector has not been without its problems for Beijing. Several Chinese entities were sanctioned for their involvement in the Iranian ballistic missile programme.[63] According to OFAC, these comprised a 'China-based network that is supporting Iran's military by supplying millions of dollars' worth of missile-applicable items and an Iran-based entity that is assisting Iran's ballistic missile programme.'[64] These items included US-origin products, supplied to an entity designated by the US Treasury Department, known as the Shiraz Electronics Industries, which had produced electronics for Iran's military, including missile guidance technology.[65] The Chinese challenged these sanctions, highlighting in particular that they disagree with the imposition of unilateral sanctions, especially when they hurt a third party, and harm relations based on mutual respect between countries.

Beyond Arms: Joint Military Ventures

China traditionally focused much of its military assistance to Iran on arms sales. But this is changing fast. In addition to being an important weapons supplier to Tehran, Beijing is also becoming a critical partner for the country in other defence spheres. Iran views China as an important counterpart in its 'defence diplomacy' and describes military cooperation with the power as one of its top defence priorities.[66] The high-level military exchanges and joint military drills in the Persian Gulf and the Yellow Sea symbolise the importance of this partnership.[67] Since 2010, the two countries have discussed and increased their cooperation on a range of matters, including intelligence sharing, counterterrorism, anti-piracy, disaster relief operations, and technical expertise.[68] The two countries first held a joint maritime exercise in 2014, including maritime rescue, shortly after the Iranian Navy helped release a Chinese cargo ship from pirates in the Gulf of Aden.[69] Later, Iran's Navy Commander Rear Admiral Habibollah Sayyari stated that his country would be launching joint-anti-piracy missions in the Gulf of Aden with the Chinese.[70] Since then, the two countries' navies have visited each other. For example, Iran sent its destroyer Sabalan and helicopter carrier Kharg to the Jiangsu province in China, while the Chinese sent out their own destroyer, the Changchun and the frigate Changzhou to Bandar Abbas, the port city on the Strait of Hormuz.[71] As we will see later, the two countries have also expanded their joint counter-terrorism efforts with Russia.

Iran–Russia Defence Cooperation

As we have seen, Iran–Russia relations have been complicated. This is especially the case in the realm of defence, characterised by both conflict and cooperation. Russia played a key role in modernising Iran's military, while also being an adversarial force, responsible for some of the country's most significant defeats in the past few centuries. But despite deeply rooted distrust on both sides and the perceived Russian foot-dragging on the delivery of the S-300 missile defence system, Tehran and Moscow increased their defence cooperation once the nuclear talks resumed. For Iran, rebuilding ties with Russia became a question of necessity following its international isolation. But Russia also sought to rebuild its military and security relationship with Iran for a number of reasons.

First, the Russians aimed to reinforce their presence in Iran as they anticipated the emerging nuclear agreement to open the door to new partners for the Iranians, and wanted to ensure they had a head start. The new Rouhani government did not mince its words: Tehran's top priority was the West, and Europe in particular.[72] This deeply concerned the Russians, who tried to strengthen their foothold in the country before the P5 + 1 and Iran reached an agreement.[73] But a more assertive and confident Iran, on the verge of openness, was no longer allowing Russia to leverage its privileged position in the country to dictate the terms of the relationship, as it once had.[74] All this meant that, as Moscow saw it, it had to move fast to resume security cooperation or it would lose out once Iran emerged from isolation post-JCPOA.

Secondly, drastic changes in the broader regional landscape also worried Moscow: Most notably, the Arab Spring was weakening Russian influence in the region.[75] As a result, as the conflicts that emerged from the Arab Spring deepened – notably in Syria – and other regional crises began to brew in key strategic areas for the two countries – including the rise of ISIS and its offshoot in Afghanistan – it made sense for Moscow and Tehran to deepen their military cooperation. Indeed, the two countries' interest aligned in many key theatres, including in Syria and Afghanistan, as noted by Russia's Defence Minister Sergei Shoigu during his trip to Tehran.[76] Russia believes that by working with Iran, it is afforded political cover for its activities in the Middle East and Afghanistan, because it operates with a regional power.

In addition, Russia sees Iran as a stable and important power in an otherwise volatile region: Iran has 25 centuries of 'mostly unbroken statehood' under its belt, an important benefit to Moscow, which sees much of its southern border as unstable.[77] Iran also has influence from Afghanistan to the eastern Mediterranean, and from the Caucuses to the Arabian Peninsula. This makes it an important player for Moscow to leverage in its own efforts in those areas.[78] Finally, in Syria, especially, Iran has provided Russia with ground support, which has made the Russian air campaign there more effective. In fact, Putin stated that without Iranian ground troops – and its support for local ground forces – the Russian air campaign there would not have been possible.[79]

Lastly, Tehran's access to the central authorities, various groups and militias, and knowledge of the region make it an important intelligence partner. These benefits add to the obvious economic gains of military assistance to Iran. And the Russians see these benefits as long-lasting. Even after the sanctions and arms embargo are lifted, Tehran will struggle to gain access to the Western arms market because of its lasting pariah reputation as well as its nefarious activities in the region and beyond. As a result, Rosoboronexport, the Russian state arms export intermediary, will continue to have a stronghold in Iran,[80] and Russia's military industrial complex stands to gain from Russo–Iranian relations.[81]

As we noted, Shoigu visited Iran just months before the JCPOA was concluded in January 2015. The visit led to the conclusion of an agreement between him and his Iranian counterpart, Dehqan, which provided the framework for cooperation. The agreement was meant to build up the capabilities of the two parties, and covered counterterrorism, drug trafficking, information exchanges, exchanges of military personnel for training purposes, and an increase in the number of reciprocal port visits by the Iranian and Russian navies.[82] It also called for increased delegation exchanges, more dialogue, and exchanges best practices on peace-building efforts. Just three months later, Putin lifted the ban on the transfer of the S-300 that had been installed by Medvedev.[83] Following all these events, Nikolai Kozhanov, described the 'intensity of contact' between the two countries as 'unprecedented' since the collapse of the Soviet Union.[84]

In February 2016, during a two-day visit to Moscow, Iranian Defence Minister Hossein Dehqan made it clear that Iran was interested in purchasing a number of different weapons systems from Russia, with a special focus on boosting Iran's air force and fighter jets.[85] Up until then, Iran's efforts to modernise its air force meant upgrading old technologies such as the old Soviet MiGs, American F-14A Tomcats from the 1970s, and Chinese F-7s, because it could not acquire new systems. The Iranians were keen to finalise new agreements rather than focus on the implementation of old ones, with the acquisition of Su-30SM tactical aircraft seemingly top of the list.[86] Russian defence sources suggested that the Iranians were interested in purchasing $8 billion worth of kit.[87] Other possible purchases were rumoured to include Yak-130 advanced training aircraft, Hip family multi-role helicopters, the K-300P Bastion coastal defence missile system previously supplied to Syria and new frigates and diesel electric submarines.[88] The discussions also covered land-based military gear. The Russian company Uralvagonzavod, the world's largest main battle tank manufacturer, offered to organise the licensed production of the T-90S main battle tank in Iran, should the UN Security Council restrictions be lifted.[89] In addition, the supply of some these technologies will require training by Russian forces, something Iranian troops have already taken part in, increasing the back and forth between the two military organisations. In July 2016, Iranian officials went to Moscow to discuss increased cooperation in the procurement of military goods, as well as training and drills.[90] In November, the Russian news agency

TASS reported that Russian officials estimated the worth of the package of contracts covering the sale of Russian weaponry to Iran at $10 billion.[91] The Russians did, however, reiterate that they would not complete these contracts should the Security Council veto them in accordance with resolution 2231. Instead, Moscow would revisit the package in 2020, after the lifting of the conventional weapons ban on Iran.

As with China, the growing security relationship between Iran and Russia has not translated into a more comprehensive strategic alliance. The lack of trust between the two countries is significant. Instead, they prefer to expand their ties without any strings attached: By keeping the relationship flexible and only working together where their interests align, Tehran and Moscow manage expectations. The Russians worry about the optics of their relationship with the Iranians: They do not want to be seen as developing comprehensive ties with the country, instead opting to keep them 'situational' – a sentiment echoed by the Iranians.[92] This also allows Russia to preserve relationships with the other regional powers, predominantly Israel and the Gulf Arabs. For Iran, as Zarif put it,

> I view Russia as a very close neighbour that can play different roles in various areas. But we must always have a very close relationship based on constructive engagement and partnership with Russia. The reason why I do not use any of those terms [partner, collaborator, ally, or rival] to describe Russia is that I believe coalitions are passing in the world. Coalitions are not permanent and comprehensive, Coalitions are topical. [...] It is possible that we have different viewpoints in certain areas [with Russia]. It is possible that we sometimes have different interests. It is possible that we have some rivalry with one another on certain issues, such as oil and gas. But all this leads to us having the essence of a strong and strategic relationship between Iran and Russia. Likewise,

this applies to China and we can and must create a strategic relationship with China.[93]

Defence Equipment and Arms Sales

After the collapse of the Soviet Union, the end of the Iran–Iraq War, and particularly, the imposition of sanctions on Iran for its nuclear programme, Moscow and Tehran started to increase their defence ties. Following Iran's initial turn to China for weapons imports during the war, Tehran turned its attention to Russia by the end of the 1980s, with weapons imports peaking at $772 million in 1991.[94] But with the imposition of restrictions by the Security Council with Resolution 1747 (2007), which included an arms embargo, Russia severely drew down its sales. It even suspended the delivery of the S-300, following pressure from the United States in particular, but neither side stopped security relations completely.

As we have seen, during the Iran–Iraq War, Iran imported most of its weapons from China. But by the end of the war, Russia overtook China and became a significant weapons supplier for Iran, with sales peaking at $772 million in 1991 and at $559 million in 1993.[95] Throughout the 1990s, Russian sales to Iran included tanks, anti-tank missiles, submarines, and surface-to-air missile systems. Already throughout this period, relations were strained, as the Russians did not always deliver the promised number of ordered items. Although there has been a great deal of speculation over what happened exactly, in 1991, Iran ordered 1,000 T-72M1 tanks from Russia, but the Russians reportedly only delivered 422 of them, including a significant number that were assembled in Iran.[96]

Throughout the early 2000s military and security ties continued, with another peak in Russian weapons sales to Iran in 2006, amounting to $368 million.[97] At the turn of the century, Iran received items such as the MiG-29 fighter aircraft, Su-24 fighter bombers, T-72 tanks and Kilo class attack submarines.[98]

But, as we have noted, the sale of weapons to Iran took a hit after the imposition of international sanctions on Iran with UNSC resolution 1737, and following US pressure. At first, Moscow tried to continue the existing level of sales, but unlike China, Russia chose to draw down some of its sales to Iran following sanctions. For example, in 2007, Russia sold Iran the surface-to-air missile S-300 as part of an $800 million contract, but suspended the sale of the system in 2010 until 2016, after the nuclear deal. The delay in the delivery reinforced Iran's perceptions that no foreign power, including its friends, could be trusted to resist Western pressure to isolate Iran and that the country must take steps to become increasingly self-reliant, in order to neutralise efforts to isolate it. At the time, it was also announced that Russia was interested in exploring the potential sale of fighter jets, tanks, and ships, with the potential for Iran to be involved in the production of the jets.[99] Today, Iran is pursuing the option of building capacity while engaging in procurement efforts more actively with Russia.

Russia is also heavily involved in dual-use areas. As we saw, the Russians held a quasi-monopoly on the Iranian nuclear programme starting at the end of the Iran–Iraq War, and until the signing of the JCPOA. Despite distrust of the Iranians, the Russians are continuing to provide dual-use technology to Iran. In particular, both Tehran and Moscow have expressed an interest in cooperating to develop the Iranian space programme.[100] The Iranians are hoping that the programme will serve both civilian and military purposes. In terms of its military aspects, the space programme would be used for intelligence, counter-intelligence, and counterterrorism. Iran is hoping to build its signals intelligence (SIGINT) capabilities, which it would use for both defensive and offensive counterintelligence, as well as its domestic intelligence activities.[101] In this context, Tehran expressed interest in acquiring communications and remote sensing satellites from Moscow, as well as access to the GPS-equivalent GLONASS positioning and navigation system.[102]

More recently, the two countries also started cooperating in the cyber-realm. For its part, Russia has extensive and wide-ranging cyber-capabilities, with the goal of gathering data, espionage or developing offensive capabilities against specific targets.[103]

Beyond Arms: Joint Military Ventures

Iranian–Russian defence cooperation goes beyond simple arms sales. It covers more exhaustive defence cooperation, including joint military drills, especially in the Caspian, and on the ground coordination, particularly in Syria. The two countries also cooperate in the South Caucasus and Afghanistan.[104]

The first joint exercises between Russia and Iran were held in 2009, and Deputy Commander of Russia's Caspian Flotilla Nikolai Yakubovsky announced further joint drills after Iranian ships were dispatched to Russian ports in 2013.[105] They took place a year later in October 2014, when Russian ships were dispatched to the port of Anzali, in northern Iran.[106] Since the nuclear deal between the P5 + 1 and Iran, the pace of these drills picked up. In the Caspian basin, the two countries leveraged their respective positions to assert themselves as the key players in the region and push back against potential NATO presence there. As a result, in August 2015, a mere month after finalising the nuclear deal, Moscow and Tehran conducted joint military exercises in the Caspian basin. Russian ships docked in the Anzali port for three days of training and exercises involving the Iranian Navy destroyer, Damavand, and missile armed fast attack craft Joshan and Peikan, as well as 200 Iranian naval forces, with Russia's Volgodonsk and Makhachkala corvettes.[107] Both countries repeated the exercise a few months later in October 2015, with Iranian ships making the journey to the Russian port of Astrakhan for joint drills.[108]

In Syria, Iran became involved in the conflict by sending advisors and putting boots on the ground and propping-up various militias to help ensure the Assad regime's survival. For its part, Russia did not become overtly involved in Syria until later, when it began to offer intelligence, material support, and air power to provide cover for these ground forces in 2015.[109] Russia was able to leverage Iranian presence in Syria in a number of ways. First, Iran had boots on the ground fighting alongside Assad's forces. Secondly, Tehran's extensive ties to various militias in the country and throughout the region became an asset for Russia. Syrian and Iraqi militias, as well as the Pakistani and Afghan militias Tehran deployed to Syria – known as the Zeynabiyoun and Fatemiyoun, respectively – and its proxy, Hezbollah, were all involved, but also influential and effective in the conflict. Thirdly, Iran's relationship with Baghdad was also a benefit to Russia. While Iran welcomed Russian assistance, which was key in re-capturing territories that the Syrian government had lost to the rebels, it also came at a cost to Iran. Prior to Russian involvement in the conflict, Iran's influence in Damascus was unparalleled; Assad was indebted to Tehran for its support at a time when important players within the international system, particularly the West, were calling for him to step down. In addition, Iran's involvement in the conflict in Syria bought it a 'seat at the table' in the same way the negotiations with the P5 + 1 on its nuclear programme had done. With Russia's growing involvement in Syria however, Iran saw its influence in Damascus, as well as on the Syrian conflict in international fora, diminished.[110]

A noteworthy escalation of tensions in the Russo–Iranian partnership in Syria occurred in the aftermath of the Russian use of an Iranian military base in August 2016. The Iranian Nojeh base – located outside the city of Hamedan, which is the closest facility to the air corridor between Tehran and Damascus – is the third Tactical Air Base (TAB-3) of the Iranian Air Force,[111] considered Iran's main combat air base. The base was designed and completed by the United States in the 1960s, when the two countries were still allies. At the time, Nojeh – then known as the Shahrokhi Airbase – was built to counter the potential threat of a Soviet invasion across the Zagros Mountains – a mountain range spanning approximately 1,500 km from the northwest of Iran down the country's Western boarder and into Fars province – and also Iraqi aggression from the west. During the Iran–Iraq War, Nojeh was the main hub from which the country conducted deep strike missions inside Iraq. Iran granted Russian long-range Tu-22M3 bombers access to the base, which is far closer to Syria than bases in Russia, allowing the aircraft to carry less fuel and more munitions as they struck rebel forces and positions in Aleppo, Dair Alzour and Idlib provinces in Syria.

Prior to being granted access to the base, Russian long-range bombers conducted airstrikes in Syria from a southwestern Russian base in Mozdok. But this meant that they had to cover a distance of about 2,000 km to get to Syrian airspace. That distance was greatly reduced, to approximately 700 km when the bombers took off from Nojeh, thus both reducing the cost of the strikes and ensuring their timeliness. At the time, the Russian Defence Ministry said the strikes eliminated five major terrorist weapons depots and training compounds, as well as three command posts and a 'significant number of terrorists'.[112] Granting access to the Iranian airbase was part of the agreement signed in January 2016, expanding Russian–Iranian military cooperation.[113]

But the Iranians did not want the details of this arrangement to be made public. Indeed, Iranians are particularly sensitive to foreign presence on their soil. The Iranian constitution under the Islamic Republic specifically refers to this: Article 146 forbids 'establishing any kind of foreign military base on Iran's territory, even for peaceful purposes.'[114] And critics of the move were quick to point this out. But there were domestic disagreements over the interpretation of this provision, especially as pertaining to the temporary use of Iranian bases for refuelling purposes. Nevertheless, a number of Iranian lawmakers questioned the decision to grant Russians access to the base. This group included the influential Speaker of the Majles Ali Larijani, who criticised Dehqan for failing to discuss it with parliament and not observing 'the ethics of governing.'[115] Iranian officials, however, were quick to dismiss the criticisms. The Chairman of the Parliament's National Security and Foreign Policy Commission, Alaeddin Boroujerdi, pointed out that the Russians had not established a presence on the Iranian base. Their warplanes had merely used it for refuelling.[116] Other Iranian officials went further and outlined the parameters of the Russia–Iran partnership in Syria, and how the decision to grant Russia access to the airbase was part of the fight against terror. Ali Shamkhani, Secretary of the Supreme National Security Council and Khamenei's representative there stated, 'Iranian–Russian cooperation to fight terrorism in Syria is strategic. We must unite our potential and capabilities.'[117]

What critics had judged problematic was the reported overnight stay of the Russian jets on the base. High-ranking Western military officials said that they believed this was a miscalculation on the part of the Iranian defence establishment, which no longer had the expertise to judge the amount of time the Russians would require to refuel.[118] Nevertheless, although they defended the decision, Iranian officials were outraged that the Russians leaked the information. A week after members of parliament criticised the Iranian government's decision to grant Moscow access to the Iranian base and the Iranian media reported it, Dehqan criticised the Russians for excessively publicising the whole event, stating that, ' [the] Russians are interested to show they are a superpower to guarantee their share in political future of Syria and, of course, there has been a kind of show-off and ungentlemanly [attitude] in this field'.[119] He also criticised Iranian parliamentarians for involving themselves in matters that did not fall within their mandate as lawmakers. This was not entirely unreasonable given that the Supreme National Security Council (SNSC) and its secretary had approved of the decision to grant the Russians access to the base – one presumably approved at the highest levels. Dehqan was forced to apologise for his comments, after Larijani criticised him for it in an open letter to parliament.[120]

As the debate over whether the decision was constitutional or not reached fever pitch, the Iranian government overturned the access granted to Moscow, barring Russian jets from refuelling in Iranian facilities.[121] The Russians downplayed Iran's decision to rescind their access to the airbase by stating that the aircraft had completed the mission they had set out to achieve.[122] The public criticism of the decision by Iranian lawmakers, the media coverage, and the apparent uncoordinated responses from Iranian officials suggested that this arrangement was meant to remain secret. Iran perceived the Russian move as one designed to bolster its image as the lead partner in this collaboration effort and a force to be reckoned with as it displayed its military capabilities. There was also disbelief at the Russian lack of understanding or simple disregard for the sensitive and difficult internal political scene in Iran.

Nevertheless, and to great surprise, given the controversy and criticism this incident attracted in Iran, the government indicated in the first half of 2017 that it would be assessing Russian requests to use its bases for refuelling purposes on a case by case basis, and potentially granting them access to these facilities.[123] This was an important step and the overall incident was significant for a few reasons. First, this was the first time a foreign power had used an Iranian military facility since the end of World War II. Secondly, throughout the nineteenth century and first decades of the twentieth century, the Persians worked to minimise Russian influence in their country and to limit Moscow's access to their resources and territories. Thirdly, this precedent was important, as a key driver of the revolution was ending what Iranians viewed as their country being used and exploited by foreign powers, particularly the United States. But while Tehran accepted granting Moscow access to its air bases on an ad hoc basis, it made it clear that authorisation would not constitute blanket access – although such a blank check would increase Russia's operational flexibility and effectiveness by boosting its firepower and manoeuvering space.[124] The air base incident illustrated the complex nature of Iran–Russia defence and security cooperation once again: Increased military cooperation against a backdrop of tensions.

In Afghanistan, Tehran and Moscow's coordination is also underpinned by tension. In 1996, when the Taliban gained control of Kabul and took the reins of power, Iran and Russia started operating together there together. When the United States and its allies entered Afghanistan in 2001, their interests aligned with those of Washington and NATO. As a result, despite their disagreements on a number of other issues, Russia and Iran cooperated with America and its NATO allies. But while US and NATO presence was helpful in combatting mutual threats, such as Al-Qaeda, it also created some anxiety in both Tehran and Moscow. This is because both countries see Afghanistan as their backyard.[125] Yet, as the war continued without an end in sight and the volatile country once again descended into more instability, the Russians and Iranians took matters into their own hands and started working with the Taliban. Indeed, although both Tehran and Moscow view the Taliban as a threat, they see the groups as the 'lesser of two evils' when weighed against ISKP, whose ideology, brutality, and recruitment efforts pose a greater threat to the two nations. Hence, Iran and Russia have provided support to Taliban groups since ISKP began to make gains in Afghanistan following the rise of ISIS in Iraq. And as we will see, in these efforts, they are joined by China.

Iran–China–Russia Joint Military Ventures

As we have seen so far, bilateral defence cooperation and procurement activities between Iran and Russia, on the one hand, and Iran and China, on the other, afforded Tehran the opportunity to circumvent Western limits on its military acquisition. In addition to equipping and arming Iran, Russia and

China both allowed the country to develop its knowhow to advance towards its objective of self-reliance by involving it in the production process. This partnership also extended to training and military drills.

Counterterrorism Efforts

As we saw, most of Iran, Russia, and China's defence activities were focused on bilateral efforts: Russia and China, Iran and Russia, and Iran and China developed their bilateral defence cooperation. But since the rise of ISIS and its offshoot in Afghanistan, ISKP, the three countries have seen counterterrorism as an area where they can all work together to better focus their efforts.

In Syria, Iran has been involved on the side of the Assad regime in the conflict since it started. It committed ground troops, including the IRGC and Artesh, as well as recruits from Afghanistan and Pakistan.[126] Russia committed air power to supporting Assad and Iran's ground forces later. China did not join these efforts officially until the second half of 2016, when it began to overtly support the Assad regime. Since then, China has provided Damascus with military advisers and personnel, as well as material support, such as sniper rifles and rocket launchers.[127]

Russia and Iran have constructed a careful narrative in justifying their efforts and their cooperation in Syria. As established, one major stated goal of their cooperation efforts in Syria is to counter terrorism. Moscow and Tehran have made this another pillar of their relationship. Russia believes that the chaos in a post-Assad Syria would result in the rise of Islamism and Islamist terrorism, which it wants to avoid, including in Russia. The country has a small, but growing Muslim minority. Assessments of the Muslim population's integration differ. Some posit that Russia under Putin made an effort to ensure that a patronage system is fostered with Russian Muslims and that they are brought into the military, for example,[128] while others argue that Putin fostered ultra-nationalism, which alienated the Muslim minority.[129] Nevertheless, Russia's growing nationalism and role in Syria helped the spread of extremist Islamist ideologies within the Russian Muslim minority, including the Caucasus Emirate, a group responsible for a number of terrorist attacks in Russian cities.[130] In recent years, these attacks have increased the fear of Islamist extremism in Russia. These include the April 2017 bombing in the St. Petersburg subway, which caused 14 deaths and 50 injured, reportedly committed by a young man with ties to radical Islamist entities.[131] Such attacks are also likely to worsen as Russia's efforts in Syria continue, with ISIS pledging to retaliate for Russia's strikes against it in Syria.[132] In addition, Russia does not nuance the different Islamist groups, like the United States and other countries do. For example, Washington differentiates between ISIS and Al-Nusra, viewing ISIS as an extreme Sunni jihadist threat it must fight and al-Nusra as a more moderate Islamic force that fights the Assad government, while Moscow aims to eliminate both.[133] Interestingly, Russia does differentiate between ISIS and the Taliban in Afghanistan, and works with the latter – a departure from its previous position on the matter.[134]

Iran, for its part, is acutely aware of the threat presented by ISIS.[135] The group put Shia Iran at the top of its target list and believes that Shia Islam is a 'deviation' from true Islam.[136] Iranian fears of ISIS were confirmed when Iran's Intelligence Ministry unveiled and defused an ISIS plan to conduct a large-scale terrorist attack on Tehran.[137] The plan was to hit 50 targets using 100 kg of explosives across the Iranian capital. ISIS paid the operatives hundreds of thousands of dollars for these attacks. A year later, in June 2017, ISIS hit two symbolic sites in the Iranian capital, the mausoleum of Ayatollah Khomeini and the Majles, killing a dozen and wounding many more.[138] This was the group's first successful attack against Iranian targets. While Tehran feels the ISIS threat more severely on its border with Iraq, it believes the organisation must be countered in all regional arenas, including in Syria.

Both Russia and Iran believe that the only way to prevent the growth of terror in Syria is to maintain the Assad regime in place as a bulwark against it. In addition, it is their perspective that having a government structure and bureaucracy in place allows them to coordinate more effectively with someone on the ground in order to make the fight against terror more effective. But there are inconsistencies in the Russian and Iranian position on the Syrian conflict and their counter-ISIS efforts. While Iran and Russia support Assad, Assad continues to be lenient on ISIS to present himself as a better alternative to the Syrian people and international community. Likewise, while ISIS represents a critical threat to both Iran and Russia, it also serves as a convenient excuse for the two countries' operations in Syria in support of Assad, even as he massacres civilians and uses chemical weapons. Finally, Russia seems to be avoiding targeting ISIS in its efforts in Syria, which is inconsistent with its stated goal of fighting the group. Interestingly, and in an effort to present itself in a positive light, Russia highlighted that none of the cooperation with Iran on fighting terrorism was at any point, against Security Council resolution 2231, which endorsed the nuclear deal with Iran.[139]

China, for its part, upped its involvement in the crisis in Syria when it hosted Syrian government officials and members of the opposition (at different times) and then appointed a special envoy for Syria, to support the UN mediation efforts in September 2016. As promised, it reportedly sent special advisors and military personnel to Syria after Chinese Rear-Admiral Guan Youfei, the head of the Office for International Military Cooperation under the Central Military Commission that oversees China's armed forces, went to Syria to meet Syrian Defence Minister Fahd Jassim Al Freij and Russian Lieutenant-General Sergei Chvarkov, head of the ceasefire monitoring mission in Syria, as well as Russian commanders at the Hmeimim military base.[140] A few months later, the Governor of Aleppo Hussein Diab thanked Russia,

China, and Iran for their efforts supporting the Syrian government in their 'fight against terror'.[141]

In Afghanistan, all three countries have been working together to fight the growing terror threat posed by ISKP. For Iran, ISKP poses critical challenges. As a result, starting in 2014, Iranian officials were worried about the rise of an offshoot of ISIS in Afghanistan, and warned that ISIS operatives were active there.[142] Afghan and NATO officials did not view the threat as pressing, as they did not believe ISIS to be a viable player in Afghanistan. But for Tehran, the possibility of ISKP gaining ground in its Eastern border, therefore sandwiching Iran between two volatile regions with substantial ISIS presence was and remains a critical concern.

In Russia, ISIS and ISKP are increasingly viewed as a threat, as the organisation gained ground not just in Afghanistan but also in Central Asia, a key area of interest to Moscow. And ISIS also penetrated another critical region to Russia: Chechnya. In 2016, Chechen law-enforcement estimated 3,000 to 4,000 Chechens had gone to Iraq or Syria to join ISIS.[143] For its part, China has long struggled with its Muslim minority, the Uighur, predominantly concentrated in the Xinjiang province in western China. In fact, Beijing has been criticised for oppressing cultural and religious rights and freedoms in the area under the pretext of national security and counterterrorism, while at the same time exacerbating its terrorism problem.[144] These tensions provided ISIS with fodder for its propaganda, which rallied 114 Uighurs to join ISIS in 2016.[145] These operatives predominantly came from Xinjiang, which they call Turkestan or East Turkestan. As a result, the rise of ISKP in Afghanistan and Central Asia was a key concern to China, which it viewed as a threat to stability and security in the vulnerable Xinjiang province. But the threat has gained more urgency and Beijing now views its scope as much broader. In the first quarter of 2017, ISIS released a video threatening China, promising to retaliate by making Chinese 'blood flow in rivers'.[146] As a result, the Chinese, who traditionally had a more hands off and wait and see approach to Afghanistan, became more involved there following these developments.

Iran allocated substantial resources to the fight against ISIS and adapted its counterterrorism apparatus and policies to fight this threat. And as Russia and China have each begun to see ISIS and ISKP as a more serious threat to their own territories, populations, and interests, the three countries have increased their cooperation in counterterrorism. As all three countries feel the threat posed by ISIS and ISKP acutely, they all try to neutralise the group in Afghanistan by working individually, with Kabul and various insurgent groups in the country, together, and with other international players, such as India. Iran works with the central government in Afghanistan, while also funding Taliban groups to counter ISKP, as it views Kabul as too weak and the Taliban as gaining ground in the country regardless.[147] Similarly, the Russians work with the Taliban.[148] And China has sent armed forces to Afghanistan and conducted law enforcement operations with the Afghan police in the border areas.[149] The three countries have also held several multilateral meetings on countering ISKP in Afghanistan, including with India and Pakistan.[150]

Conclusion

After all ties between Iranian and Western security apparatuses were broken off following the revolution and the hostage crisis in particular, the Iranian military establishment began working closely with the Russians and the Chinese to develop the country's capabilities. As a result, today's generation of Iranian military cadres have extensive experience working with the Russian and Chinese militaries. Iran's military has limited contact with Western military personnel. Indeed, Iran's armed forces have worked with Western military personnel in a few cases – such as the Iranian Navy's limited but regular contacts with the US Navy in the Persian Gulf,[151] Tehran's cooperation with Washington to secure the future of Afghanistan and its government after the 2001 Bonn conference, and the limited tactical coordination with America in pushing back ISIS in Iraq. But military and security relations with Russia and China have remained extensive, despite the ban on the sale of weapons systems to Iran under the Security Council resolutions prior to the JCPOA.

Iran's experience of dealing with Russia and China, which it deemed as untrustworthy partners, was a driver behind its decision to embark on the nuclear negotiations with the P5 + 1. It also served to emphasise the development of a 'resistance economy', based on self-sufficiency in key 'strategic sectors', including the sciences and the military.[152] Tehran understood, however, that it would not be able to wean itself off partners such as Russia and China for some items such as defence systems. Today, the two countries allow Iran to acquire systems it cannot buy from other sources. Defence cooperation with Russia and China is not just useful for Iran as it pertains to procurement. Instead, both countries afford Tehran the opportunity to also be part of the production process, allowing it to develop its knowhow and, thus, take steps towards its goal of boosting indigenous manufacturing and, ultimately, self-reliance.

CHAPTER 5

POST-JCPOA: FUTURE PROSPECTS

As we have seen, Iran leveraged its relations with China and Russia to overcome international political and economic isolation during the nuclear crisis. But as Western efforts to isolate the country continued, finally culminating in Trump's decision on 8 May 2018 to withdraw America from the JCPOA, China and Russia further consolidated their presence and influence in key sectors in Iran. Tehran came to the negotiating table with the objective to normalise its relations with the rest of the international community, especially the West, terminate international sanctions impeding its economy, and to diversify its partners. But even though the JCPOA opened a number of doors for Iran to resume relations with other countries, it did not afford the country the ability to replace Russia and China as key partners, especially in light of Trump's efforts to increase the uncertainty surrounding the deal starting in January 2017. Instead, the JCPOA served as a catalyst for broader and deeper partnerships between Tehran and Beijing, on the one hand, and Tehran and Moscow, on the other. Today, despite numerous points of tension and disagreement, Iran's relationship with Russia and China runs deep and spans a wide range of issues, including foreign policy, trade and finance, energy, and security and defence.

Iran was expected to become a business 'El Dorado' after the lifting of sanctions. But while interest was high and many delegations rushed to sign MOUs, the actual increase in business and the exchange of money was still few and far between in the aftermath of the nuclear agreement. This was especially the case for larger Western businesses with significant brand recognition – the type of business that the Iranian economy required to show growth and resultant credibility to attract more business and foreign investment. The slow pace of sanctions relief, coupled with the uncertainty brought upon the JCPOA by political changes in the United States and the shortcomings in the Iranian regulatory landscape and economic environment – including corruption, mismanagement, and the lack of transparency – stymied business attraction to Iran.[1]

To make matters worse, processing payments for deals made with Iranian businesses remained complicated, and major banks, especially those based in Europe, refused to expose themselves to third party US sanctions and risk their access to the American market.[2] But these were precisely the major European banks the Iranian economy needed to attract, as they were the ones that could process major payments and open significant lines of credit of the type the Iranians sought to offset their economic woes. But only institutions with no business exposure in the United States could afford to conduct business in Iran. As a result, only the small to medium-sized financial institutions of Europe were willing to take the risk of entering Iran, including Raffeisen of Switzerland and Erste Bank of Austria.[3] Iranian businesses and their foreign counterparts found it difficult to find banks to process payments for their deals, which made it difficult to rush back into Iran. While some European firms jumped at the chance to explore the Iranian market once the dust settled after the nuclear deal, the general risk aversion by major companies and US firms, in particular, was only exacerbated by the uncertainty following Trump's election.

Initially, upon taking office, Trump's campaign rhetoric, combined with his administration's hawkish stance on Iran, increased the questions surrounding the future of the deal. In October 2017, he failed to recertify the nuclear deal,[4] and in January 2018, he renewed US sanctions waivers but stated it would be for the last time,[5] placing the deal's future in even more doubt. Finally, in May 2018, Trump announced his decision to withdraw the United States from the JCPOA. As a result, in the aftermath of the nuclear deal, neither Tehran nor European businesses were able to reach their objectives of Iran opening up and establishing ties with European businesses, banks, and investors.

While some smaller to medium-sized foreign businesses re-explored the Iranian market and took their time to familiarise themselves with what had become an unfamiliar environment, Russia and China needed no additional time to understand the Iranian economy. As we saw, both had maintained a presence in Iran. And both understood the inner workings of the Iranian economy: The 'who's who', what to avoid, and how to navigate the murky obstacles in place to establish a presence. Most importantly, because of their sustained presence, both had the necessary contacts for successful business ventures, and this, despite the mistrust between them and Iranians. As a result, Russia and China were able to meet their objectives: Expanding, their strong presence in Iran. In some ways, the post-JCPOA environment afforded them opportunities that surpassed their expectations, allowing them to further consolidate their presence in Iran and preserve or create quasi-monopolies in key sectors. The nuclear deal created an ideal environment for the two powers: Thanks to Russia and China's continued presence in Iran, their firms were free to navigate the Iranian market and expand their presence, unconstrained by international regulations. But now, they could do so without the barriers that existed prior to the JCPOA like their European counterparts.

As we highlighted throughout this book, a key advantage for Russia and China in Iran was their continued presence in the country throughout the sanctions period, which allowed them to build and preserve human relationships and better understand the opaque Iranian economic environment. Today, a generation of entrepreneurs, bankers, investors, and other businessmen on both sides have become accustomed to dealing with each other, in a way that Iranians have not done with Westerners for many years. And the same can be said for other sectors. It is noteworthy that the majority of Iran's population is under 35 years of age,[6] meaning most Iranians were was born and raised after the Islamic Revolution. This is significant because Iran's ties and extensive exchanges with the West occurred prior to the power grab by the revolutionaries in 1979. After the collapse of the Shah, Tehran was rapidly cut off from the United States and, to a lesser extent, Europe. As a result, different sectors in Iran were forced to adapt to this new reality. Iran's human resources in the business, political, and defence sectors increasingly shifted towards Russia and China.

Iran–Russia Relations Post-JCPOA: Bitter Friends in Need

Future of Defence Cooperation

Russia is likely to remain a key partner for Iran in defence and security. Since the JCPOA, both countries expressed their desire to boost military and defence cooperation. The aforementioned 2016 bill requiring the Iranian government to spend 5 per cent of its annual state public budget on defence, significantly boosted defence spending for the foreseeable future.[7] This made the Iranian market a potentially lucrative one for Russia, the world's second largest supplier of military arsenal.[8]

But Russia–Iran military cooperation post-JCPOA was not limited to the sale of weapons and defence systems; it also extended to conducting joint exercises – an area in where more activity is likely to occur in the future. In February 2017, Iran announced its intention to intensify naval cooperation with Russia in the future during the visit of an Iranian flotilla in the port of Makhachkala, the capital city of the Republic of Dagestan in Russia.[9] These exercises are part of a joint effort for Russia and Iran to assert themselves as the two main powers in the Caspian, and consequently, capable of handling security in those waters and region without foreign intervention. But the relationship is not without its difficulties, as the Nojeh airbase access incident demonstrated.[10] In fact, as Iranian and Russian interests in Syria increased and solidified and the fight against ISIS wound down, and everyone considered reconstruction efforts, the tensions worsened.[11] Both parties wanted to ensure they had a bigger cut of the pie when it came to economic deals and contracts for reconstruction, and Iran felt as though it was being left behind in favour of Russia.[12] Nevertheless, neither state will walk away from the other in the context of this conflict. The two countries' aligned interests in Syria include asserting themselves in the conflict to avoid a potential Western brokered solution that would exclude them, propping Bashar al-Assad's regime, and counter-ISIS efforts. In fact, despite their differences, Russia and Iran continued to present a unified front. Differences with others in Syria,[13] and President Trump's intensifying offensive on the Iran deal, resulted in Russia increasingly defending Iran.[14] In late 2017 and early 2018, the Russians vigorously defended Iran and the nuclear deal, including during a number of UNSC meetings.[15] In fact in February 2018, Russia went so far as to veto a UN Security Council Resolution targeted at Iran for its assistance to the Houthi rebels in Yemen, clearly demonstrating that Moscow was not afraid to use its seat on the Council to stand up for its partner.[16] In early 2018, the Iranians and Russians continued their regular high-level meetings discussing regional security, with a meeting between Hossein Jaberi Ansari, senior assistant to Iran's Foreign Minister and Russian Deputy Foreign Minister Mikhail Bogdanov, who also served as Vladimir Putin's special envoy for the Middle East.[17]

But Syria was not the only arena where Russia and Iran coordinated their fight against terrorism. After the ISIS-sponsored terrorist attack in St. Petersburg in early 2017, President Rouhani was quick to extend condolences to the Russians and call for further cooperation in anti-terror efforts between the two states.[18] Today, both countries are on the same side in Afghanistan. As we have seen, Tehran and Moscow see ISKP as a prominent threat, and believe it is gaining ground in Afghanistan. As the Taliban began to regain territories they had lost to NATO, Iran and Russia began to work with Taliban groups. Neither Moscow nor Tehran sees the Taliban as a friend or an ally, and both see it as a destabilising force. However, the threat of ISKP, coupled with the Taliban's growing influence in key rural areas in Afghanistan, have led Iran and Russia to see working with the groups as almost inevitable.

Another area where Russia and Iran have indicated a desire to intensify cooperation is in cyber-security. During Rouhani's visit to Moscow in March 2017, a joint statement outlining the outcomes of the meeting with Putin addressed growing concerns over cyber-security – and, in particular, the spread of cyber-attacks for 'criminal, terrorist, military and political goals.' Cyber-security and countering cyber-attacks will clearly be an area of further cooperation between Russia and Iran, who highlighted, 'the need to elaborate under the UN aegis the rules of the states' responsible behaviour in the information space and noted the readiness of Russia and Iran to develop cooperation in this direction.'[19] Once again, it is noteworthy that both governments stated their desire to work within the existing international UN-led order to develop a legal framework on cyber-security applicable to all. Nevertheless, as we have seen, the two countries continue to build their offensive cyber-capabilities and have a track record of using the cyberspace for intelligence-gathering purposes – an activity that will only gain in importance.

Cooperation between Iran and Russia in the aftermath of the nuclear deal was not limited to the realm of military efforts. The two countries also boosted trade relations in a number of sectors, a trend that will only increase and intensify over time, particularly as sanctions relief remained slow and patchy.

Resources, Technology, and Infrastructure

In the aerospace industry, Russia courted the Iranian government as early as December 2015, to deliver the medium range passenger plane the Sukhoi Superjet and establish a production facility in Iran to cover partial localisation of production.[20] This is significant because Iranians view the Russian aerospace sector negatively and had hoped to boost cooperation with the West following the JCPOA. The Iranian negotiators wanted the purchase of civilian aircraft from the West to be a clear component of the JCPOA.[21] As a result, Boeing was specifically named in the agreement. And Tehran was also permitted to work with Boeing's European rival, Airbus, the joint European consortium of aerospace manufacturers, without contravening international sanctions. Indeed, after decades of being limited to flying an aging American fleet purchased prior to the revolution and Russian Tupolev and Illyushin planes, which have been prone to accidents – from 2005 to 2015 alone, Iranian airlines experienced 16 incidents that resulted in 586 deaths[22] – Iranians wanted to gain access to top-notch Western technology.

But the slow pace of sanctions relief and the sluggish confirmation of the deals with Boeing and Airbus, which occurred against the backdrop of US Congressional efforts to block the deals,[23] meant that Iran was once again open to discussions with

Russia on the sale of planes and aircraft parts. The long-running negotiations between the two on the sale of the Sukhoi Superjet are an indication of the difficulty of negotiations between Iran and Russia. In February 2017, Tehran and Moscow were still negotiating the sale of these aircraft, and only reached an MOU on the sale in April 2018.[24] Interestingly, Russia reportedly decided to avoid requesting OFAC's permission for the deal by reducing the proportion of US parts in the planes to less than ten per cent. Iran typically accuses Russia of dragging its feet in completing and delivering projects. But in this case, given both the Iranian public's negative view of Russian aircraft and the government's desire to update the country's civilian fleet with reliable Western technology, it is possible Iran stalled the negotiations in order to buy time to finalise purchases from Western firms. This afforded Tehran the opportunity to keep Moscow on the backburner as the deals with Boeing and Airbus stalled, while prioritising those two deals nonetheless. However, Washington's withdrawal from the JCPOA, coupled with the announcement by the US Treasury that Airbus and Boeing's licences would be revoked further signalled to Tehran that its aerospace sector would remain dependent on Moscow for the foreseeable future.

Iran and Russia also discussed collaboration in a number of projects in areas such as energy, infrastructure, and technology, in some cases, expanding on existing infrastructure development projects. A year after the 2015 nuclear deal, Russia's state firm Rostec became the first foreign company to win a major contract with Iran.[25] In November 2016, the two countries finalised and signed the agreement on the construction of a thermal power station, including four 250 MBT reactors and a desalination plant by the city of Bandar Abbas in southern Iran, by the Strait of Hormuz.[26] The agreement, between the open joint-stock company Technopromexport – a Russian power engineering construction firm part of Rostec – and the Iranian holding company for the production of electric energy at thermal power stations, is still ongoing and will be financed as an inter-state loan by the Russian side, as part of the 2.2 billion euros that Moscow is allocating to all Russo–Iranian energy projects.[27] Cooperation also extended to areas of significance for Iran. In late 2016, a Russian delegation of oil and gas executives visited Tehran and met with representatives from the NIOC to discuss the development of various Iranian oil fields. Russia's Lukoil, Tatneft, and Zarubezhneft signed several MOUs with the Iranians.[28]

It is well known that Iran has a severe water scarcity crisis on its hands, due to drying water sources and decades of poor water management by the government.[29] In November 2015, Russia's Rosgeologia, and the Water and Waste Water Macro Planning Bureau of the Ministry of Energy of Iran signed an agreement on the execution of exploration and evaluation of deep underground water reserves on Iranian territory.[30] In addition, the Russians agreed to train Iranian personnel in exploration and evaluation, thereby boosting Iranian capacity in this domain – allowing the country to become more self-reliant and build capacity. In Agriculture, Iran and Russia in March 2018 also drafted an MOU on the purchase of wheat from Russia, to be milled into flour and exported out of Iran, placing Iran in the top ten buyers of Russian wheat.[31]

When Rouhani announced a trip to Russia in March 2017 – his last before he was re-elected later that spring – observers made a flurry of predictions on the budding Russo–Iranian alliance. Prior to the visit, it was announced that the two leaders would discuss key bilateral, regional, and international issues, and expand cooperation in legal and judicial sectors, roads and urban development, technology and communications, energy, and sports.[32] While the visit focused on security cooperation in the Middle East, including on counterterrorism efforts in Afghanistan and maintaining the territorial integrity of Iraq, the two leaders and Rouhani's accompanying delegation also discussed a number of other areas of collaboration, effectively setting the tone for the future of the relationship. The visit resulted in the signature of 14 documents on expanding cooperation in the political, economic, scientific, legal, and cultural arenas.[33]

In the energy sector, Russia and Iran pledged to work together to stabilise the global energy markets and address the falling price of oil. They hoped to do so within the Gas Exporting Countries Forum aimed at balancing the interests of gas producers and consumers and promoting a wider application of a more efficient and eco-friendly fossil fuel in the global energy balance, particularly for purposes of reducing greenhouse gas emissions'.[34] Importantly, the two countries have discussed much-needed foreign investment in the development of the ageing Iranian oil and gas infrastructure, building on Russia's existing involvement in other infrastructure development projects in Iran. The final statement on the March 2017 meeting between Rouhani and Putin outlined that Russia and Iran would work together in the 'exploration, production and transportation of raw hydrocarbons, including to third countries, technology transfers, swaps and construction of related infrastructure'.[35]

Russia's involvement in the Iranian energy sector is likely to be significant moving forward. Given the lasting difficulty of processing payments for contracts with Iranian counterparts and the continued risk associated with doing business with Iran, Russia will continue to have a privileged understanding of and access to the Iranian energy market. It also continues to have a more advantageous financial access, as the basis for it already exists. Indeed, Russia approved a government export credit extension, permitting Russian funds to finance a large part of several projects in Iran, including the construction of a thermal power plant in Bandar Abbas and the extension of a railway line.[36] This forms the basis of increased funding flows now that the links have been established. Both parties highlighted the 'importance of more active interbank cooperation, including between central banks, and the importance of using national currencies in mutual settlements'.[37] This is a clear effort on Iran's part to overcome the remaining restrictions and difficulties of payment processing. During Rouhani's visit to Russia in March 2017, both countries reiterated their focus on increasing trade, reportedly up by more than 70 per cent in 2016.[38]

Moving Forward

The relationship between Russia and Iran can only continue to build in strength and layers, not least because of the shared desire by both capitals to boost ties. But looking forward, a number of problem areas could potentially cause further tension in the relationship between the two.

The first problem area for the immediate future and possibly, the medium term, lies in the US factor: the Trump administration and Russian involvement in US elections, and its effect on US–Russia and, consequently, US–Iran relations. On the US–Russia front, Trump seemed to be the Kremlin's preferred candidate for President, to replace President Barack Obama who, together with Congress, condemned Moscow's military support to the Assad government and prior to that, established wide-ranging sanctions on Russia for its annexation of Crimea in 2014.[39] Aside from allegations of Russian interference in the US elections,[40] it was anticipated that a Trump administration would focus on improving US relations with Russia and focusing on shared interests. After a call between Trump and Putin in January 2017, the White House seemed to confirm this, calling the exchange a 'start to improving the relationship' between their two countries and focused on 'issues of mutual concern'.[41] But the first few months of the Trump presidency saw the new administration's Russia policy evolve. While the White House had wished to improve relations with the Kremlin, US officials have also become more vocal in their commitment to international norms and to challenging Russia's flouting of international law.[42] Moreover, the alleged ties of members of the Trump campaign to Russia and its interference in the 2016 US presidential elections, have also made it difficult for the Trump administration to mend US–Russia ties to the degree they had originally planned. While the Trump administration spoke of mending ties with Russia, it insisted on 'putting Iran on notice' for its ballistic missile testing, nefarious activities in the Middle East, and its continued sponsoring of terror.[43] While the administration signalled its intent to uphold the implementation of the Iran deal until its policy review was finalised, the rhetoric towards Iran became increasingly confrontational and President Trump did not hesitate to inject doubt into whether the US would continue to uphold its end of the bargain. Indeed, in July 2017, in an interview with the *Wall Street Journal*, the US President expressed doubt over whether the United States would certify Iran's compliance of the JCPOA in the autumn of 2017.[44] He followed through by not certifying the deal in October 2017,[45] but nevertheless, renewed US sanctions waivers in January 2018.[46] Trump's policy on Iran seemed to be to extend and entrench the mood of uncertainty as much as possible, knowing that this would have a similar effect on Iran as the US openly walking away from the deal.[47] In May 2018, the Trump administration pulled out of the agreement, thus leaving the burden of preserving the deal to the Europeans, Russia, China, and Iran.

The option of an improvement in relations between the United States and Russia has made the Iranians nervous about the possibility that Moscow could abandon them in favour of the United States.[48] In this context, Iranian officials began to emphasise the strength and stability of their relationship with Russia, while Russians highlighted their ability to work with anyone whose interests aligned with their own, displaying the first hints of a difference in perspective on the importance of the relationship to each capital. The increasing disagreements over a number of issues between Russia and the United States over the course of 2017 somewhat allayed the Iranians' fears. But the possibility that Russia could shift to the

United States or another party, highlighted the Russians' lack of loyalty to their partners, exacerbating the sense that the Russians are not trustworthy partners, the civil nuclear relationship is another factor that could stir tensions between Iran and Russia. As we have seen, both countries have worked closely together to develop Iran's nuclear programme, but delays in delivery and Iranian obfuscation have fed tensions between the two sides. As a result, Iran began to look to other suppliers, including China, in order to secure the development of its civilian nuclear programme. This too, will cause further tensions between the two partners.

Finally, it is not inconceivable that disagreements emerge in areas where the two countries seemingly work well together today. The fact that both Iran and Russia compete for the European gas market, for example, most obviously pits them against one another. Russia, however, does not prioritise this as a concern for now, because it is aware of the shortcomings plaguing the Iranian energy industry, including gas, which impede on Tehran's ability to become a critical competitor. And unless significant investment allows Iran to update and upgrade its energy infrastructure, it cannot boost exports.[49] But Iran's government is making the modernisation and expansion of its energy industry a priority, including by developing its LNG capability, in order to boost jobs in the sector and help Iranian firms develop capability.[50] As the Iranian market opens up, however, and foreign investment slowly trickles in, Iran could eventually become the competitor Russia dreads.

In addition, the greater the joint effort to tackle a crisis like terrorism in the Middle East, the greater the scope for disagreements. Russia and Iran strongly disagree on which countries constitute a viable partner in the region. Russia is willing to work with both Turkey and Israel, Iran's key rivals in the neighbourhood. While Iran is willing to be pragmatic and work with Turkey, any relation with Israel is inconceivable for the Islamic Republic. Coupled with the previously mentioned divergent visions for Syria, it is not inconceivable that growing conflicting interests plague their efforts in the region.

Nevertheless, given the history and patterns in the two countries' relations, it is safe to bet that minor tensions will exist without derailing the broader pragmatic partnership Iran and Russia have cultivated. The transactional nature of the relationship means that, while it is possible for tensions to unsettle aspects of Iran–Russia collaboration, it is unlikely to fully torpedo all areas of cooperation. Rather, Russia and Iran will continue to work together pragmatically, by separating the different components of their collaboration, effectively shielding each issue from problem areas to ensure their continued partnership for as long as it is needed.

Iran–China Relations Post-JCPOA: Tehran, Buckle of the Belt

Russia is not the only country enhancing its cooperation with Iran; China too, has been taking advantage of the post-JCPOA context to further its relations with Iran. Like Russia, China, having largely maintained its presence in the Iranian market throughout the period Iran was under sanctions, was able to draw on its advanced knowledge of the Iranian landscape and the internal political and economic dynamics. As a result, China took advantage of the sanctions relief to increase its presence and reap the benefits of a more open Iranian economy. But as was the case with Russia, for Iran, the post-JCPOA context was an opportunity to turn away from China, or at least minimise reliance on it, and look towards Western firms. Former Deputy Oil Minister and Chairman of Iran's Development and Renovation Organisation Mansour Moazami, captured the widespread sentiment vis-à-vis the Chinese when he said, 'China has done enough investment in Iran (. . .) We will provide opportunities and chances for others'.[51] In an interview with the *Financial Times*, Mohsen Safaei Farahani, former deputy economy minister, went a step further, asserting that, 'what is definite is that the speed of growth of trade with China will decrease as of 2017, when the risks of business with Iran will decline, and hence there will be less room for China to manoeuvre'.[52] As we have seen, this sentiment was due to the growing frustration of Iranian businesses of dealing with Chinese firms, which capitalised on the fact that they had faced little competition in Iran because of the sanctions. 'In the absence of rivals, Chinese groups imposed conditions by increasing prices and delaying deliveries', explained Farahani.[53]

But some within the Iranian political and economic establishments remained more grounded than others, warning all along that Iran would not be completely turning away from China. As Majid-Reza Hariri, deputy head of the Iran–China chamber of commerce, explained just weeks after the JCPOA's signing: 'The psychological atmosphere against China is because of too much excitement about the return of Western companies [...]. The dust will settle. Neither our economic interests allow us to put aside China, nor are we able to ignore one of the world's biggest economies.'[54] And this coincided with China elevating the OBOR to a top priority: in October 2017, China enshrined the initiative in its constitution during the party congress.[55] This has added pressure on the government, and on Xi himself, to ensure the initiative succeeds. Much of the initiative centres on energy deals, in geographies where Tehran has significant interests, and also in Iran itself, making Tehran even more important to its implementation.

Initially, the post-JCPOA environment led to the equalisation of the field between Iran and China. Tehran was no longer desperate for China's business. Rather, Beijing wanted to work with Tehran, as much as Tehran wanted the expansion of ties with China.[56] But some of this shift eroded when it became clear that the hundreds of MOUs that Iran had signed with Western businesses would not all lead to contracts, and those that did, would materialise slowly. This only worsened with each successive statement by the Trump administration, culminating with his decision to pull out of the deal in May 2018. As a result, wary of the West and the promised gold-rush after sanctions relief, many Iranians began to change their minds about China and its potential investments. As Moazimi put it, 'We need investment. What we expected has not happened yet.'[57] As a result, much like with Russia, for Iran, enhancing its relationship with China became essential as it became obvious that the JCPOA would not result in the anticipated boost in exchanges and trade with the West. Beijing also served as a useful counterweight to an increasingly belligerent Washington. Despite tensions in the relationship and Iranian distrust of the Chinese, Rouhani made the improvement of Iran–China ties another foreign policy priority after his election.[58] As a result, he undertook to expand the relationship on multiple levels, as he did for Iran's partnership with Russia. In the years following the nuclear deal, Iran and China expanded their economic, political, military, and even nuclear ties, a trend that is likely to continue for the foreseeable future.

A few months after the nuclear deal, in January 2016, and, importantly, a short week after the nuclear-related sanctions on Iran were lifted, Xi visited his counterpart in Tehran to discuss growing bilateral ties. Ahead of his visit, he penned an open letter to Iranians highlighting the long history of ties between China and Iran, the continuing Chinese presence in Iran despite international efforts to isolate it, and the 'mutual understanding and mutual trust' that exists between the two countries.[59] The visit set the tone for economic relations between the two countries for the medium term. During Xi's visit, the two sides agreed to expand trade to $600 billion over the following ten years, an optimistic target.[60] Much of that will constitute the continuation and expansion of trade in crude oil. China was also Zarif's first stop on his diplomatic tour to other P5 + 1 countries following Trump's announcement that the US would no longer be party to the deal. The visit aimed to clarify the economic impact of Trump's decision and what the remaining states party to the deal would offer Iran to ensure its continued implementation of its nuclear commitments.

Energy

China has made it no secret that as a leading global consumer, and net importer, of oil, it aims to both diversify its imports and negotiate them at the most favourable rates, something which international sanctions made possible with Iran. In addition, the dramatic increase in Chinese imports of LNG in recent years make China's involvement in the development of Iran's natural gas fields all the more important.[61] For its part, as we have seen, Iran's energy sector, after being abandoned by Western firms, is still in dire need of foreign investment and extensive re-development. According to the Director General of Strategic Planning in the Ministry of Petroleum, Said Qavampur, the Iranian oil sector needs $150 billion of foreign investment over the five-year period beginning in December 2015, to meet the government's goals of boosting production and increasing revenue.[62] At that time, Iranian officials were aware that development of Iran's energy sector had to occur rapidly in order to bring in money and provide the ailing economy with a much-needed boost. In January 2017, Iran's Deputy Oil Minister Abbas Kazemi announced that China would invest $3 billion to upgrade Iran's oil refining facilities, including a major investment in the Abadan facility. The Iranians noted that they would expand the venture to the construction of joint-refineries.[63]

China's involvement in the Iranian energy industry is not likely to recede, at least not while Western firms continue to be wary of becoming involved in Iran. But, as discussed previously, the reticence of Western firms was not just a product of sanctions, it was due to a number of internal and external factors. For example, Iran's onerous contract system added a layer of difficulty for companies looking to enter the Iranian energy market. The new Iranian Petroleum Contract (IPC), drafted under Oil Minister

Zangeneh, offered foreign firms more flexible and lucrative terms, including the right to book reserves in Iran and the possibility of buying stakes in Iranian oil companies.[64] But these changes have not gone unnoticed among the conservative factions in Tehran who criticised the government for selling the country's natural resources on the cheap.[65] As a result, the IPCs implementation has been consistently delayed, adding a layer of complication to Iran's ability to attract foreign, and in particular, Western investment into its energy sector. This became increasingly urgent as discontent with the country's poor economic state has grown within the population, which took to the streets in late December 2017 and early January 2018 to call for change. Rouhani's December 2017 speech during the unveiling of his government's 2018–19 budget highlighted some areas of corruption, shadow economic activities, and mismanagement that had long plagued Iranian economics, and drew the ire of Iranians.[66] The protests did not lead to any substantive changes or reforms, but they spurred the government to re-examine its traditional response to public discontent, leading to a cautious consideration of protesters' demands by Iranian officials.[67] While it was expected that after a few years questions surrounding the uncertainty of the permanent nature of sanctions relief and the future of the JCPOA would have been clarified, leading to more certainty for Western businesses seeking to enter the Iranian market, President Trump's Iran policy prevented that. In fact, the environment of uncertainty even prompted firms who had committed to doing business with Iran to re-examine their commitment. For example, in July 2017, a consortium led by the French energy giant Total, signed a $4.8 billion deal with Iran to develop its the South Pars gas field.[68] But after Trump's refusal to certify the deal and the increased environment of uncertainty brought on by the Trump's decision to walk away from the deal, Total announced it might have to reconsider its plans.[69] As a result, China's CNPC, already involved in the Iranian energy market, is already poised to take over Total's share of the investment, as per the terms of the agreement.[70] In addition to this, China has taken steps to wean the world off the dollar for transactions involving oil. Indeed, because of the constraints associated with trading in dollars, which became apparent as the US increased its sanctions regimes against other countries, including Russia and North Korea, China began to explore ways to ensure that it would not be bound by US rules in oil trading. At the end of 2017, it announced it would begin its own yuan-based oil futures contract in 2018, which would challenge the US dollar.[71] In March 2018, it was also reported that China would develop a pilot programme to pay for crude oil imports in yuan instead of dollars,[72] and would also facilitate dealings with countries that are restricted in their ability to use dollars in their transactions, including Iran. In fact, China has taken an increasingly active role in circumventing the challenges posed by lack of financing for deals in Iran. In March 2018, Beijing offered to finance Iran Air's new aircraft purchases. This type of offer is significant because an inability to finance major deals through traditional financing vehicles is a major reason why Iran cannot reap the benefits of the JCPOA.[73]

As a result, for Iran, Chinese presence in their energy industry has become a fact of life. Likewise, Chinese investments - which have mainly focused on large upstream projects - are also likely to grow. In addition, as with the Russians, maintaining the link with Chinese state-owned firms in the energy sector allows Iran to also deepen political ties with the government, which in itself is valuable to Tehran.

Beyond Energy: Iran–China Economic Ties

Iran's growing economic relationship with China is not restricted to the energy sector, although it is centred on it. In August 2016, during a visit to Beijing, Iranian Minister of Economy and Financial Affairs Ali Tayyebnia stated that he welcomed Chinese investments in non-energy related sectors. He also noted that Iran wished to maintain 'an active role' in China's OBOR initiative, highlighting its potential benefits for his country's and Iran's potential contributions to the project, including its ample resources and strategic location.[74] China exports a wide range of products to Iran, including machinery, electrical and electronic equipment, vehicles, and lighting. As part of Iran's efforts to build a 'resistance economy',[75] Iran sought to diversify its non-oil exports, and boosted exports of iron ore to China.[76] This is a trend that Iran is eager to maintain.

In February 2017, Iran announced that China was the biggest purchaser of Iranian goods in the preceding 11 months, with $7.29 billion sales – an almost 7 per cent increase from the previous year.[77] As part of its efforts to diversify its economy away from hydrocarbons, Tehran sought foreign investment in other sectors. China's development investment vehicles, including the China Development Bank and the Asian Infrastructure Investment Bank, provide key funding for developing economies for projects not only related to energy, but to core areas including infrastructure and construction. China proposed, for example, to construct a high-speed rail network from Urumqi in China's northwest, through Kazakhstan and Tajikistan, amongst others, and ending in Iran's capital, both for passengers and cargo.[78] In March 2016, it was announced that China's government-run China National Transportation Equipment and Engineering Co Ltd (CTC) would finalise a $3 billion project to connect Tehran and Mashhad by high-speed rail, the majority of which would be funded by China's Export and Import Bank.[79] China also signed an MOU with Iran to help it develop the planned tramway system in the city of Tabriz.[80] More recently, China sold Iran subway cars for Mashhad's underground system.[81] Iran has made the development of its antiquated and underdeveloped railway system a priority, pledging to expand it to cover 25,000 km by 2025 from 15,000 km in 2015.[82] Iran also aims to expand the metro system in its major cities – in particular, Tehran – to tackle their significant traffic and pollution problems. China has been key to this development, because while some European firms, such as Germany's Siemens,[83] signed contracts with Iran, to tackle such large-scale infrastructure projects remaining financing problems again have played in China's favour. Chinese firms are also involved in discussions on building Iran's tanker fleet and shipping industry,[84] as well as in Iran's telecommunications network.

Nuclear Power

One interesting non-oil sector that China is attempting to make an inroad into in Iran is the civilian nuclear sector. While Moscow has had a near monopoly on the Iranian nuclear programme since the late 1980s, Beijing expressed an interest in the market. Shortly after Iran was declared to be in compliance with the JCPOA on Implementation Day, Chinese interest turned into a concrete plan prior to Xi's visit to Tehran in January 2016. The Head of the AEOI, Ali Akbar Salehi, announced that China had signed a contract with Iran to build his country's fourth nuclear power plant on the country's south-eastern coast of Makran, near the port city of Chabahar, an area Iran has prioritised in its development plans, with significant (but slow) ventures with India.[85] After this announcement outlining the project, which had a total budget of $10 billion, Salehi stated that Chinese engineers visited the region to select the site of the new power plant.[86] Iran also announced that it planned to build small 100 MW plants along the same coast for the desalination of seawater and to generate electricity, which it had also discussed with China but was pending final agreement. These plans fit into Rouhani's broader development objective, which would update infrastructure, utilise resources, and create jobs in the country's most underdeveloped areas. These are often border areas, populated by minorities, traditionally ignored by the central authority. But Rouhani, who received support from these populations, hopes to develop them to promote security and utilise their potential. The development of the Chabahr port falls under these plans.

Aside from discussions on building new plants, China and Iran signed a preliminary agreement on the re-design of the Arak reactor, as warranted by the JCPOA, during Xi's visit to Tehran in January 2016.[87] The two countries were in discussions following the stipulation by the nuclear agreement that Iran would have to remove the core vessel of the Arak heavy water reactor, which it completed by Implementation Day. In return, Iran would receive foreign assistance to re-design the reactor to significantly cut the amount of plutonium it produces, while allowing the country to continue to use it for research and medical purposes. On 24 April 2017, Iran and China finalised and signed the first commercial agreement on the re-design of the reactor. According to the initial agreement between the P5 + 1 and Iran signed in 2015, Tehran would be the project manager, while Beijing would 'participate in the redesign and the construction of the modernized reactor'. For its part, Washington would 'provide technical support and review of the modernized reactor design'. Paris, London, and Berlin would also participate by reviewing the design suggestions for the plant's redesign, while Moscow would provide consultative services.[88]

China aiming to become a nuclear supplier for Iran coupled with its work on the Arak redesign means that it will be involved in the Iranian nuclear programme for the foreseeable future. In fact, although there is little or slow progress on the promised power plants, China's involvement in the Arak re-design is engrained in the JCPOA and will result in greater Chinese–Iranian interactions in this domain, potentially opening the door to further collaboration. In fact, Iran and China held a nuclear cooperation workshop in April 2018, where they discussed expanding their ties in this area. Held as part of the cooperation outlined in the JCPOA, events such as this one strengthened the motivation to uphold the deal for the countries involved.[89]

China's efforts in the field of nuclear energy in Iran are in line with Beijing's objectives to expand its nuclear industry and become a key international nuclear supplier. In 2015, China declared nuclear power as one of its 16 'national science and technology projects', with substantial government financial backing.[90] The purpose was to make the Chinese nuclear industry – still reliant on foreign parts and components – fully self-sufficient, and to allow it to export its nuclear technology and expertise internationally. As a result, China's interest in the growing Iranian nuclear industry is likely to continue.

Military and Defence Cooperation

China and Iran also deepened their military and defence ties following the JCPOA. As established, China was a major provider of advanced weapons to Iran in the 1980s and early 1990s, driven in part by a desire to strengthen the Islamic Republic as a buffer against a growing US presence in the Middle East. After a significant decrease in sales of military equipment to Iran beginning in the late 1990s, as the sanctions were strengthened, and as part of its efforts to expand its influence in the Middle East, China aimed to regain its footing in the Iranian defence market. This coincided with President Xi's military reform programme, to turn the Chinese military into an elite fighting force capable of winning wars; signalling a move to a more offensive capability.[91] Indeed, China's military-to-military exchanges with other countries have been on the rise, and it has expanded its military presence globally. Military relations with Iran fit into these plans. This coincided with Iran being on the lookout for arms suppliers in anticipation of the arms embargo being lifted, once the IAEA deemed it in compliance of the JCPOA. As discussed, arms sales to Iran continue to be subject to UNSC approval until 2020 at the earliest, but Iran could still begin to build its supply network and purchase some items, provided there is UNSC approval.

In late 2016, Dehqan stated that, 'The upgrading of relations and long-term defense-military cooperation with China is one of the main priorities of the Islamic Republic of Iran's defence diplomacy'.[92] As a result, during Xi's visit to Tehran in January 2016, the two countries agreed to boost cooperation on military and defence issues. They later expanded these ties during Chinese defence minister General Change Wanquan's visit to Tehran in November 2016, where the two countries inked an agreement outlining a boost in military and defence cooperation and exchanges.[93] China's development of its A2/AD capabilities – designed to counter US presence in its backyard – could prove useful for a country like Iran, which is keen to push back American forces and presence in the Persian Gulf, especially in the event of a crisis. Iran's desire to improve and expand its military arsenal will continue. Iran and China also pledged to increase cooperation and collaboration in fighting terrorism and cybercrime, including training, technology, and intelligence sharing.

China and Iran increased collaboration in a concrete manner in Syria after 2016, when the former joined the civil war after the government passed a law to authorise counterterrorism efforts abroad.[94] Finally, as part of growing Sino–Iranian security ties, Beijing (and Moscow) supported Tehran's application for full membership in the SCO. It is likely that whether within the SCO, or on a bilateral level, relations between Iran and China will continue to grow for the foreseeable future, and especially as long as the risk of doing business with Iran remains considerable for Western firms. The Trump administrations insistence on scrapping the Iran deal further pushed China and Iran closer together. Throughout 2017 and 2018, Beijing reiterated its support for the nuclear deal with Iran and highlighted that Iran was complying with the agreement - a statement it reiterated right after Trump walked away from the deal.[95] As a result, even if the risk of doing business with Iran lessened, while Iran will likely diminish its dependence on China, it is unlikely to turn away from it.

Iran's mistrust of the West will not evaporate any time soon because it is inherent to parts of the Islamic Republic. Many in Iran are also thankful for China's presence in Iran at a time where other powers isolated it. In addition, even those who are weary of the Chinese in Iran, gradually overcame their distrust as the Trump administration made it unlikely that Iran could eventually turn West. Finally, China's economic might is a force to be reckoned with, and while Iran has not had a wholly positive experience of dealing with the Chinese, it needs the trade and the foreign investment from China in order to offset its economic isolation and boost growth.

***

Despite the potential for greater opening towards the West in a post-JCPOA environment, Iran will pragmatically continue to seek greater ties and collaboration with both Russia and China. One of the reasons why Tehran embarked on the nuclear negotiations with the P5 + 1 was that parts of the Islamic Republic believed it was necessary for the country to emerge out of political and economic isolation, and to no longer be forced to rely on Moscow and Beijing. And the Iranian public, who remain outward-looking and eager to resume decent relations with the international community, and the West, in particular, share this sentiment.

But the disappointment over the slow pace of promised sanctions relief, as well as the resumption of hostile rhetoric emanating from Washington, has made the Islamic Republic cautious in its vision of alliance building. Iran has also learned the lessons of the past. It believes that the United States will ultimately seek regime change regardless of what direction the Islamic Republic takes, and the rhetoric out of Washington culminating in the US withdrawl from the nuclear deal, have served to confirm these suspicions. While this sentiment is not shared by all quarters of the Islamic Republic – including many within the Rouhani government who are more favourably inclined towards building long-term ties with Europe and America – the system as a whole remembers what it viewed as countless disappointments by the West. These experiences included the West siding with or turning a blind eye to Saddam Hussein's use of chemical weapons during the Iran–Iraq War, and on a smaller scale, the gradual withdrawal of Western businesses from Iran following the 1979 revolution, including by abandoning existing contracts and deals. President Trump added the JCPOA to the list of Iran's grievances with America when he announced that his country would withdraw from it and reimpose sanctions on the Middle Eastern nation.

Iran is also wary of both Russia and China. Tehran's experience of working with both capitals has been far from smooth. Iran remembers past experiences of untrustworthiness, such as Russia dragging its feet in building and launching the Bushehr power plant, as well as the delayed delivery of the S-300 system, and China exploiting Iran's isolation to obtain more favourable trade terms for itself. But Iran remains pragmatic and understands it cannot evolve and grow without the political and economic backing of the two powers. It is also aware that neither Moscow nor Beijing condition their ties to Tehran to a change in aspects of the government, its behaviour, or the regime itself, but rather what they can obtain out of the relationship. It is notable, for example, that neither Beijing nor Moscow comment on domestic upheavals in the country, for example, refraining from calling on the regime to respect human rights during the 2017–18 unrests.

In the eyes of Iranian officials, this makes it easier to negotiate and work with Beijing and Moscow than the Europeans, for example. The two countries provide Iran with what it needs with no strings attached. Russian and Chinese willingness to ignore Iran's remaining semi-pariah status means that Tehran can discuss expanding ties in areas that other countries would be unwilling to discuss, such as weapons sales, which are subject to UNSC approval until Iran's nuclear programme is deemed totally in compliance with the JCPOA. Finally, the desire of all three countries to stand up to a US-led Western order is unlikely to diminish for the foreseeable future. As a result, they are likely to continue pragmatically working together to diminish Western, and US presence in particular, in the Middle East.

The endurance of these growing ties has an impact on the United States and Europe's ability to set policy on Iran. Russia and China offer Iran a cushion to fall back on should the path of attempted dialogue with the West backfire, as some hardliners in Iran have warned. When America led the charge in expanding UN sanctions against Iran in 2010, it took deft negotiations to bring Russia and China on board, especially after Iran had agreed to a new fuel swap deal with Turkey and Brazil shortly before the UNSC Resolution 1929 was passed. Iran's intransigence on aspects of its nuclear programme made it easier for then US President Obama to negotiate the tightening of international sanctions on Iran. Today, Iran has agreed to curb its nuclear programme in exchange for sanctions relief in the JCPOA. In the eyes of the Europeans, Russia, and China, the international sanctions have fulfilled their goal: to coax Iran to the negotiating table and to obtain major concessions from it. As a result, any re-imposition of international sanctions on Iran's nuclear programme will require a significant and obvious violation on Tehran's part to convince more reticent players, including Moscow and Beijing, to come back on board. This became increasingly visible after Trump's decision to reimpose US sanctions on Iran. The unpopular decision created divisions between the US and its allies, which only served to further make universal sanctions on Iran an idea of the past.

Having both Moscow and Beijing on board is vital to ensuring the effectiveness of sanctions, which required the universality of their implementation.[96] Iran's growing ties with both countries will increase the sympathy from both capitals towards it, as well as to increase the number of shared interests, and consequently, the costs of Russia and China abandoning their partner. This means that the bar for the re-imposition of sanctions is much higher, and Moscow and Beijing will likely want proof of clear and substantial violations of the nuclear deal by Tehran, rather than the likely wider approach to what constitutes a violation from Brussels and Washington's perspectives. The result of both the nuclear deal, but perhaps more importantly, Iran's growing ties with Russia and China, is that Tehran seems to have emerged from isolation for good. Indeed, potential future Western efforts to constrain Iran by re-imposing some form of isolation may no longer be as effective as they were in the past. And they will also be much more difficult. This is because Iran is able to more effectively offset the effects of Western efforts at isolating it through the relationships it has built, and continues to nurture and expand, with Russia and China.

CONCLUSION AND RECOMMENDATION

As we have seen throughout this book, Iran's relations with Russia and China go back centuries, and span the rise and fall of empires in those countries, lasting the test of time, wars, diplomacy, and commerce. Today, Iran's relationship with the two powers is a complex one, characterised by deep, and in the case of Russia, historically rooted, distrust. But eight years of a devastating interstate war, followed by decades of sanctions and political isolation propelled a reluctant Tehran into the arms of Beijing and Moscow. As a result, in the twenty-first century, China and Russia established themselves as key political, economic, and military partners for Iran. As the years went by and Tehran increasingly found itself at the mercy of Russia and China, it aimed to overcome the costly political isolation and economic sanctions. To do so, in 2015, it concluded the JCPOA, which would allow it to diversify its partnerships. But as the agreement's implementation progressed, it became clear that the European businesses and investors Iran had so highly coveted would not rush back into its market because of remaining obstacles and because of the lingering environment of uncertainty, further entrenched by President Trump's Iran policy. Economic recovery was slower than the Rouhani government promised and the Iranian people had hoped. Politically, however, the JCPOA bore some dividends: Building on the personal channels of communication created during the negotiations, Zarif conducted comprehensive talks with EU High Representative Mogherini to settle other areas of concern, while deescalating tensions between his country and the United States with then State of Secretary John Kerry.

With the election of Donald Trump in the United States, the JCPOA entered a more uncertain and fragile state just a year into its implementation. In the beginning, Trump's Iran policy was largely incoherent. The administration's rhetoric was more belligerent than that of the Obama team, having put Iran 'on notice' and calling it out multiple times as a state-sponsor of terror and a destabilising force in the Middle East.[1] Key members of the administration, including Secretary of State Tillerson, went as far as openly condoning regime change by supporting 'elements' in the country vowing to topple the Islamic Republic.[2] Yet throughout his first year in office, many of Trump's policies targeting or dealing with Iran were a continuation of those pursued by Obama. For example, the additional designations made by the new administration throughout 2017 were no different to Obama's policy of sanctioning Iran despite the more positive undertones in US–Iran relations. More generally as time went on, the Trump team adopted a much more hawkish stance towards Tehran. Close advisors to the president made appearances at the rally of the Mujahedin-e Khalgh (MeK) in Paris in July 2017, a terrorist group that presents itself as an alternative to the Iranian regime.[3] Some of the more mainstream figures appointed by the president, including Secretary of Defense Mattis, National Security Advisor H.R. McMaster, and Secretary of State Rex Tillerson, harboured more ideologically inclined views of Iran. A number of them were replaced by well-known Iran hawks in 2018, including Mike Pompeo as Secretary of State and John Bolton as the National Security Advisor. It seemed the administration's general Iran policy was to increase pressure on the country and to isolate it once again, although it was not clear to what degree or what would be considered success. And to justify its stance, the administration, backed by decades of conventional wisdom in foreign policy circles in the United States, painted Iran as an existential threat, rather than just a nuisance, to America. In line with his policy of containment, President Trump also gave his unwavering support to the US Gulf Arab partners, and particularly Saudi Arabia, sparking their renewed confrontation with Tehran, and among themselves.[4] In January 2018, French President Emmanuel Macron warned America and its Israeli and Saudi allies against deploying a belligerent rhetoric, which, he noted, could pave the way to war.[5] However, both Saudi Arabia and Israel increased their anti-Iran rhetoric. Most notable, was a speech delivered by Israeli Prime Minister Benjamin Netanyahu on 1 May 2018, where he reiterated that Iran had lied about the military dimensions of its nuclear programme, likely intended to sway Trump to walk away from the nuclear deal, which he did a few days later. The result was that the administration drastically increased the uncertainty surrounding the JCPOA and its continued implementation, as well as broader security concerns in the Persian Gulf. The environment of uncertainty meant that for Iran, it was impossible to fully reap the benefits of the deal it agreed to in 2015.

As we argued throughout this book, Iran has neither the intention nor the capabilities to fundamentally challenge the United States and the Western order. Instead, the country presents some tests to Western, particularly, US, interests. But Tehran can also align with certain Western interests and cooperate with Brussels and EU member states and Washington in specific areas. Afghanistan is perhaps the most prominent example of such cooperation – as Tehran and Washington did during the Bonn Conference in 2001,[6] and securing the future of the Iraqi state in the post-ISIS environment is another. But the Trump administration refused to pursue either.

Against this backdrop, the EU, led by Mogherini, who had extensive experience of working with Iran, wanted to solve outstanding disagreements through dialogue and reliance on institutions, and to increase economic interdependence between the bloc and Iran, especially following the US decision to unilaterally violate the terms of the nuclear deal. As a result, it took the leadership role in ensuring the JCPOA's continuation and broader engagement with Tehran, especially once President Trump came to office. Individual member states too, took on a more active role in promoting the benefits of the JCPOA and doing their part to ensure it would remain. France, under President Macron, took a leading role in this, looking for ways to ensure the deal's longevity. For example, its parliament, traditionally in the background on foreign policy issues, took a more active role in finding ways to ensure that Iran would feel the benefits of the JCPOA.[7] It helped the French state investment bank decide to finance projects for French companies in Iran in 2018.[8] Macron also took a leading role in attempting to convince President Trump to stay in the deal during a trip to Washington in April 2018, where the two men discussed extending the current agreement to cover a number of problematic areas, including Iran's missile arsenal, the so-called 'sunset clauses' of the JCPOA and inspection procedures. When these efforts failed and Trump pulled out of the deal, French officials were vocal critics of the US president's decision: French Finance Minister Bruno Le Maire said that Europe is not a 'vassal' of the US, and that the block should not accept the US as the 'world's economic policeman'.[9] For its part, the Iranian government undertook a robust outreach effort to European capitals in order to safeguard the deal and ensure regime stability and survival. Zarif led these efforts, driven by the idea that only Europe could serve as a bulwark against US efforts to leave the agreement.[10] For example, just weeks before the JCPOA's second anniversary in June 2017, Zarif travelled to key European cities to discuss the deal's future, economic and business ties between his country and Europe, and regional security issues.[11]

He repeated the exercise immediately after Trump's announcement to exit the nuclear deal in May 2018, only this time, he began his trip in China and Russia, and went to Europe last.[12] Iranian officials, somewhat rightly, believed that Europe stood to gain the most from the JCPOA's smooth implementation given the restrictions that continue to exist on US companies. As a result, they saw the EU and its member states as a force in preserving and sustaining the deal. Indeed, while America under President Trump was increasingly isolating itself, renegading on its traditional leadership role, and ultimately, violating the terms of the nuclear deal by withdrawing from the agreement. Europe's interests were diverging from those of America. Iranian officials emphasised that the EU must, therefore, lead on a number of fronts.[13] And while Russia and China worked fast to secure their interests in the early years of the JCPOA's implementation, they were not the champions the agreement needed during Trump's tenure. But European leadership came with a number of challenges and shortcomings, which allowed Russia and China to continue filling the vacuum.

For decades, European capitals and Brussels took on a backseat role on the international stage. They merely followed Washington's lead. In a handful of cases and, at most, they served as an opposition force to counterbalance America. This was the case of France during the lead up to the 2003 US invasion of Iraq, where then President Jacques Chirac bore the flag of Western nations opposing President Bush's use of WMD and the September 11 attacks to wage war on Saddam Hussein. There, Europe was divided. While London followed Washington, Paris stood firmly against it. Indeed, for decades, even when EU and US interests diverged – as they did during the Iraq War – America served as the flag-bearer of the post-World War II international order and championed its key values. But with the growing differences with the US under the Trump administration, the Europeans faced a new challenge: They could no longer afford to either take a backseat and let America lead or be content with merely serving as the opposition to the United States. What America represented under a President Trump leadership, in many instances, went against European values and President Trump made it no secret he did not believe in the Trans–Atlantic relationship, preferring instead to call on Europe to pay for its 'fair share' of the security burden, for example.[14] As a result, Europe recognised that it had to take on a proactive role to protect its interests, especially when they diverged from those of the United States. And with the strong leadership of German Chancellor Angela Merkel, Macron, and Mogherini, Europe and its member states began to do just that. In particular, in the days leading to Trump's 12 May 2018 deadline to make a decision on the future of the JCPOA, European leaders, particularly Macron and Merkel, traveled to Washington to convince him to remain in the deal to no avail. But Europe's learning curve to fill the void left by the United States will be significant, as it has changed a decades-long policy and tried to overcome the blow inflicted to it by the United Kingdom's choice to exit the union in the summer of 2016. As a result, at times, it still lacks the political will to effectively stand up to the United States, as was the case with the negotiations over maintaining US participation in the Iran deal in the run up to President Trump's 12 May deadline. It will take time for Europe to lead fully and effectively in key areas where America renegades its traditional leadership role.

On Iran, Europe must ensure the JCPOA is preserved and sustained without the United States. This will require it to serve as an intermediary between the different concerned parties and to ensure that small bumps during the implementation process neither turn into full violations on the Iranian side, nor lead to the deal being. These bumps can stem directly and indirectly from the JCPOA. For example, they can stem from delays in the delivery of certain provisions or licences, small excesses in stockpiles, or unrelated events leading to complications in the implementation process, such as the imposition of non-nuclear sanctions on Iran.

Prior to the Trump administration, Washington and Tehran directly managed this type of hiccup in the deal's implementation. In November 2016, for example, Iran accumulated too much heavy water – beyond what it was allowed in the JCPOA. After direct negotiations between concerned parties, the crisis was swiftly resolved when Iran sent its excess heavy water to Oman. But Europe's role cannot be limited to managing bumps along the road. It will also have to make sure Iran receives the dividends of its compliance with the JCPOA. This includes navigating America's secondary sanctions, new designations, and other actions designed to pressure Iran.[15] The Europeans will also have to be ready to deescalate general tensions between America and Iran. Indeed, Trump's temperament and his decision to withdraw from the nuclear deal, and IRGC activities in the region increased the likelihood of escalation due to miscalculation. Economically, European businesses were slow in taking advantage of the JCPOA. As we saw in previous chapters, this is due to both internal and external factors. The slow pace allowed Russian and Chinese businesses to navigate the Iranian market with less competition than many expected. And as Iranians became more impatient and frustrated with the course of economic recovery, they once again turned to Russia and China for business, while keeping a watchful eye on Europe as a potential partner.

Nevertheless, European businesses and investors can expect bumps along the way. As we saw, Russian and Chinese businesses, backed by their governments, built and expanded their presence in Iran – affording them relationships and knowledge of the market, which provide them with an advantage the Europeans lack. However, unlike Russian and Chinese goods and services, European investors and businesses enjoy a good reputation, making them more attractive to Iranians. Moreover, as Russia and China grew and deepened their presence in key sectors of the Iranian economy, many in Iran questioned whether their country had not become too dependent on the two powers. As a result,

Iranian businesses and the government sought to diversify their partners to make sure they do not put all their eggs in two baskets: Those of Russia and China.[16]

On defence and security, the West and Iran have a number of overlapping interests, ranging from Afghanistan to the South Caucasus. There, the European Union must capitalise on the opportunities afforded to it by the JCPOA to engage Iran on areas of mutual concern and cooperation. This is something the EU began to do following the JCPOA, with the establishment of the EU–Iran Comprehensive Dialogue, which covered a range of issues and areas of joint concern, as well as the EU–Iran High Level Political Dialogue, which established a regular forum for Zarif and Mogherini to meet directly. For decades, Europe took a backseat on these matters and areas, such as the resumption of the frozen conflict in Nagorno–Karabakh and the increase in Afghan refugee flows, both of which directly impact Europe. Iran, like the EU, has an interest in maintaining the status quo or remedying the Nagorno–Karabakh issue and bringing some level of security and stability in Afghanistan. This is not to say that Iranian activities are without challenges. Iran notoriously funds and supports nefarious actors in its neighbourhood, as it does the Taliban in Afghanistan. But working with Iran in those areas is critical to any solution to the instability and insecurity there. It can also allow the West to engage with and have a role shaping Iranian policies on those fronts.[17]

If Europe fails to build on the JCPOA, Russia and China will continue to grow their presence in Iran. The duration of the JCPOA's implementation process thus presents a key opportunity to shape the future of Iranian foreign policy for the West. Today, despite recognising Russian and Chinese shortcomings in the economic sphere as in defence and foreign policy, Tehran sees Beijing and Moscow as viable bulwarks against Western, and particularly, US efforts to isolate it once more. In fact, even the Supreme Leader said that it was time Iran focused its attention on the East in a speech in February 2018, highlighting Tehran's growing frustrations with the West in the post-deal environment.[18] Iranian leaders know that neither Russia nor China will use its political capital or jeopardise its interests and relationships for Iran. And, Iranians believe that to some degree, both countries benefit from Iranian isolation. But, as we have seen throughout the book, ever-growing political, economic, and security ties to Iran have led Russia and China to oppose the isolation of Iran. Instead, they want Iran to gradually re-integrate itself into the international community, especially financially and in terms of how it is perceived. This would allow Moscow and China to continue to expand ties with it. From Beijing and Moscow's point of view, the ideal situation is one where Iran is no longer isolated or subject to stringent international sanctions, but harbours continued mistrust of the West, ensuring that Tehran will continue to turn to them as partners. Ideally, for the two countries, however, Iran's mistrust of and lack of sustained political ties with the West would continue, making Russia and China Tehran's favoured partners. And even though neither Russia nor China will serve as a champion of the JCPOA, they are unlikely to join America's efforts to isolate Iran again in light of the Trump administration's unilateral withdrawal from the process.

It is important to note that the Trump administration upped the ante with China, especially in the South China Sea, and the US Congress pushed to pressure and sanction Russia after its interference in the 2016 elections. The growing tensions in America's bilateral relations with China and Russia will make it even more difficult for the country to convince them to jump on board to isolate Iran should Tehran no longer implement the JCPOA. Indeed, as Moscow is being subjected to sanctions for its invasion of Crimea and meddling in the American elections, and Chinese banks and firms are designated for their cooperation with Iranian and North Korean sanctioned entities, they are more inclined to oppose US sanctions on other individuals and entities, including in Iran, and to stand up to perceived US hegemonic behaviour. All this makes already reluctant powers even less inclined to work with America to isolate Iran, especially if they believe that the latter is abiding by its end of the bargain.

The difficulty of keeping isolation as a policy option for the West is likely to increase over time. Tehran's ties with Moscow and Beijing show no signs of abating. If anything, they are on a clear upward trajectory, aided by the slow pace of promised sanctions relief and Iranian economic recovery. Additionally, both Beijing and Moscow increasingly see Tehran as a critical part of their own agendas. For Russia, Iran is an ally in Syria and a fellow sanctioned country by America. For China, the Middle Eastern power serves as a vital component of the OBOR initiative.[19] Moreover, as the gap widens between Washington and Brussels on the one hand, and Washington and EU capitals, especially Paris and Berlin, on the other, the United States will find it more difficult to present a united Western front against Iran. Likewise, the growing tensions between America and Russia and complicated relations between America and China also increase the difficulty of galvanising the major international players to pressure or isolate Iran, especially if the JCPOA's implementation process continues without the United States. And American leadership on the global stage has also taken a blow since President Trump's inauguration, decreasing once abundant political capital and ability to shape narratives and policies around the world.[20]

Today, isolating Iran is a difficult task. Tehran has drawn on its growing ties with Russia and China to ensure that it would no longer find itself in the same position it did at the end of the 1990s and until the 2013 negotiations began in earnest. As its relationship with Moscow and Beijing deepens, Tehran continues to ensure that Western-imposed isolation is no longer an option. This, as we have seen, does not come without challenges, however, as Iranians worry about becoming too dependent on Russia and China, two powers they do not fully trust to begin with. But as established, the ties between Tehran and Moscow and Tehran and Beijing are not traditional alliances. They are pragmatic relationships, based on mutual interests and necessities. This comes with both advantages and disadvantages for Iran. On the one hand, this pragmatic relationship means that Russia and China will never abandon Iran because of the Islamic Republic's human rights record or controversial interventions in the region, for example. But, on the other hand, it also means that both Russia and China will not hesitate to walk away from Iran should economic, political and/or military ties no longer be useful to them. China and Russia's willingness to ignore Iranian regional activities or its human rights record for example, is why pragmatic elements of the Islamic Republic continue to call for ever-growing ties to Russia and China, especially as the benefits of the JCPOA are slow to come by. Tehran's logic is driven by the idea that further deepening the ties will mean that more is at stake. This, in turn, will translate into more intertwined interests, and as a result, greater difficulty in walking away from Iran should Russia and China want to. And the growing increase in intertwined interests and ties will effectively make any future Western attempts to isolate Iran unfeasible.

NOTES

Introduction

1. President George W. Bush, 'The President's State of the Union Address', The United States Capitol Washington, DC, 29 January 2002, https://georgewbush-whitehouse.archives.gov/news/releases/2002/01/20020129-11.html.
2. 'President Trump's Speech to the Arab Islamic American Summit', The White House, Office of the Press Secretary, 21 May 2017, https://www.whitehouse.gov/the-press-office/2017/05/21/president-trumps-speech-arab-islamic-american-summit.
3. 'Democratic debate: Which Enemy are You Most Proud of?', CBS News, 14 October 2015, http://www.cbsnews.com/news/democratic-debate-which-enemy-are-you-most-proud-of/.
4. Mark Perry, 'James Mattis' 33-year Grudge Against Iran', *Politico*, 4 December 2016, http://www.politico.com/magazine/story/2016/12/james-mattis-iran-secretary-of-defense-214500.
5. Ibid.; Stephen Graubard, 'Lunch with the FT: Henry Kissinger', *Financial Times*, 23 May 2008, https://www.ft.com/content/6d4b5fb8-285a-11dd-8f1e-000077b07658.
6. Author interviews with US officials and lawmakers, Washington, DC, 2014–17.
7. For more on the Iran–Iraq War's impact on Iran's feeling of isolation see, Ariane Tabatabai and Annie Tracy Samuel, 'Dealing with History,' *International Security*, Vol. 42, No. 1, Summer 2017, doi:10.1162./ISEC_a_00286.

8. Ayatollah Khomeini, 'Government of the Jurist', The Institute for Compilation and Publication of Imam Khomeini's Works, http://www.iranchamber.com/history/rkhomeini/books/velayat_faqeeh.pdf.

9. 'The Latest: Iran: UN meeting on US Protests is "Bullying"', Associated Press, 5 January 2017, https://www.washingtonpost.com/world/europe/the-latest-us-ambassador-world-will-be-watching-iran/2018/01/05/0d5d559c-f259-11e7-95e3-eff284e71c8d_story.html?utm_term=.b0663b96ca5d.

10. Ben Blanchard and David Lawder, 'China Launches WTO Complaint Against US, EU over Dumping Rules', Reuters, 12 December 2016, http://www.reuters.com/article/us-china-trade-wto-idUSKBN14112M.

11. Jane Perlez, 'Tribunal Rejects Beijing's Claims in the South China Sea', *New York Times*, 12 July 2016, https://www.nytimes.com/2016/07/13/world/asia/south-china-sea-hague-ruling-philippines.html.

12. Xi Jinping, 'Work Together for a Bright Future of China-Iran Relations', Full text in English in *China Daily*, 21 January 2016, http://www.chinadaily.com.cn/world/2016xivisitmiddleeast/2016-01/21/content_23189585.htm.

13. 'Global Trading Giants Dip Toes in China Oil Futures on Debut Day', Bloomberg News, 25 March 2018, https://www.bloomberg.com/news/articles/2018-03-26/china-s-first-ever-yuan-oil-futures-begin-trading-in-shanghai. China also announced plans to pay for crude oil imports in Yuan in 2018, see Sumeet Chatterjee and Meng Meng, 'Exclusive - China taking first steps to pay for oil in yuan this year - sources', Reuters, 29 March 2018, https://uk.reuters.com/article/uk-china-oil-yuan/exclusive-china-taking-first-steps-to-pay-for-oil-in-yuan-this-year-sources-idUKKBN1H51M5.

14. Chen Aizhu and Meng Meng, 'Russia Beats Saudi Arabia as China's Top Crude Oil Supplier in 2016', Reuters, 23 Janaury 2017, http://www.reuters.com/article/us-china-economy-trade-crude-idUSKBN1570VJ.

15. Alec Luhn and Terry Macalister, 'Russia Signs 30-year Deal Worth $400bn to Deliver Gas to China', *Guardian*, 21 May 2014, https://www.theguardian.com/world/2014/may/21/russia-30-year-400bn-gas-deal-china.

16. Andrew E. Kramer, 'Russia Reaches Deal with Iran to Construct Nuclear Power Plant', *New York Times*, 11 November 2014, https://www.nytimes.com/2014/11/12/world/europe/russia-to-build-2-nuclear-plants-in-iran-and-possibly-6-more.html.

17. Felicia Schwartz, 'US Sanctions Chinese Entities, Others, for Aid to Iran, North Korea, Syria', *Wall Street Journal*, 24 March 2017, https://www.wsj.com/articles/u-s-sanctions-chinese-entities-others-for-aid-to-iran-north-korea-syria-1490373607.

18. Paul D. Shinkman, 'The Hidden Message for China in Trump's Iran sanctions', *US News*, 3 February 2017, https://www.usnews.com/news/

politics/articles/2017-02-03/trumps-iran-sanctions-list-included-hidden-message-for-china-experts-say; on the links between North Korea and China, see reports by Project Alpha, King's College London and 'North Korea's proliferation and illicit procurement apparatus', Project Alpha, 6 June 2017, https://projectalpha.eu/north-koreas-proliferation-illicit-procurement-apparatus-within-china/, see also, Anthony Ruggiero, 'Severing China-North Korea Financial Links', CSIS, 3 April 2017, https://www.csis.org/analysis/severing-china-north-korea-financial-links.

19. Author interview with Iranian official from the Ministry of Foreign Affairs, email, June 2017.

20. Shawn Donnan and Najmeh Bozorgmehr, 'US Puts Iran "On Notice" After Weekend Missile Test', *Financial Times*, 2 February 2017, https://www.ft.com/content/98aeee34-e8ba-11e6-893c-082c54a7f539.

21. 'Remarks by Federica Mogherini on the Implementation of the Joint Comprehensive Plan of Action (Iran Nuclear Deal)', European External Action Service, 16 October 2017, https://eeas.europa.eu/headquarters/headquarters-homepage_en/33997/Remarks%20by%20Federica%20Mogherini%20on%20the%20implementation%20of%20the%20Joint%20Comprehensive%20Plan%20of%20Action%20(Iran%20nuclear%20deal), see also, Robin Emmot, 'European Powers urge Trump to Preserve Nuclear Deal', Reuters, 11 January 2018, https://www.reuters.com/article/us-iran-nuclear-eu/european-powers-urge-trump-to-preserve-iran-nuclear-deal-idUSKBN1F00XN.

22. For the full text of the JCPOA see, Joint Comprehensive Plan of Action, 14 July 2015, https://www.state.gov/e/eb/tfs/spi/iran/jcpoa/.

23. Joint statement by the High Representative/Vice-President of the European Union, Federica Mogherini and the Minister of Foreign Affairs of the Islamic Republic of Iran, Javad Zarif, Brussels, 16 April 2016, http://europa.eu/rapid/press-release_STATEMENT-16-1441_en.htm.

24. Statement by Federica Mogherini on the first Anniversary of the Implementation of the JCPOA, Brussels, 16 January 2017, https://eeas.europa.eu/headquarters/headquarters-homepage_en/18609/Statement%20by%20Federica%20Mogherini%20on%20the%20first%20Anniversary%20of%20the%20Implementation%20of%20the%20JCPOA.

25. Article 146 of the constitution states: 'The Establishment of Any Kind of Foreign Military Base in Iran, even for Peaceful Purposes, is Forbidden', Article 146, Chapter 9, Constitution of the Islamic Republic of Iran, http://www.iranonline.com/iran/iran-info/government/constitution-9-3.html.

Chapter 1   Iran and the World Order: Russia and China as a Bulwark Against the West

1. Annabelle Sreberny-Mohammadi and Ali Mohammadi, *Small Media, Big Revolution: Communication, Culture, and the Iranian Revolution* (Minneapolis: University of Minnesota Press, 1994), p. 148.
2. Terms associated with 'exporting the revolution'.
3. See, Ariane Tabatabai and Annie Tracy Samuel, 'The Legacy of the Iran–Iraq War and Its Implications for the Iranian Nuclear File', *International Security* (Vol. 42, No. 1, Summer 2017).
4. Ibid.
5. See: Ray Takeyh, 'Iran's "Resistance Economy" Debate,' 7 April 2016. https://www.cfr.org/expert-brief/irans-resistance-economy-debate.
6. 'The General Policy of "Resistance Economy" was Announced', ISNA, 20 February 2013, http://www.isna.ir/news/92113020882/%D8%B3%DB%8C%D8%A7%D8%B3%D8%AA-%D9%87%D8%A7%DB%8C-%DA%A9%D9%84%DB%8C-%D8%A7%D9%82%D8%AA%D8%B5%D8%A7%D8%AF-%D9%85%D9%82%D8%A7%D9%88%D9%85%D8%AA%DB%8C-%D8%A7%D8%A8%D9%84%D8%A7%D8%BA-%D8%B4%D8%AF.
7. Author interview with Ali Asghar Soltanieh, Tehran, July 2014.
8. Glenn Kessler, 'In 2003, US Spurned Iran's Offer of Dialogue', *Washington Post*, 18 June 2006, http://www.washingtonpost.com/wp-dyn/content/article/2006/06/17/AR2006061700727.html.
9. President George W. Bush, 'The President's State of the Union Address', The United States Capitol Washington, DC, 29 January 2002, https://georgewbush-whitehouse.archives.gov/news/releases/2002/01/20020129-11.html.
10. Final Assessment on Past and Present Outstanding Issues Regarding Iran's Nuclear Programme, Report by the IAEA Board of Governors, GOV/2015/68, 2 December 2015, https://www.documentcloud.org/documents/2631873-IAEA-document.html.
11. Author interviews with US officials and former officials, Vienna and Washington, DC, 2014–16.
12. 'Iran's President Rouhani addresses Davos', President Hassan Rouhani, *Telegraph*, 23 June 2014, http://www.telegraph.co.uk/finance/financetopics/davos/10590192/Irans-President-Rouhani-addresses-Davos.html.
13. Author interviews with senior Iranian officials, Tehran, Vienna, Lausanne, Geneva, and New York, 2014–16.
14. Ibid.

15. Ervand Abrahamian, *Iran Between Two Revolutions* (Princeton, NJ, Princeton University Press: 1982), p. 278; 'Foreign Relations of the United States, 1952-54, Iran, 1951-1954. 307. Record of Meeting in the Central Intelligence Agency, TPAJAX,' 28 August 1953, https://history.state.gov/historicaldocuments/frus1951-54Iran/d307; 'Foreign Relations of the United States, 1952-54, Iran, 1951-1954. 363. Memorandum Prepared in the Directorate of Plans, Central Intelligence Agency. Campaign to Install Pro-Western Government in Iran', 8 March 1954, https://history.state.gov/historicaldocuments/frus1951-54Iran/d363.

16. Author interviews with senior Iranian officials, Tehran, Vienna, Lausanne, Geneva, and New York, 2014-16.

17. Michael Birnbaum and Carol Morello, 'European Companies Beat US to Iran Business after Nuclear Deal Reached', *Washington Post*, 25 August 2015, https://www.theguardian.com/business/2015/aug/25/europe-us-iran-business-nuclear-deal-sanctions.

18. Antonella Cinello and Crispian Balmer, 'Deals and Warm Words Flow as Iran President Visits Europe', Reuters, 26 January 2016, http://www.reuters.com/article/us-iran-europe-rouhani-idUSKCN0V31DJ.

19. Parisa Hafezi, 'Iran's Khamenei says US, "evil" Britain can't be trusted: state TV', Reuters, 3 June 2016, http://www.reuters.com/article/us-iran-usa-khamenei-idUSKCN0YP0MA.

20. 'Iran's Khamanei blames U.S. for regional instability, creation of Islamic State', Reuters, 12 June 2017; 'Khamenei: US wants regime change in Iran', Al Jazeera, 9 February 2014.

21. Author interviews with Iranian officials, New York, Vienna, Geneva, Berlin, Tehran, 2014–18.

22. John W. Graver, 'China and Iran: An Emerging Partnership Post-Sanctions,' Middle East Institute Policy Focus Series, February 2016, http://www.mei.edu/sites/default/files/publications/Garver_ChinaIran.pdf, p. 3.

23. Abbas Amanat, *Pivot of the Universe: Nasir al-Din Shah and the Iranian Monarchy* (London: I.B.Tauris, 2008), p. 1.

24. Jonathan D Spence, *The Search for Modern China* (New York: Norton Paperback, 1991).

25. Robert Lawrence Kuhm, 'Xi Jinpeng's Chinese Dream', *New York Times*, 4 June 2013, http://www.nytimes.com/2013/06/05/opinion/global/xi-jinpings-chinese-dream.html.

26. Brandon Fite, 'US and Iranian Strategic Competition: The Impact of China and Russia', CSIS, March 2012, p. 5.

27. Edward Burman, *China and Iran: Parallel History, Future Threat?* (Stroud: The History Press, 2009).

28. Scott Warren Harold and Alireza Nader, 'China and Iran: Economic, Political, and Military Relations' RAND Corporation, 2012.

29. John W. Garver, *China and Iran: Ancient Partners in a Post-Imperial World* (Seattle: University of Washington Press, 2006), pp. 4–5.

30. Ibid., p. 53.

31. Ibid., p. 60.

32. Brandon Fite (2012), p. 8.

33. John W. Garver, 'China and Iran: Expanding Cooperation under conditions of US domination', in Nov Horesh (ed.), 'Toward Well-Oiled Relations: China's Presence in the Middle East following the Arab Spring', the Nottingham China Policy Institute Series', p. 195.

34. Brandon Fite (2012), p. 7.

35. Author interviews with Iranian officials, Vienna, Geneva, Lausanne, 2014–16.

36. Javad Tabatabai, *Maktab-e Tabriz va mabani-ye tajjadod-khahi*, 151.

37. Morgan Schuster, *The Strangling of Persia*, xvii.

38. Ishaan Tharoor, 'A Russian Ambassador was Murdered. The apology came in the shape of a huge diamond', *Washington Post*, Dec. 22, 2016, https://www.washingtonpost.com/news/worldviews/wp/2016/12/22/a-russian-ambassador-was-murdered-the-apology-came-in-the-shape-of-a-huge-diamond/?utm_term=.0f2d15478acb.

39. Clément Therme, 'Iran and Russia: A Tactical Entente', in Stephanie Cronin (ed.), *Iranian–Russian Encounters: Empires and Revolutions Since 1800* (Oxon: Routledge, 2013).

40. Aras, Bulent and Ozbay, Faith, 'The Limits of the Russian–Iranian Strategic Alliance: Its History and Geopolitics, and the Nuclear Issue', *Korean Journal of Defense Analysis*, Vol. 20, No.1, 2008.

41. Clément Therme, 'Iran and Russia: A Tactical Entente,' in Stephanie Cronin (ed.), *Iranian–Russian Encounters: Empires and Revolutions Since 1800* (Oxon: Routledge, 2013), p. 385.

42. 'Global views of Iran Overwhelmingly Negative', Pew Research Center, 11 June 2013.

43. Robert F. Worth and Nicola Clark, 'Plane Crash Leaves 168 Dead in Iran', *New York Times*, 15 July 2009, http://www.nytimes.com/2009/07/16/world/middleeast/16plane.html.

44. 'Are the Russians and Iranians Friends?', World Policy Blog, 6 February 2015, http://www.worldpolicy.org/blog/2015/02/06/are-russians-and-iranians-friends.

45. Dennis Lynch, 'Russia, Iran Expand Military Ties With New Deal To "Confront" The US', *International Business Times*, 20 January 2015, http://www.ibtimes.com/russia-iran-expand-military-ties-new-deal-confront-us-1788410.

46. M. Ehsan Ahrari, 'Iran, China, and Russia: The Emerging Anti-US Nexus?', Security Dialogue, 2001, Vol. 32(4), pp. 453–66.
47. Author interviews with senior Iranian officials, Tehran, Vienna, Lausanne, Geneva, and New York, 2014–16.
48. Author interviews with senior Iranian officials and junior diplomats, Tehran, Vienna, Lausanne, Geneva, and New York, 2014–16.
49. Katie Sanders, 'Bob Schieffer says Iran President Hassan Rouhani has More Cabinet Members with American Ph.D.s than Obama', Politifact, 16 December 2013, http://www.politifact.com/punditfact/statements/2013/dec/16/bob-schieffer/bob-schieffer-says-iran-president-hassan-rouhani-h/.
50. Author interviews with US officials and former officials, Vienna and Washington, DC, 2014–16.
51. Author interviews with US officials and lawmakers, Washington, DC, 2014–17.
52. Press statement following the Fourth Caspian Summit, The Kremlin, 29 September 2014, http://en.kremlin.ru/events/president/transcripts/46689.
53. 'Iran, Russia to Stage Joint Naval Drills in Caspian Sea Today,' Fars News, October 15, 2014, http://en.farsnews.com/newstext.aspx?nn=13930723000616.
54. Shanghai Cooperation Organisation. For more, see SCO's main website, http://eng.sectsco.org/.
55. 'China Supports Iran's Application for Full Membership of SCO', Xinhua, 23 January 2016, http://news.xinhuanet.com/english/2016-01/23/c_135038723.htm.
56. For a comprehensive account of the Iran–Iraq War see, Williamson Murray and Kevin M. Woods, The Iran–Iraq War: a Military and Strategic History (Cambridge: Cambridge University Press, 2014).
57. For example: See Shireen Hunter, Iran's Foreign Policy in the Post-Soviet Era: Resisting the New International Order (Oxford: Praeger, 2010); for a more textured, constructivist approach, see, Maaike Warnar, Iranian Foreign Policy During Ahmadinejad: Ideology and Actions (New York: Palgrave Macmillan, 2013).
58. Alistair Iain Johnston, 'Is Chinese Nationalism Rising?' International Security, Vol. 41, No. 3 (Winter 2016/17), pp. 7–43; Richard Arnold, 'Surveys Show Russian Nationalism is on the Rise. This Explains a Lot about the Country's Foreign and Domestic Politics', Washington Post – Monkey Cage, 30 May 2016, https://www.washingtonpost.com/news/monkey-cage/wp/2016/05/30/surveys-show-russian-nationalism-is-on-the-rise-this-explains-a-lot-about-the-countrys-foreign-and-domestic-politics/?utm_term=.52e5c044e76d; Author interviews in Iran, 2009–14.

59. Embodied by the power struggle between Bani-Sadr and Khomeini; see Shaul Bakhash, *The Reign of the Ayatollahs* (New York: Basic Books, 1984), Chapter 5 (Bani-Sadr: The 'Devoted Son' as President).
60. For a brief analysis of the political machinations behind this, see Ali M. Ansari, *Iran, Islam and Democracy: The Politics of Managing Change* (London: Royal Institute of International Affairs, 2006), pp. 45–6 (titled 'Religious Nationalism').
61. 'Timeline of Iran's nuclear programme', *Guardian*, https://www.theguardian.com/world/2013/nov/24/iran-nuclear-timeline.
62. 'Inalienable Right to Enrich' can be attributed to Sirous Naseri, then head Iranian negotiator. 'This World: Iran's Nuclear Secrets', *BBC*, 3 May, 2005, http://news.bbc.co.uk/1/shared/spl/hi/programmes/this_world/transcripts/irans_nuclear_secrets_03_05_2005.txt.
63. While the NPT does provide non-nuclear weapon states with the right to the peaceful use of nuclear technology, it is actually silent on the specifics and scope of the technology. In other words, fuel cycle activities, including its front and back ends, enrichment and reprocessing, are not explicitly allowed or prohibited by the NPT.
64. Article 49 of Iran's Safeguards Agreement requires that information on LOFs be provided 'on a timely basis'. Implementation of the NPT safeguards agreement in the Islamic Republic of Iran', *IAEA*, 19 June, 2003, http://www.securitycouncilreport.org/atf/cf/%7B65BFCF9B-6D27-4E9C-8CD3-CF6E4FF96FF9%7D/Disarm%20GOV200340.pdf.
65. See Wyn Bowen, Matthew Moran and Dina Esfandiary, *Living on the Edge: Iran and the Practice of Nuclear Hedging* (London: Palgrave Macmillan, 2016), Chapter 4; Ariane Tabatabai and Annie Tracy Samuel, 'The Legacy of the Iran–Iraq War and Its Implications for the Iranian Nuclear File', *International Security* (Vol. 42, No. 1, Summer 2017).
66. President Ahmadinejad's speech to the UN General Assembly, New York, 18 September 2005, http://news.bbc.co.uk/1/hi/uk_politics/4257278.stm.
67. 'Ahmadinejad Says Sanctions Won't Stop Iran's Nuclear Advancements', Associated Press, 18 December 2012, http://www.foxnews.com/world/2012/12/18/ahmadinejad-says-sanctions-wont-stop-iran-nuclear-advancements.html.
68. See Rebecca Shimon Stoil, 'Rice: Total End to Iranian Enrichment is "Unachievable Ideal"', *Times of Israel*, 3 March 2015, https://www.timesofisrael.com/rice-total-end-to-iranian-enrichment-is-unachievable-ideal/.
69. Author interviews with US and EU officials, Washington, DC, Brussels, Vienna, 2015.
70. The JCPOA was also largely popular in Iran despite widespread misconceptions about sanctions relief in the deal. Mehdi Khalaji (2015)

'Great Expectations: Iran after the Deal', *Washington Quarterly*, 38:3, 61–77, DOI: 10.1080/0163660X.2015.1099025.

71. James Palmer, 'China Really Isn't Joking About Taiwan,' *Foreign Policy*, December 5, 2016, http://foreignpolicy.com/2016/12/05/china-really-isnt-joking-about-taiwan/.

72. Christopher Hughes, *Taiwan and Chinese Nationalism* (London: Routledge, 1997), p. 2.

73. As rural modernity became a component of the statism adopted by the nationalist regime. Yongnian Zheng, *Discovering Chinese Nationalism in China* (Cambridge: Cambridge University Press, 1999).

74. Christopher Hughes, *Taiwan and Chinese Nationalism* (London: Routledge, 1997), p. 7.

75. For discussion of the trends in Chinese nationalism, see Alistair Iain Johnston, 'Is Chinese Nationalism Rising?' *International Security*, Vol. 41, No. 3 (Winter 2016/17), pp. 7–43.

76. Richard Arnold, 'Surveys Show Russian Nationalism is on the Rise. This Explains a Lot about the Country's Foreign and Domestic Politics,' *Washington Post*, May 30, 2016, https://www.washingtonpost.com/news/monkey-cage/wp/2016/05/30/surveys-show-russian-nationalism-is-on-the-rise-this-explains-a-lot-about-the-countrys-foreign-and-domestic-politics/?utm_term=.b00aa6947e0a.

Also see: Pål Kostø and Helge Blakkisrud, *The New Russian Nationalism: Imperialism, Ethnicity and Authoritarianism 2000-15* (Edinburgh: Edinburgh University Press, 2016).

77. Richard Arnold, 'Surveys Show Russian Nationalism is on the Rise. This Explains a Lot about the Country's Foreign and Domestic Politics,' *Washington Post*, 30 May 2016, https://www.washingtonpost.com/news/monkey-cage/wp/2016/05/30/surveys-show-russian-nationalism-is-on-the-rise-this-explains-a-lot-about-the-countrys-foreign-and-domestic-politics/?utm_term = .b00aa6947e0a.

78. Masha Lipman, 'Putin's Nationalist Strategy,' *The New Yorker*, March 2, 2014, http://www.newyorker.com/news/news-desk/putins-nationalist-strategy.

79. Paul Goode, 'How Russian Nationalism Explains—And Does Not Explain—the Crimean Crisis,' *Washington Post*, March 3, 2014, https://www.washingtonpost.com/news/monkey-cage/wp/2014/03/03/how-russian-nationalism-explains-and-does-not-explain-the-crimean-crisis/?utm_term=.f04986a27049.

80. Richard Arnold, 'Surveys Show Russian Nationalism is on the Rise. This Explains a Lot about the Country's Foreign and Domestic Politics,' *Washington Post*, 30 May 2016, https://www.washingtonpost.com/news/

monkey-cage/wp/2016/05/30/surveys-show-russian-nationalism-is-on-the-rise-this-explains-a-lot-about-the-countrys-foreign-and-domestic-politics/?utm_term=.b00aa6947e0a.

81. Dmitri V. Trenin, *Getting Russia Right* (Carnegie Endowment For International Peace: 2007), p. 4.

82. 77 Henry E. Hale, 'Russian Nationalism and the Logic of the Kremlin's Actions on Ukraine,' *Guardian*, 29 August 2014, https://www.theguardian.com/world/2014/aug/29/russian-nationalism-kremlin-actions-ukraine

83. Aghaie, Kamran Scot, and Marashi, Afshin (eds), *Rethinking Iranian Nationalism and Modernity* (Austin: University of Texas Press, 2014).

84. Paul Goode, 'How Russian Nationalism Explains—And Does Not Explain—the Crimean Crisis,' *Washington Post*, 3 March 2014, https://www.washingtonpost.com/news/monkey-cage/wp/2014/03/03/how-russian-nationalism-explains-and-does-not-explain-the-crimean-crisis/?utm_term=.f04986a27049; Alistair Iain Johnston, 'Is Chinese Nationalism Rising?' *International Security*, Vol. 41, No. 3 (Winter 2016/17), pp. 7–43.

85. Author interviews with Iranian officials, Vienna, Geneva, Lausanne, New York, 2014–16.

86. Author interviews, Tehran, July 2014.

87. Author interviews with senior Iranian officials and the nuclear negotiating team, Tehran, New York, Vienna, Geneva and Lausanne, 2014–16.

88. Ibid.

89. Ibid; Wyn Bowen, Matthew Moran and Dina Esfandiary, *Living on the Edge: Iran and the Practice of Nuclear Hedging* (London: Palgrave Macmillan, 2016).

90. Zhao, Suisheng, 'Foreign Policy Implications of Chinese Nationalism Revisited: The Strident Turn', *Journal of Contemporary China* 22, no. 82 (2013), p. 537; Wang, Zheng, 'The Legacy of Historical Memory and China's Foreign Policy in the 2010s' in Gilbert Rozman (ed.), *Misunderstanding Asia* (New York: Palgrave Macmillan, 2015), pp. 227–39, p. 233.

91. Daniel Treisman, 'Why Putin took Crimea', *Foreign Affairs*, May/June 2016, https://www.foreignaffairs.com/articles/ukraine/2016-04-18/why-putin-took-crimea.

92. J. Dumbrell, 'The Bush Administration, US public diplomacy and Iran', Working Paper, Durham University, School of Government and International Affairs, Durham (2007).

93. Some even assert that the Revolutionary Guards have eclipsed most of Iran's politicians in power. Elliot Hen-Tov and Nathan Gonzalez, 'The Militarization of Post-Khomeini Iran: Praetorianism 2.0', *Washington Quarterly*, 17 Dec. 2012 (published online).

94. H. E. Chehabi, 'The Political Regime of the Islamic Republic of Iran in Comparative Perspective', *Government and Opposition*, 36: 48–70. doi: 10.1111/1477-7053.00053 (2001).

95. Ibid.

96. Ariane Tabatabai, 'Where Does the Islamic Revolutionary Guard Corps Stand on Nuclear Negotiations?' *Bulletin of the Atomic Scientists*, 11 March 2015, http://thebulletin.org/ where does islamic revolutionary guard corps stand nuclear negotiations 8084.

97. Qassem Soulemani, head of the Quds Force, maintains an active social media presence for this purpose.

98. Dina Esfandiary and Ariane Tabatabai, 'A Comparative Study of US and Iranian Counter ISIS Strategies', *Studies in Conflict and Terrorism*, Vol. 40, Iss. 6 (2017).

99. Indeed, Iranian factionalism has been a widely observed phenomenon since the waning years of the Iran–Iraq War. Maziar Behrooz, 'Factionalism in Iran under Khomeini', *Middle Eastern Studies* (1991), 27:4, 597–614. https://doi.org/10.1080/00263209108700879.

100. R. K. Ramazani, 'Ideology and Pragmatism in Iran's Foreign Policy', - *Middle East Journal* 58, no. 4 (2004), pp. 549–59, http://www.jstor.org/ stable/4330062.

101. Author interviews with Iranian, US, EU, and Gulf Arab officials, Tehran, New York, Washington, DC, Brussels, London, Muscat, Dubai, 2014–17.

102. Author interviews with Iranian officials, New York and Berlin, 2016–17.

103. Lu Ning, *The Dynamics of Foreign-Policy Decision-making in China* (Boulder, CO: Westview Press, 2000), p. 7.

104. Ibid., p. 8.

105. Ibid., p. 9.

106. Jacopo Detoni, 'Russia and Iran Lock NATO Out of Caspian Sea', *The Diplomat*, 1 October 2014, http://thediplomat.com/2014/10/russia-and-iran-lock-nato-out-of-caspian-sea/.

107. See Kenneth Katzman, 'Iran Sanctions', *Congressional Research Service*, Nov. 16, 2016.

108. Author interviews with US, EU, and GCC lawmakers and officials, New York, Washington, DC, Brussels, London, Paris, Dubai, Abu Dhabi, Muscat, Doha, and Kuwait City, 2014–17.

109. Michael Eisenstadt, 'Iran Primer', *Washington Institute*, 13 September 2015, https://www.washingtoninstitute.org/uploads/Documents/opeds/ Eisenstadt20150913-IranPrimer.pdf.

110. The 'campfire strategy' is diverting jihadists onto someone else. Daniel Byman, 'US Counter Terrorism Options: A Taxonomy', *Global Politics and Strategy* (Vol. 49, Issue 3, 2007), pp. 121–50.

111. Dina Esfandiary and Ariane Tabatabai, 'A Comparative Study of US and Iranian Counter ISIS Strategies', *Studies in Conflict and Terrorism*, Vol. 40, I. 6 (2017).

112. Stephen J. Cimbala, 'Forward to Where? US–Russian Strategic Nuclear Force Reductions', *Journal of Slavic Military Studies*, 22:1, 68–86, DOI: 10.1080/13518040802695266 (2009).

113. 'Nuclear arsenals', *ican*, http://www.icanw.org/the-facts/nuclear-arsenals/.

114. Brad Lennon and Katie Hunt, 'China, Russia, Begin Joint Exercises in South China Sea', CNN, 12 September 2016, http://www.cnn.com/2016/09/12/asia/china-russia-south-china-sea-exercises/.

115. 'China Trade Statistics', *World Integrated Trade Solution*, https://wits.worldbank.org/CountryProfile/en/CHN.

116. See, Hugh White, *The China Choice: Why America Should Share Power* (Oxford: Oxford University Press, 2013).

117. Ali Vaez, 'Spider Web: the Making and Unmaking of Iran Sanctions', Middle East Report No. 138, International Crisis Group, 25 February 2013, https://d2071andvip0wj.cloudfront.net/138-spider-web-the-making-and-unmaking-of-iran-sanctions.pdf, p. i.

118. Resolution 1737 (2006), adopted by the Security Council at its 5612th meeting, 23 December 2006, https://www.iaea.org/sites/default/files/unsc_res1737-2006.pdf.

119. US Executive Order NO. 12170, 14 November 1979, https://www.treasury.gov/resource-center/sanctions/Programs/Documents/Executive%20Order%2012170.pdf.

120. Vaez, 'Spider Web', p. 6.

121. Both in 1993 (S. 1583, Public Law) and in 1996 with the Iran and Libya Sanctions Act of 1996 (H.R. 3107, Public Law).

122. For example, the Comprehensive Iran Sanctions Act of 1993 (S. 1583).

123. Executive Order 12957, Prohibiting Certain Transactions with Respect to the Development of Iranian Petroleum Resources, 15 March 1995 and Executive Order 12959, Prohibiting Certain Transactions With Respect to Iran, 6 May 1995.

124. Iran Sanctions Act, Public Law 104-172, 6 August 1996.

125. 'H.R. 2194 – Comprehensive Iran Sanctions, Accountability, and Divestment Act of 2010,' Public Law, https://www.congress.gov/bill/111th-congress/house-bill/2194?q=%7B%22search%22%3A%5B%22Iran+Sanctions%2C+Accountability+and+Divestment+Act%22%5D%7D&r=2.

126. Comprehensive Iran Sanctions, Accountability, and Divestment Act of 2010 (CISADA), Public Law: 111–195, 1 July 2010.

127. Iran Freedom and Counter-Proliferation Act of 2012 (IFCPA).

128. Hillary Rodham Clinton and Timothy F. Geithner, 'Announcement of Japanese Autonomous Sanctions on Iran', 3 September, 2010, https://geneva.usmission.gov/2010/09/03/announcement-of-japanese-autonomous-sanctions-on-iran/.

129. Council Conclusions on Iran, 2776th EU External Relations Council meeting, Brussels, 22 January 2007 and Council Common Position 2007/140/CFSP, Concerning restrictive measures against Iran, 27 February 2007.

130. For more on EU measures on Iran see, 'EU restrictive measures on Iran' fact sheet, EU Consilium, http://www.consilium.europa.eu/en/policies/sanctions/iran/.

131. Dina Esfandiary, 'Assessing the European Union's Sanctions Policy: Iran as a Case Study', Non-Proliferation Papers, No. 34, December 2013, https://www.nonproliferation.eu/web/documents/nonproliferationpapers/dinaesfandiary52b41ff5cbaf6.pdf.

132. Farnaz Fassihi and John M Biers, 'EU Bans Import of Iran's Oil, Raising Pressure on Iran', *Wall Street Journal*, 24 January 2012, https://www.wsj.com/articles/SB10001424052970203718504577178231285985826.

133. Nearly all economic indicators support this statement. For detail, see 'Iran, Islamic Rep', World Bank Data, https://data.worldbank.org/country/iran-islamic-rep.

134. US Executive Order 13660, 10 March 2014, https://www.treasury.gov/resource-center/sanctions/Programs/Documents/ukraine_eo.pdf.

135. For a list of all the measures, see the EU's website on EU sanctions against Russia over Ukraine crisis, https://europa.eu/newsroom/highlights/special-coverage/eu-sanctions-against-russia-over-ukraine-crisis_en.

136. Jeremy Herb and Ashley Killough, 'Senators Reach Russia Sanctions Deal', CNN, 13 June 2017, http://edition.cnn.com/2017/06/13/politics/senate-russia-sanctions-deal/index.html.

Chapter 2   Iranian Political Relations with the Two Powers

1. Iranian–American cooperation on nuclear research began with the Atoms for Peace Initiative during the Eisenhower administration, which lasted from 1959–1964 as a cooperative research project. Richard G. Hewlett and Jack M. Holl, *Atoms for Peace and War, 1953–1961: Eisenhower and the Atomic Energy Commission* (University of California Press: 1989). See p. 581. US–Iranian military cooperation was extensive throughout the Shah's reign, but came to its zenith in the 1970s, after the implementation of the Nixon Doctrine – it was from the US that the Shah acquired the

meat of his air force, the F-4 Phantom Fighter-Bomber, and the F-14 Tomcat.

2. See Roham Alvandi, 'The Shah's Détente with Khrushchev: Iran's 1962 Missile Base Pledge to the Soviet Union', *Cold War History*, Volume 14, Issue 3 (2014).

3. Ibid.

4. Ibid.

5. Alexander Orlov, 'The U2 Program: A Russian Officer Remembers: A "Hot" Front in the Cold War', https://www.cia.gov/library/center-for-the-study-of-intelligence/csi-publications/csi-studies/studies/winter98_99/art02.html.

6. See Roham Alvandi, 'The Shah's Détente with Khrushchev: Iran's 1962 Missile Base Pledge to the Soviet Union', *Cold War History*, Volume 14, Issue 3 (2014).

7. Rouhollah K. Ramazani, 'Iran's Changing Foreign Policy: A Preliminary Discussion', *Middle East Journal* 24, no. 4 (1970): 421–37. http://www.jstor.org/stable/4324642.

8. Such as a committee on economic cooperation, a gas pipeline, and multiple shared economic ventures.

9. Guang Pan, 'China's Success in the Middle East', *Middle East Quarterly* (Vol. 4 No. 4, Dec. 1997) pp. 35–40.

10. Although unofficial trade had continued for more than a decade prior, at a value of $2.5 million across the span of the 1950s. Mohamed Bin Huwaidin, *China's Relations with Arabia and the Gulf: 1949–1999* (London: Routledge, 2002), p. lxxv.

11. Both Ashraf and Fatimeh Pahlavi visited China in April, 1971. Mohamed Bin Huwaidin, *China's Relations with Arabia and the Gulf: 1949–1999* (London: Routledge, 2002), p. lxxvii.

12. Ibid.

13. John W. Garver, *China's Quest: The history of the foreign relations of the People's Republic of China* (Oxford: Oxford University Press, 2016), p. 339.

14. Garver (2006).

15. Harris, Lillian Craig, 'China's Response to Perceived Soviet Gains in the Middle East', *Asian Survey* 20, no. 4 (1980): 362–72, doi:10.2307/2643863.

16. Ibid., p. 54.

17. Ibid., p. 64.

18. Ibid., p. 60.

19. In 1979 changing course from their support for the Shah. See: Mark N. Katz, 'Iran and Russia', *The Wilson Center*, https://www.wilsoncenter.org/sites/default/files/Iran%20and%20Russia.pdf; Abrahamian, Ervand,

'Iran in Revolution: The Opposition Forces', *MERIP Reports*, no. 75/76 (1979): 3–8, doi:10.2307/3012310.

20. Author interview with Iranian official, phone, 4 July 2017.

21. Ray Takeyh, *Guardians of the Revolution: Iran and the World in the Age of the Ayatollahs* (Oxford: Oxford University Press, 2009), p. 20.

22. 'Soviet–Iranian Relations after Khomeini', US Directorate of Intelligence, 23 June 1989, https://www.cia.gov/library/readingroom/docs/DOC_0000602666.pdf, p. 3.

23. USSR–Iran: Prospects for a Troubled Relationship – An Intelligence Assessment, US Directorate of Intelligence, January 1987, https://www.cia.gov/library/readingroom/docs/CIA-RDP89B00224R000903140008-2.pdf, p. 3.

24. Ibid., p. 1.

25. Ibid., p. 5.

26. Ibid., p. 4.

27. 'USSR–Iran: Prospects for a Troubled Relationship – An Intelligence Assessment', US Directorate of Intelligence, p. 4.

28. Elaine Sciolino, 'Soviet Proposes talks in Gulf War but Iran is reported to reject call', *New York Times*, 3 July 1987.

29. Elaine Sciolino, 'Soviet–Iraqi Ties Hit Snag on Iran', *New York Times*, 3 October 1987, http://www.nytimes.com/1987/10/03/world/soviet-iraqi-ties-hit-snag-on-iran.html.

30. USSR–Iran: Prospects for a Troubled Relationship – An Intelligence Assessment, US Directorate of Intelligence, January 1987, https://www.cia.gov/library/readingroom/docs/CIA-RDP89B00224R000903140008-2.pdf, p. 3.

31. 'Soviet–Iranian Relations after Khomeini', US Directorate of Intelligence, 23 June 1989, https://www.cia.gov/library/readingroom/docs/DOC_0000602666.pdf.

32. Ibid., pp. 2–3.

33. Ibid., pp. 6–7.

34. John M Broder, 'Despite a Secret Pact by Gore in '95, Russian Arms Sales to Iran Go On', *New York Times*, 13 October 2000, http://www.nytimes.com/2000/10/13/world/despite-a-secret-pact-by-gore-in-95-russian-arms-sales-to-iran-go-on.html.

35. 'Velayati on Visit to Soviet Republics,' IRIB Television First Program Network, 8 December 1991, in Brenton Clark, 'Iran and the Civil War in Tajikistan', Orta Asya ve Kafkasya Arastirmalari, Vol. 9, Issue 18 (2014), p. 89.

36. For a discussion of Iran's involvement in the conflict see, Brenton Clark, 'Iran and the Civil War in Tajikistan', Orta Asya ve Kafkasya Arastirmalari, Vol. 9, Issue 18 (2014).

37. Robert O. Freedman, 'Russian-Iranian Relations in the 1990s', *Middle East Review of International Affairs*, Vol. 4, No. 2, June 2000, http://www.rubincenter.org/2000/06/freedman-2000-06-05/.

38. Jeffrey Mankoff, *Russian Foreign Policy: The Return of Great Power Politics* (New York: Rowman & Littlefield Publishers, Inc, 2012), p. 124.

39. Jon Lee Anderson, 'Rabbani Assassination: An Afghan Understanding', *The New Yorker*, 20 September 2011, http://www.newyorker.com/news/news-desk/rabbani-assassination-an-afghan-understanding.

40. Fiona Symon, 'Afghanistan's Northern Alliance', BBC News 19 September 2001, http://news.bbc.co.uk/2/hi/south_asia/1552994.stm.

41. James Dobbins, 'How to Talk to Iran', *Washington Post*, 22 July 2007, http://www.washingtonpost.com/wp-dyn/content/article/2007/07/20/AR2007072002056.html.

42. Mark N. Katz, 'Iran and Russia', *The Wilson Center*, https://www.wilsoncenter.org/sites/default/files/Iran%20and%20Russia.pdf.

43. See multiple sub-sections in 'The Iranian Revolution at 30', *The Middle East Institute*, https://www.mei.edu/sites/default/files/publications/2009.01.The%20Iranian%20Revolution%20at%2030.pdf.

44. Brandon Fite (2012), p. 7.

45. Ibid., p. 65.

46. Karen DeYoung, 'Soviets Veto Sanctions By U.N. Against Iran', *Washington Post*, 14 January, 1980, https://www.washingtonpost.com/archive/politics/1980/01/14/soviets-veto-sanctions-by-un-against-iran/9d6b8b82-e415-4d14-b421-3b620ecdb88a/?utm_term=.86bf1bbaa615.

47. List of agreements on mutual visa exemptions, China Ministry of Foreign Affairs, http://cs.mfa.gov.cn/zlbg/bgzl/cgqz/P020140821530413680590.pdf.

48. Richard Halloran, 'The Downing of Flight 655', *New York Times*, 4 July 1988, http://www.nytimes.com/1988/07/04/world/downing-flight-655-us-downs-iran-airliner-mistaken-for-f-14-290-reported-dead.html?pagewanted=all.

49. Karen DeYoung, 'Soviets Veto Sanctions by U.N. Against Iran', *Washington Post*, 14 January 1980, https://www.washingtonpost.com/archive/politics/1980/01/14/soviets-veto-sanctions-by-un-against-iran/9d6b8b82-e415-4d14-b421-3b620ecdb88a/?utm_term=.e345dan, 'The Downing of Flight 655', *New York Times*, 4 July 1988.

50. Garver (2006), p. 109.

51. Elaine Sciolino, 'China will build A-Plant for Iran', *New York Times*, 11 September 1992, http://www.nytimes.com/1992/09/11/world/china-will-build-a-plant-for-iran.html.
52. Garver (2006), p. 109.
53. Ibid., p. 110.
54. For a description of the dual containment policy, see 'The Clinton Adminstration's Approach to the Middle East', Speech by Martin Indyk, Soref Symposium, Washington Institute for Near East Policy, 1993, http://www.washingtoninstitute.org/policy-analysis/view/the-clinton-administrations-approach-to-the-middle-east.
55. David E. Sanger, 'On Russian–Iranian Oil Deal, US Sanctions May Backfire', *New York Times*, 16 October 1997, http://www.nytimes.com/1997/10/16/world/on-russian-iranian-oil-deal-us-sanctions-may-backfire.html.
56. Garver (2006), p. 113.
57. Ibid.
58. Ibid., p. 114.
59. Kenneth Daines, 'Sino–Iranian Relations: History and Nuclear Proliferation Implications', *Sigma: Journal of Political and International Studies* (2013): Vol. 30, Article 6, Available at: https://scholarsarchive.byu.edu/sigma/vol30/iss1/6.
60. Garver (2006), p. 119.
61. James Dobbins, 'How to talk to Iran', *Washington Post*, 22 July 2007, http://www.washingtonpost.com/wp-dyn/content/article/2007/07/20/AR2007072002056.html.
62. Shaohua Hu, 'Russia and Cross Straight Relations', 2008, https://www.soas.ac.uk/taiwanstudies/eats/eats2008/file43181.pdf.
63. Culminating in the Iran Freedom Support Act of 2006, which codified many extant sanctions born of executive order (12957, 12959, and 13059). 'Sanctions Against Iran: A Guide to Targets, Terms, and Timetables', Belfer Center for Science and International Affairs, June 2015, https://www.belfercenter.org/sites/default/files/legacy/files/Iran%20Sanctions.pdf.
64. Russia subsequently restarted work on the Bushehr reactor, 'Chronology of Iran's Nuclear Programme, 1957–2007', Oxford Research Group, http://www.oxfordresearchgroup.org.uk/oxford_research_group_chronology_irans_nuclear_programme_1957_2007.
65. 'China Disapproves Use of "Axis of Evil" in International Relations', *People's Daily Online*, 5 February 2002, http://en.people.cn/200202/04/eng20020204_89911.shtml.
66. Garver (2006), p. 122.
67. Ibid.

68. Given the framework set by the Israel lobby, Iran's fears seemed justifiable. John J. Mearsheimer and Stephen M. Walt, 'The Israel Lobby and US Foreign Policy', *Middle East Policy*, Vol. 13 No. 3, Autumn 2006, http://mearsheimer.uchicago.edu/pdfs/IsraelLobby.pdf.

69. 'Analysts: Russia, China Ready to Block New UN Sanctions on Iran', *VOA*, 10 November 2011, https://www.voanews.com/a/analysts-russia-china-ready-to-block-new-un-sanctions-on-iran-133720178/148047.html.

70. Michael Wines, 'China's Ties with Iran Complicate Diplomacy', *New York Times*, 29 September 2009, http://www.nytimes.com/2009/09/30/world/asia/30china.html.

71. Thomas Juneau and Sam Razavi, *Iranian Foreign Policy Since 2001: Alone in the World* (London: Routledge, 2013), p. 171.

72. Ahmadinejad even challenged Rouhani to a debate after Rouhani succeeded him in 2013. Robert Tait, 'Mahmoud Ahmadinejad Challenges Hassan Rouhani to Debate', *Telegraph*, 3 December 2013, http://www.telegraph.co.uk/news/worldnews/middleeast/iran/10491468/Mahmoud-Ahmadinejad-challenges-Hassan-Rouhani-to-debate.html.

73. As we have seen, first the USSR and then Russia frequently vetoed sanctions against Iran, and China frequently abstained from voting.

74. Thomas J Christensen, *The China Challenge: Shaping the Choices of a Rising Power* (New York: WW Norton and Company, 2016).

75. Dina Esfandiary, 'Assessing the European Union's Sanctions Policy: Iran as a Case Study', Non-Proliferation Papers, No. 34, https://www.files.ethz.ch/isn/175467/EUNPC_no%2034.pdf.

76. MehdParvizi Amineh, *Towards the Control of Oil Resources in the Caspian Region* (New York: St. Martin's Press, 1999), p. 145.

77. Joshua Kussera, 'Did the Caspian Summit Do Anything to Improve Caspian Security?', Eurasia.net, 19 November 2010, http://www.eurasianet.org/node/62409.

78. Bruce Pannier, 'Caspian Summit Fails to Clarify Status, Resource Issues', RFERL, 19 November 2010, https://www.rferl.org/a/Caspian_Summit_Fails_To_Clarify_Status_Resource_Issues/2225159.html.

79. Vladimir Isachekov, 'No Deal at Caspian Sea Summit on Sharing Sea', *Washington Post*, 16 October 2017, http://www.washingtonpost.com/wp-dyn/content/article/2007/10/16/AR2007101601416.html.

80. Ibid.

81. Ibid.

82. Speech by President Vladimir Putin at the Press Statement following the Fourth Caspian Summit, 29 September 2014, http://en.kremlin.ru/events/president/transcripts/46689#sel=3:17:m6o,3:40:vxo;4:27:62q,4:50:w8x,

see also statement by Iranian President Rouhani, http://217.218.67.229/detail/2014/09/29/380453/no-foreign-force-in-caspian-region/.

83. Tony Paterson, 'Ukraine Crisis: NATO to Step Up Military Cooperation with Russia's Neighbours', *Telegraph*, 1 April 2014, http://www.telegraph.co.uk/news/worldnews/europe/ukraine/10736834/Ukraine-crisis-Nato-to-step-up-military-cooperation-with-Russias-neighbours.html.

84. Yelena Nikolayevna Zabortseva, *Russia's Relations with Kazakhstan: Rethinking ex-Soviet Transitions in the Emerging World System* (London: Routledge, 2016), p. 109.

85. Elmir Murad, 'Azerbaijan, Kazakhstan Sign Military Cooperation Plan 2016', Trend News Agency, 4 November 2015, http://en.trend.az/azerbaijan/politics/2452640.html.

86. 'Sagem and Kazakhstan Engineering Sign an Agreement to Create Joint Venture for Drones', Safran Group press statement, 2 November 2010, https://www.safran-electronics-defense.com/media/20101102_sagem-and-kazakhstan-engineering-sign-agreement-create-joint-venture-drones.

87. 'Oil and Natural Gas Production Growing in the Caspian Sea', Economist Intelligence Unit, 11 September 2013, https://www.eia.gov/today inenergy/detail.php?id=12911.

88. Ebrahim Gilani, 'Tehran Struggles to Claim Share of the Caspian', Tehran Bureau – PBS, 18 December 2010, http://www.pbs.org/wgbh/pages/frontline/tehranbureau/2010/12/tehran-struggles-to-claim-share-of-caspian.html.

89. 'Resolution 1929', UN Security Council, 9 June 2010, https://www.iaea.org/sites/default/files/unsc_res1929-2010.pdf.

90. As we have seen, given the World Bank data already presented and referenced, the Iranian economy struggled in key sectors under new sanctions.

91. For a detailed account of Iranian perceptions of the negotiations, see Seyed Hossein Mousavian, *The Iranian Nuclear Crisis: A Memoir* (Washington DC: Brookings Institution Press, 2012).

92. Author interviews with Iranian, European, and US officials, Vienna, Lausanne, Geneva, Brussels, London, Paris, New York, Washington, DC, Tehran, 2014–16.

93. 'Russia told US It Will Not Attend 2016 Nuclear Summit', Reuters, 5 November, 2014, https://www.reuters.com/article/us-nuclear-security-usa-russia/russia-told-u-s-it-will-not-attend-2016-nuclear-security-summit-idUSKBN0IP24K20141105.

94. Author interviews with US and European officials, Paris, London, Brussels, and Washington, DC, 2014–16.

95. For a comprehensive assessment of the nuclear deal, see Dina Esfandiary and Marc Finaud, 'The Iran Nuclear Deal: Distrust and Verify', GCSP Geneva Paper n18, April 2016, http://www.gcsp.ch/News-Knowledge/Publications/The-Iran-Nuclear-Deal-Distrust-and-Verify.

96. The Obama administration had to use Executive Waivers because it became clear that Congress, under a Republican majority, would not pass any legislation ending US sanctions on Iran.

97. 'German Delegation Aims to Renew Trade Ties on Trip to Iran', *Deutsche Welle*, 19 July 2015, http://www.dw.com/en/german-delegation-aims-to-renew-trade-ties-on-trip-to-iran/a-18594348. 'French FM Fabius in Iran for Talks with Senior Officials', Press TV, 29 July 2015, http://presstv.com/Detail/2015/07/29/422337/Iran-French-Foreign-minister-Laurent-Fabius -. Fabrice Node-Langlois, 'Les entreprises francaises se ruent dur l'Iran', *Le Figaro*, 22 September 2015, http://www.lefigaro.fr/societes/2015/09/20/20005-20150920ARTFIG00203-les-entreprises-francaises-se-ruent-sur-l-iran.php.

98. Saeed Kamali Dehghan, 'Iran's Dealmaking with Europe: The Seven Biggest Contracts', *Guardian*, 29 January 2016, https://www.theguardian.com/world/2016/jan/29/irans-dealmaking-europe-seven-biggest-contracts.

99. Author interviews with Iranian officials, Berlin, 26 June 2017.

100. The level of Iranian involvement in Syria has been the subject of debate, with some analysts confirming numbers in the thousands by the end of 2013 and others disputing that. See Jonathan Saul and Parisa Hafezi, 'Iran boosts military support in Syria to bolster Assad', Reuters, 21 February 2014, https://www.reuters.com/article/us-syria-crisis-iran-idUSBREA1K09U20140221. Jubin Goodarzi, 'Iran and Syria at the Crossroads: The Fall of Tehran-Damascus Axis?', Wilson Center Viewpoints, No.35, August 2013, https://www.wilsoncenter.org/sites/default/files/iran_syria_crossroads_fall_tehran_damascus_axis.pdf.

101. 'Syria Crisis: Where Key Countries Stand', BBC News, 30 October 2015, http://www.bbc.com/news/world-middle-east-23849587.

102. See Chapter 4.

103. See for example, Supreme Leader Ayatollah Khamenei's speech to the member of Ahlul Bayt World Assembly and Islamic Radio and TV Union, 17 August 2015, http://english.khamenei.ir/news/2109/Leader-s-speech-to-members-of-Ahlul-Bayt-World-Assembly-and-Islamic.

104. Author interview of Iranian expert, Montreux, 12 December 2017.

Chapter 3   It's the Economy, Stupid

1. 'Blocking Iranian Government Property', US Presidential Executive Order 12170, 14 November 1979, https://www.treasury.gov/resource-center/sanctions/Programs/Documents/Executive%20Order%2012170.pdf.

2. Author interviews with former US officials and European officials, Washington, DC, Paris, London, Brussels, 2014–16.

3. UN Security Council Resolution 1929, 9 June 2010, https://www.iaea.org/sites/default/files/unsc_res1929-2010.pdf.

4. Patrick Clawson, 'Knitting Iran Together: The Land Transport Revolution, 1920–1940.' *Iranian Studies* 26, no. 3/4 (1993): 235–50. http://www.jstor.org/stable/4310856.

5. Ehlers Eckart and Willem Floor, 'Urban Change in Iran, 1920–1941.' *Iranian Studies* 26, no. 3/4 (1993), pp. 251–75, http://www.jstor.org/stable/4310857.

6. Ibid.

7. See, Ervand Abrahamian, *Iran Between Two Revolutions* (Princeton: Princeton University Press, 1982).

   Said Amir Arjomand, *The Turban for the Crown: The Islamic Revolution in Iran* (Oxford: Oxford University Press, 1988); Ali M. Ansari, 'The Myth of the White Revolution: Mohammad Reza Shah, "Modernization" and the Consolidation of Power,' *Middle Eastern Studies* 37, no. 3 (2001), pp. 1–24, http://www.jstor.org/stable/4284172.

8. Richard G. Hewlett and Jack M. Holl, *Atoms for Peace and War, 1953–1961: Eisenhower and the Atomic Energy Commission.* (Berkeley, CA: University of California Press, 1989), p. 581.

9. Ervand Abrahamian, *A History of Modern Iran* (Cambridge: Cambridge University Press, 2008), Chapter 5, Table 8.

10. Richard Butler, Wantanee Suntikul, *Tourism and Political Change* (Oxford: Goodfellow Publishers, 2017), p. 190.

11. Juan De Onis, '$1-Billion for Poor Lands is Pledged by Shah of Iran', *New York Times*, 22 February 1974, http://www.nytimes.com/1974/02/22/archives/1billion-for-poor-lands-is-pledged-by-shah-of-iran-special-to-the.html.

12. Gawdat Bahgat, 'Nuclear Proliferation: The Islamic Republic of Iran.' *Iranian Studies* 39, no. 3 (2006), pp. 307–27, http://www.jstor.org/stable/4311832.

13. Author phone interview with Akbar Etemad, October 2014.

14. Author phone interview with Akbar Etemad, October 2014 and Aliasghar Soltanieh, Tehran, July 2014.

15. Author phone interview with Akbar Etemad, October 2014.

16. David Kinsella, 'Conflict in Context: Arms Transfers and Third World Rivalries during the Cold War', *American Journal of Political Science* 38, no. 3 (1994), pp. 557–81. doi:10.2307/2111597.

17. C. D. S. Drace-Francis, 'Irano–Soviet economic relations 1962–1983', *Asian Affairs* (1985), 16:1, pp. 54–68, http://dx.doi.org/10.1080/03068378508730173.

18. Ibid., footnote 26.

19. 'Economic Implications of Soviet–Iranian Agreements Involving Oil and Gas', CIA Intelligence Memorandum, June 1967, https://www.cia.gov/library/readingroom/docs/DOC_0000381440.pdf.

20. Ibid.

21. Ibid., p. 14, para 26.

22. Manochehr Dorraj and Carrie L. Currier, 'Lubricated with Oil: Iran–China Relations in a Changing World', *Middle East Policy Council* (Vol. XV, Summer No. 2, 2008).

23. Ibid.

24. Parviz Mohajer, 'Chinese–Iranian Relations v. Diplomatic and Commercial Relations, 1949–90', *Encyclopædia Iranica*, V/4, pp. 438–441, available online at http://www.iranicaonline.org/articles/chinese-iranian-v.

25. Manochehr Dorraj and Carrie L. Currier, 'Lubricated with Oil: Iran–China Relations in a Changing World', Middle East Policy, Vol. XV, No. 2, http://www.mepc.org/lubricated-oil-iran-china-relations-changing-world.

26. President Carter, 'Sanctions Against Iran Remarks Announcing US Actions Against Iran', The American Presidency Project, 7 April 1980, http://www.presidency.ucsb.edu/ws/?pid=33233.

27. *Xinhua News Bulletin*, 7 August 1987, pp. 51–2.

28. See: 'Implementation of the NPT Safeguards Agreement and Relevant Provisions of Security Council Resolutions in the Islamic Republic of Iran', Report by the Director General, IAEA GOV/2011/65, 8 November 2011, https://www.iaea.org/sites/default/files/gov2011-65.pdf.

29. For more on President Ahmadinejad's economic policies, see Nader Habibi, 'The Economic Legacy of Mahmoud Ahmadinejad', *Middle East Brief* – Brandeis University, No. 74, June 2013, https://www.brandeis.edu/crown/publications/meb/MEB74.pdf.

30. Kamiar Mohaddes, M. Hashem Pesaran, 'One Hundred Years of Oil Income and the Iranian Economy: A Curse or a Blessing?' (Cambridge: Cambridge University Press, Dec. 2012), p. 5, Table 1.

31. Author interview with Akbar Etemad, phone, October 2014.

32. Brandon Fite (2012), p. 11.

33. Ibid.

34. 'Iran's Joint Fields Offer Development, Partnership Opportunities', *Oil and Gas Journal*, 1 February 2017, http://www.ogj.com/articles/print/volume-115/issue-1/exploration-development/iran-s-joint-fields-offer-development-partnership-opportunities.html.

35. Fareed Mohammadi, 'The Oil and Gas Industry', *Iran Primer*, August 2015, http://iranprimer.usip.org/resource/oil-and-gas-industry.

36. IEA, *World Energy Outlook: China and India Insights,* 2007.

37. Manouchehr Dorrakj and Carrie L Currier, 'Lubricated with Oil: Iran–China Relations in a Changing World', Middle East Policy Council, Vol. XV, No. 2, http://www.mepc.org/lubricated-oil-iran-china-relations-changing-world.

38. China analysis, US Energy Information Administration, 14 May 2015, https://energy.gov/sites/prod/files/2016/04/f30/China_International_Analysis_US.pdf; Yu Guoqing, 'China's Foreign Policy Toward Iran', IIAS Newsletter, No. 62, Winter 2012, http://www.iias.asia/sites/default/files/IIAS_NL62_27.pdf.

39. John S Park, Cameron Glen, 'Iran and China', *Iran Primer*, 2010, http://iranprimer.usip.org/resource/iran-and-china.

40. 'China Launches Massive Gas Pipeline Campaign', *Oil and Gas Journal* Volume 98, Issue 23, 5 June 2000.

41. Yu Guoqing, 'China's Foreign Policy Toward Iran', *IIAS Newsletter*, No. 62, Winter 2012, http://www.iias.asia/sites/default/files/IIAS_NL62_27.pdf.

42. Ken Koyama & Mgoichi Komori, 'Oil & Gas Development in Iran and Implications for Japan', *IEEJ,* May 2001.

43. Manouchehr Dorrakj and Carrie L Currier, 'Lubricated with Oil: Iran–China Relations in a Changing World', Middle East Policy Council, Vol. XV, No.2, http://www.mepc.org/lubricated-oil-iran-china-relations-changing-world.

44. Ibid.

45. Yu Guoqing, 'China's Foreign Policy Toward Iran', IIAS Newsletter, No. 62, Winter 2012, http://www.iias.asia/sites/default/files/IIAS_NL62_27.pdf.

46. Ibid.

47. Ibid.

48. John Calabrese, 'China and Iran: Mismatched Partners', Occasional Paper – The Jamestown Foundation, August 2006, https://jamestown.org/wp-content/uploads/2006/08/Jamestown-ChinaIranMismatch_01.pdf, p. 8.

49. Ibid.

50. See data accessed here: https://wits.worldbank.org/CountryProfile/en/Country/CHN/Year/2012/Summary.

51. Thomas Erdbrink, 'China Deepens its Footprint in Iran after Lifting of Sanctions', *New York Times*, 24 January 2016, https://www.nytimes. com/2016/01/25/world/middleeast/china-deepens-its-footprint-in-iran-after-lifting-of-sanctions.html?hp&action=click&pgtype=Homepage& clickSource = story-heading&module = second-column-region&region = top-news&WT.nav=top-news&_r=1.

52. Where Iran Exports to, MIT charts http://atlas.media.mit.edu/en/visualize/ tree_map/hs92/export/irn/show/all/2001/.

53. 'China–Iran Trade at $31.2b in 2016', *Tehran Times*, 4 February 2017, http://www.tehrantimes.com/news/410775/China-Iran-trade-at-31-2b-in-2016; Marc Champion, 'Iran is Stuck with China to Finance its Oil Dreams', *Bloomberg*, 12 October 2016, https://www.bloomberg.com/news/ articles/2016-10-12/tired-of-china-s-grip-iran-confronts-a-harsh-oil-market-reality.

54. Emma Scott, 'Defying Expectations: China's Iran Trade and Investments', Middle East Institute, 6 April 2016, http://www.mei.edu/content/map/ defying-expectations-china%E2%80%99s-iran-trade-investments#_ ftn46.

55. Can reconstruct with the data on https://wits.worldbank.org/.

56. The only exception to this being France's Total, who in November 2016 signed a preliminary $4.8bn deal to develop part of Iran's South Pars gas field. But even this preliminary agreement was not on sure footing as Total announced it may have to re-evaluate its interest following President Trump's Iran policy. It is believed that Total was keen to re-enter the Iranian market rapidly because it did not have significant exposure to the US market; see Golnar Motevalli, Hashem Kalantari, Javier Blas, 'Total, China Join Iran's First Gas Deal Since Sanctions Eased', *Bloomberg*, 8 November 2016, https://www.bloomberg.com/ news/articles/2016-11-08/total-china-share-iran-s-first-gas-deal-since-sanctions-eased.

57. Marc Champion, 'Iran is Stuck with China to Finance its Oil Dreams', *Bloomberg*, 12 October 2016, https://www.bloomberg.com/news/ articles/2016-10-12/tired-of-china-s-grip-iran-confronts-a-harsh-oil-market-reality.

58. Eric Wheeler and Michael Desai, 'Iran and Russia: A Partnership in the Making', Middle East Institute, 12 September 2016, http://www.mei.edu/ content/iran-and-russia-partnership-making.

59. Ariel Farrar-Wellman, 'Russia–Iran Foreign Relations', *Critical Threats*, 2 August 2010, https://www.criticalthreats.org/analysis/russia-iran-foreign-relations.

60. Ibid.

61. Eric Wheeler and Michael Desai, 'Iran and Russia: A Partnership in the Making', Middle East Institute, 12 September 2016, http://www.mei.edu/content/iran-and-russia-partnership-making.
62. Ibid.
63. Author interview with Akbar Etemad, phone, October 2014.
64. Ibid.
65. Ibid.
66. Ibid.
67. See Wyn Bowen, Matthew Moran and Dina Esfandiary, *Living on the Edge: Iran and the Practice of Nuclear Hedging* (London: Palgrave Macmillan, 2016).
68. Hassan Rouhani, *National Security and Nuclear Diplomacy* (Tehran: Center for Strategic Research, 2011), p. 27.
69. David Patrikarakos (2012), pp. 98–9.
70. Author interview with Akbar Etemad, phone, October 2014.
71. Steven Greenhouse, 'France and Iran Mend Rift Over Loan Granted by Shah', 26 October 1991, http://www.nytimes.com/1991/10/26/world/france-and-iran-mend-rift-over-loan-granted-by-shah.html.
72. Ibid.
73. Dina Esfandiary and Ariane Tabatabai, 'Meeting Iran's Nuclear Fuel Supply Needs', *The Bulletin of the Atomic Scientists*, 5 June 2014, http://thebulletin.org/meeting-irans-nuclear-fuel-supply-needs7224.
74. Sagan, Scott, Kenneth Waltz, and Richard K. Betts, 'A Nuclear Iran: Promoting Stability or Courting Disaster?' *Journal of International Affairs* 60, no. 2 (2007), pp. 135–50, http://www.jstor.org/stable/24357975.
75. Leonard S. Spector, Prepared Testimony before the House International Relations Committee, 12 September 1996, http://carnegieendowment.org/1996/09/12/chinese-assistance-to-iran-s-weapons-of-mass-destruction-and-missile-programs-pub-129.
76. Bushehr Nuclear Power Plant (BNPP) Factsheet, The Nuclear Threat Initiative, http://www.nti.org/learn/facilities/184/.
77. For brief summary timeline of Iranian nuclear program, see: https://www.theguardian.com/world/2013/nov/24/iran-nuclear-timeline.
78. Author interviews with Iranian officials, Vienna, Lausanne, Geneva, 2014–16.
79. Dina Esfandiary and Ariane Tabatabai, 'Meeting Iran's Nuclear Fuel Supply Needs', *The Bulletin of the Atomic Scientists*, 5 June 2014, http://thebulletin.org/meeting-irans-nuclear-fuel-supply-needs7224.
80. John Calabrese, 'China and Iran: Mismatched Partners', *The Jamestown Foundation,* August 2006, p. 5. See: http://www.frankhaugwitz.info/doks/security/2006_08_China_Energy_Iran_A_Mismatach_Jamestown.pdf.

81. Zhu Yinghuang and Wang Hao, '"Made-in-China" subway fulfils Iranian dream', *China Daily*, 12 June 2004, http://www.chinadaily.com.cn/english/doc/2004-06/12/content_338907.htm.
82. For a detailed account of the Tehran metro project, see Garver (2011), pp. 261–2.
83. Liu Jun and Wu Lei, 'Key Issues in China–Iran Relations', *Journal of Middle Eastern and Islamic Studies*, Vol. 4, no. 1 (2010), http://www.mesi.shisu.edu.cn/_upload/article/76/da/2dfaaeaa4a8b9ef6100e35c162b1/16eace5f-fe3d-45da-8d19-2c53f035f9f9.pdf.
84. 'China Delivers 4th Giant Oil Tanker to Iran', *IRNA*, 21 January 2004.
85. 'Eximbank Finances Iranian Power Plant', *Tehran Times*, 23 December 2000, http://www.tehrantimes.com/news/55554/Eximbank-Finances-Iranian-Power-Plant. For more on Chinese investments in Iran see, John Calabrese, 'China and Iran: Mismatched Partners', Occasional Paper – The Jamestown Foundation, August 2006, https://jamestown.org/wp-content/uploads/2006/08/Jamestown-ChinaIranMismatch_01.pdf.
86. The 14 non-EU member states are: Armenia, Azerbaijan, Bulgaria, Georgia, Kazakhstan, Kyrgyzstan, Iran (only joined in 2009), Moldova, Romania, Turkey, Ukraine, Uzbekistan, Tajikistan, and Turkmenistan.
87. For more on the North–South Transport Corridor, see: The International North South Transport Corridor homepage, http://www.instc-org.ir/Pages/Home_Page.aspx.
88. Regine A. Spector, 'The North–South Transport Corridor', *Brookings*, 2002, https://www.brookings.edu/articles/the-north-south-transport-corridor/. The early stages of development were largely spent designating the extant routes to be used and necessary infrastructure projects.
89. See data on https://wits.worldbank.org/.
90. Ibid.
91. Garver (2011), p. 279.
92. Note that this figure omits the goods transhipped to China via the UAE. Following the ramping up of international sanctions, Iran began to look at third party ports to tranship goods to it to contravene sanctions. 'Iran opens first overseas commerce center', *Tehran Times*, 21 November 2009, http://www.tehrantimes.com/news/208434/Iran-opens-first-overseas-commerce-center.
93. Emma Scott, 'Defying Expectations: China's Iran Trade and Investments', Middle East Institute, 6 April 2016, http://www.mei.edu/content/map/defying-expectations-china%E2%80%99s-iran-trade-investments.
94. Sajjid Talebi, 'Iran–China Relations: An Iranian Perspective', Torino World Affairs Institute Note, 29 May 2017, https://www.twai.it/wp-content/uploads/2017/05/T.note29-3.pdf, p. 2.

95. 'Iran opens first overseas commerce center', *Tehran Times*, 21 November 2009, http://www.tehrantimes.com/news/208434/Iran-opens-first-overseas-commerce-center.

96. By 2014, despite ambitious European plans, Iran imported over 49 per cent of its auto parts from China. Italian Trade Agency, 'Market Overview of Automotive Sector in Iran', http://www.ra.camcom.gov.it/eurosportello/allegati-pina-newsletter/iran-automotive.

97. Sarwant Singh, 'Iran's Automotive Industry – Can American Car Manufacturers Overcome Chinese Resistance?' *Forbes*, 11 August 2015, https://www.forbes.com/sites/sarwantsingh/2015/08/11/iran-automotive-industry-can-american-car-manufacturers-overcome-chinese-resistance/#66ebcffa556b.

98. John S. Park, Cameron Glen, 'Iran and China', *Iran Primer*, 2010, http://iranprimer.usip.org/resource/iran-and-china.

99. 'Iran, China Agree on New Oil Payments', Press TV, 1 June 2015, http://www.presstv.ir/Detail/2015/06/01/413794/Iran-china-trade-oil-money-asgarowladi.

100. Ibid.

101. Garver (2011), p. 275.

102. 'Russia Speculates on Iran's Interest in Sukhoi Superjets', 25 February 2017, https://financialtribune.com/articles/economy-business-and-markets/60260/russia-speculates-on-iran-s-interest-in-sukhoi-super-jets.

103. 'How Iran is Deploying its Drone Program at Home and Abroad', World Politics Review, 7 July 2017, http://www.worldpoliticsreview.com/trend-lines/22644/how-iran-is-deploying-its-drone-program-at-home-and-abroad.

104. Ibid.

105. 'Iran's Tech Sector Blooms under Shield of Sanctions', AFP, 25 July 2017, http://www.france24.com/en/20170725-irans-tech-sector-blooms-under-shield-sanctions?ref=fb.

106. Ibid.

107. Linda Dorigo, 'Inside Iran's "Silicon Valley"', 1 December 2016, http://www.aljazeera.com/indepth/inpictures/2016/11/iran-silicon-valley-161130094759722.html.

108. 'Nanotechnology Research Publications: Statistics and Analysis', Stat-Nano, 20 February 2017, http://statnano.com/news/57667.

109. Majles Research Center, 'Moze-ye rahbar-e moazam-e enghelab dar bare-ye tahrimha va diplomacy-e hasteh-ee-ye jomhoori-e eslami-e Iran', Tehran: Majles Research Center (2012), pp. 10–11.

110. Steve Stecklow, 'Special Report: Chinese firm helps Iran spy on citizens', Reuters, 22 March 2012, http://www.reuters.com/article/us-iran-telecoms-idUSBRE82L0B820120322.

111. 'China Floods Iran With Cheap Consumer Goods in Exchange for Oil', Guardian, 20 February 2013, https://www.theguardian.com/world/iran-blog/2013/feb/20/china-floods-iran-cheap-consumer-goods.

112. Ali Dadpay, 'A Review of Iranian Aviation Industry: Victim of Sanctions of Creation of Mismanagement?', http://iraneconomy.csames.illinois.edu/full%20papers/Dadpay%20-%20IranAviation.pdf.

113. Author interviews in Iran, 2009 and 2014.

114. Ariel Farrar-Wellman, 'Russia–Iran Foreign Relations', Critical Threats, 2 August 2010, https://www.criticalthreats.org/analysis/russia-iran-foreign-relations.

115. Ibid.

116. Author interviews with Javad Zarif and the Iranian negotiating team, Vienna, Lausanne, Geneva, 2014–16.

117. Vladimir Karnozov, 'Russia and Iran Cooperate on UAVs, UCAVs', Ainonline, 15 June 2017, http://www.ainonline.com/aviation-news/defense/2017-06-15/russia-and-iran-cooperate-uavs-ucavs.

118. Ariel Farrar-Wellman, 'Russia–Iran Foreign Relations', Critical Threats, 2 August 2010, https://www.criticalthreats.org/analysis/russia-iran-foreign-relations.

Chapter 4   Defence and Security Cooperation

1. For a helpful graph, see: Kuang Keng Kuek Ser, 'Where Did Iran Get Its Military Arms Over the Last 70 Years?' PRI's The World, 1 June 2016, https://www.pri.org/stories/2016-06-01/where-did-iran-get-its-military-arms-over-last-70-years.

2. Robert Springborg, 'Economic Involvements of Militaries', International Journal of Middle East Studies 43, no. 3 (2011): pp. 397–9.

3. Stephanie Cronin, Soldiers, Shahs and Subalterns in Iran: Opposition, Protest and Revolt, 1921–1941 (London: Palgrave MacMillan, 2010).

4. Stephanie Cronin, The Army and the Creation of the Pahlavi State in Iran, 1910–1926 (London: I.B.Tauris, 1997).

5. Ibid.

6. Gary Sick, All Fall Down (London: I.B.Tauris, 1985), p. 8.

7. Ervand Abrahamian, Iran Between Two Revolutions (Princeton: Princeton University Press, 1982), p. 436.

8. Stephen McGlinchey, 'Lyndon B. Johnson and Arms Credit Sales to Iran: 1964–1968', Middle East Journal (Vol. 67, No.2, Spring 2013), http://

www.e-ir.info/wp-content/uploads/2014/05/LBJ-and-Arms-Credit-Sales-to-Iran-McGlinchey.pdf.

9. Stephen McGlinchey, *US Arms Policies Towards the Shah's Iran* (New York: Routledge, 2014).
10. SIPRI Arms Transfer Database, Importer/Exporter TIV tables, https://sipri.org/databases/armstransfers.
11. Andrew Scott Cooper, *The Oil Kings* (New York: Simon and Schuster, 2011), p. 249.
12. Sick, *All Fall Down*, pp. 16–18.
13. Roham Alvandi, 'Nixon, Kissinger, and the Shah: The Origins of Iranian Primacy in the Persian Gulf', *Diplomatic History*, Volume 36, Issue 2, 1 April 2012, pp. 337–72, https://doi.org/10.1111/j.1467-7709.2011.01025.x.
14. Garver (2006), p. 72.
15. Ibid., p. 82.
16. Harold and Nader (2012), pp. 3–4.
17. Ibid.
18. Garver (2006), p. 82.
19. Stephen C. Pelletiere, *The Iran–Iraq War: Chaos in a Vacuum* (Santa Barbara, CA: Praeger, 1992).
20. Joel Wuthnow, 'Posing Problems Without An Alliance: China–Iran Relations after the Nuclear Deal', National Defense University Strategic Forum, SF No. 290, February 2016, http://ndupress.ndu.edu/Portals/68/Documents/stratforum/SF-290.pdf, p. 2.
21. Author interviews with US and Gulf Arab officials, Washington, DC, Abu Dhabi, Doha, Dubai, Kuwait City, Muscat, 2014–17.
22. Author interviews with senior Iranian officials, New York, Tehran, Vienna, Geneva, Lausanne, Berlin, 2014–17.
23. Tweet by Foreign Minister Javad Zarif, 26 April 2017, https://twitter.com/JZarif/status/857301748456837125.
24. Ariane Tabatabai and Dina Esfandiary, 'Sana'a: Iran's Fourth Arab Capital?' Lawfare Blog, 10 January 2016, https://www.lawfareblog.com/sanaa-irans-fourth-arab-capital.
25. Author interviews with US and Gulf Arab officials, Washington, DC, Abu Dhabi, Doha, Dubai, Kuwait City, Muscat, 2014–17.
26. 'Mossahebe-ye ekhtessassi ba Dr. Mohammad Javad Zarif', *Faslnameh-ye motaleat-e siasat-e khareji-e Tehran*, Year 2, No. 5, Summer 2017, p. 33.
27. Author interviews with Iranian officials, Tehran, New York, Berlin, Vienna, Geneva, Lausanne, 2014–17.

28. Ariane Tabatabai, 'Other side of the Iranian coin: Iran's counterterrorism apparatus', *Journal of Strategic Studies* (Vol. 41, Issue 1–2, 6 February 2017), pp. 181–207, http://www.tandfonline.com/doi/full/10.1080/01402390.2017.1283613.

29. 'Senn-e dowlat bayad kahesh yabad', *Tasnim News*, 22 May 2017, http://tn.ai/1416886.

30. Joby Warrick, 'Iran's Natanz Nuclear Facility Recovered Quickly from Stuxnet Cyberattack', *Washington Post*, 16 February 2011, http://www.washingtonpost.com/wp-dyn/content/article/2011/02/15/AR2011021505395.html?sid=ST2011021404206.

31. Ibid.

32. See Ilan Berman, 'The Iranian Cyber Threat: Revisited', Statement before the US House of Representatives Committee on Homeland Security Subcommittee on Cybersecurity, Infrastructure Protection, and Security Technologies, 20 March 2013, http://www.china.usc.edu/sites/default/files/legacy/AppImages/house-2013-berman-cyber-threats.pdf.

33. Shane Harris, 'Forget China: Iran's Hackers are America's Newest Cyber Threat,' *Foreign Policy*, 18 February 2014, http://foreignpolicy.com/2014/02/18/forget-china-irans-hackers-are-americas-newest-cyber-threat/; Sam Jones, 'Cyber Warfare: Iran Opens a New Front', *Financial Times*, 26 April 2016, https://www.ft.com/content/15e1acf0-0a47-11e6-b0f1-61f222853ff3.

34. See http://rc.majlis.ir/fa/law/show/91707?keyword=%25D9%2588%25D8%25B2%25D8%25A7%25D8%25B1%25D8%25AA%20%25D8%25AF%25D9%2581%25D8%25A7%25D8%25B9%20%25D9%2588%20%25D9%25BE%25D8%25B4%25D8%25AA%25DB%258C%25D8%25A8%25D8%25A7%25D9%2586%25DB%25.

35. See Iran Electronics Industries website, http://www.ieicorp.ir/products.

36. See Bloomberg company overview of Defense Industries Organization, https://www.bloomberg.com/research/stocks/private/snapshot.asp?privcapid=292343934.

37. See Statute of the IAIO, Islamic Republic of Iran Islamic Research Center, http://rc.majlis.ir/fa/law/show/124715.

38. See Iran Space Organisation website, http://www.isa.ir/.

39. 'Iran's Parliament Passes Bill to Boost Defense Budget', *Tasnim News*, 2 May 2016, http://tn.ai/1064569.

40. Author interviews with US and Iranian officials, Washington, DC, New York, Vienna, Lausanne, Geneva, Berlin, Tehran, 2014-17.

41. Abbas Qaidaari, 'Is Iran becoming a major regional arms producer?' *Al-Monitor*, 24 March 2016, http://www.al-monitor.com/pulse/originals/2016/03/iran-weapons-arms-experts-iraq-syria-lebanon.html.

42. UNSCR 1737 (2006), https://www.iaea.org/sites/default/files/unsc_res1737-2006.pdf.

43. UNSCR 1929 (2010), https://www.iaea.org/sites/default/files/unsc_res1929-2010.pdf.

44. UNSCR 2231 (2015), http://www.un.org/en/ga/search/view_doc.asp?symbol=S/RES/2231.

45. 'Xi Jinping Arrives in Tehran for State Visit to Iran', Ministry of Foreign Affairs of the People's Republic of China press statement, 23 January 2016, http://www.fmprc.gov.cn/mfa_eng/topics_665678/xjpdstajyljxgsfw/t1335158.shtml.

46. Joel Wuthnow, 'Posing Problems Without an Alliance: China–Iran Relations after the Nuclear Deal', National Defense University Strategic Forum, SF No. 290, February 2016, p. 3, http://ndupress.ndu.edu/Portals/68/Documents/stratforum/SF-290.pdf.

47. Scobell and Nader (2016), pp. 41 and 43.

48. Ibid., p. 45.

49. Joel Wuthnow, 'Are Chinese Arms About to Flood into Iran?' *The National Interest*, 13 January 2016, http://nationalinterest.org/feature/are-chinese-arms-about-flood-iran-14887.

50. John W. Graver, 'China and Iran: An Emerging Partnership Post-Sanctions', Middle East Institute Policy Focus Series, February 2016, p. 6, http://www.mei.edu/sites/default/files/publications/Garver_ChinaIran.pdf.

51. 'How the US became more involved in the War in Yemen', *New York Times*, 15 October 2016, https://www.nytimes.com/interactive/2016/10/14/world/middleeast/yemen-saudi-arabia-us-airstrikes.html.; Rick Gladstone, 'Cholera, Famine and Girls Sold into Marriage for Food: Yemen's Dire Picture', *New York Times*, 30 May 2017, https://www.nytimes.com/2017/05/30/world/middleeast/yemen-civil-war-cholera-famine-girls-marriage-united-nations.html.

52. Brandon Fite (2012), p. 13; Franz-Stefan Gady, 'China Wants to Deepen Military Ties with Iran', *The Diplomat*, 17 October 2015, http://thediplomat.com/2015/10/china-wants-to-deepen-military-ties-with-iran/.

53. 'Unclassified Report to Congress on the Acquisition of Technology Relating to Weapons of Mass Destruction and Advanced Conventional Munitions: 1 July Through 31 December 2003', Central Intelligence Agency, 23 November 2004.

54. Ibid.

55. Brandon Fite (2012), p. 15.

56. Andrew Scobell and Alireza Nader (2016), p. 56.

57. Ibid.

58. 'In-Depth Report: In the Blink of an Eye, Chinese Arms Exports Climbed to the World's Top', Sina, 25 June 2016, http://mil.news.sina.com.cn/2016-06-25/doc-ifxtmwei9295820.shtml.

59. Farzin Nadimi, 'Iran and China are Strengthening their Military Ties', The Washington Institute Policy Analysis, 22 November 2016, http://www.washingtoninstitute.org/policy-analysis/view/iran-and-china-are-strengthening-their-military-ties.

60. 'Iran to use Chinese BeiDou as New Navigation System', Fars News, 17 October 2015, http://en.farsnews.com/newstext.aspx?nn=13940725001120.

61. 'Chinese Admiral Visits Iran, Wants Closer Defense Cooperation', Reuters, 14 October 2015, https://www.reuters.com/article/us-china-iran/chinese-admiral-visits-iran-wants-closer-defense-cooperation-idUSKCN0S907Q20151015?feedType=RSS&feedName=topNews.

62. John W. Garver, 'China and Iran: An Emerging Partnership Post-Sanctions', Middle East Institute Policy Focus Series, February 2016, http://www.mei.edu/sites/default/files/publications/Garver_ChinaIran.pdf, p. 5.

63. 'Treasury Sanctions Iranian Defence Officials and a China-Based Network for Supporting Iran's Ballistic Missile Programme', US Treasury Department Press Center, 17 May 2017, https://www.treasury.gov/press-center/press-releases/Pages/sm0088.aspx.

64. Ibid.

65. Ibid.

66. Franz-Stefan Gady, 'Iran, China Sign Military Cooperation Agreement', The Diplomat, 15 November 2016, http://thediplomat.com/2016/11/iran-china-sign-military-cooperation-agreement/.

67. Joel Wuthnow, 'Posing Problems Without an Alliance: China-Iran Relations after the Nuclear Deal', National Defense University Strategic Forum, SF No. 290, February 2016, http://ndupress.ndu.edu/Portals/68/Documents/stratforum/SF-290.pdf, p. 2.

68. Franz-Stefan Gady, 'China Wants to Deepen Military Ties with Iran', The Diplomat, 17 October 2015, http://thediplomat.com/2015/10/china-wants-to-deepen-military-ties-with-iran/; Franz-Stefan Gady, 'Iran, China Sign Military Cooperation Agreement', The Diplomat, 15 November 2016, http://thediplomat.com/2016/11/iran-china-sign-military-cooperation-agreement/; 'Commander: Iran to Stage Large-Scale Naval Drills Soon', Fars News, 22 September 2014, http://en.farsnews.com/newstext.aspx?nn=13930631000762.

69. 'First China–Iran Joint Military Exercise Attracts Attention', Ministry of National Defense, The People's Republic of China, 23 September 2014, http://eng.mod.gov.cn/DefenseNews/2014-09/23/content_4539380.htm.

70. 'Iran, China Widen Military, Naval Cooperation', Fars News, 13 December 2015, http://en.farsnews.com/newstext.aspx?nn=13940922001301.

71. Franz-Stefan Gady, 'China Wants to Deepen Military Ties with Iran', *The Diplomat*, 17 October 2015, http://thediplomat.com/2015/10/china-wants -to-deepen-military-ties-with-iran/.

72. Author interviews with senior Iranian officials, Tehran, New York, Vienna, Geneva, Lausanne, 2014-16.

73. Николай Кожанов [Nikolai Kozhanov], 'Насколько прочен альянс России и Ирана' ['How Strong is the Alliance Between Russia and Iran'], Carnegie Moscow Center, 28 November 2015, http://carnegie.ru/ commentary/?fa=62098.

74. Nikolai Kozhanov, 'Understanding the Revitalization of Russian-Iranian Relations', Carnegie Endowment for International Peace Moscow Center Brief, May 2015, http://carnegie.ru/2015/05/05/understanding-revitalization-of-russian-iranian-relations-pub-59983.

75. Ibid.

76. 'Россия и Иран подписали соглашение о военном сотрудничестве' ['Russia and Iran Signed an Agreement on Military Cooperation'], ТАСС [TASS], 20 January 2015, http://tass.ru/armiya-i-opk/1708359.

77. Dmitri Trenin, 'Russia and Iran: Historical Mistrust and Contemporary Partnership', Carnegie Endowment for Peace Moscow Center, 18 August 2016, http://carnegie.ru/2016/08/18/russia-and-iran-historic-mistrust-and-contemporary-partnership-pub-64365.

78. Ibid.

79. 'Путин: РФ и Иран намерены укреплять взаимодействие в борьбе с терроризмом' ['Putin: The Russian Federation and Iran are determined to strengthen cooperation in the fight against terrorism'], ТАСС [TASS], 23 November 2015, http://tass.ru/politika/2464885.

80. Dmitri Trenin, 'Russia and Iran: Historical Mistrust and Contemporary Partnership', Carnegie Endowment for Peace Moscow Center, 18 August 2016, http://carnegie.ru/2016/08/18/russia-and-iran-historic-mistrust-and-contemporary-partnership-pub-64365.

81. Ibid.

82. 'Россия и Иран подписали соглашение о военном сотрудничестве' ['Russia and Iran Signed an Agreement on Military Cooperation'], ТАСС [TASS], 20 January 2015, http://tass.ru/armiya-i-opk/1708359.

83. Nikolai Kozhanov, 'Understanding the Revitalization of Russian-Iranian Relations', Carnegie Endowment for International Peace Moscow Center Brief, May 2015, http://carnegie.ru/2015/05/05/understanding-revitalization-of-russian-iranian-relations-pub-59983.

84. Ibid.

85. Ali Akbar Dareini, 'Iran's Defense Minister Says His Country will Sign a Contract With Russia for the Purchase of Sukhoi-30 Fighter Jets', *US News*, 10 February 2016, https://www.usnews.com/news/world/articles/2016-02-10/iran-to-purchase-sukhoi-30-fighter-jets-from-russia.

86. 'Russia to Sign Contract this Year to Sell Su-30SM to Iran; RIA', Reuters, 17 February 2016, http://www.reuters.com/article/us-russia-iran-idUSKCN0VQ0NF.

87. Kommersant, 15 February 2016, https://www.kommersant.ru/doc/2917271.

88. Matthew Bodner, 'Iran Seeks Russian Fire Power', *Moscow Times*, 4 March 2016, https://themoscowtimes.com/articles/iran-seeks-russian-fire-power-52050.

89. 'Russia Proposes to Iran to Organize Licensed Production of Russian T-90S Tanks,' TASS, 3 February 2016, http://tass.com/defense/854186.

90. 'Ehtemal-e bargozari-ye razmayesh-e moshtarak-e nezami-e Iran o Roussiye', BBC Persian, 2 August 2016, http://www.bbc.com/persian/world/2016/08/160802_l16_iran_russia_military.

91. 'Iran's Demand for Russian Weaponry is Estimated at $10 bln', TASS, 14 November 2016, http://tass.com/defense/912141.

92. Николай Кожанов [Nikolai Kozhanov], 'Насколько прочен альянс России и Ирана' ['How Strong is the Alliance Between Russia and Iran'], Carnegie Moscow Center, November 28, 2015, http://carnegie.ru/commentary/?fa=62098.

93. 'Mossahebe-ye ekhtessassi ba Dr. Mohammad Javad Zarif,' 32.

94. SIPRI Arms Transfer Database, Importer/Exporter TIV files.

95. SIPRI Arms Transfer Database, Importer/Exporter TIV files.

96. SIPRI Arms transfers database, Trade Register File.

97. Ibid.

98. 'Conventional Arms Transfers to Developing Nations 1990–1997', CRS reports to Congress, 31 July 2008, p. 7, https://fas.org/sgp/crs/weapons/transfers90-97.pdf.

99. Andrew Roth, 'Iran Announces Delivery of Russian S-300 Missile Defence System', *Washington Post*, 10 May 2016, https://www.washingtonpost.com/world/iran-announces-delivery-of-russian-s-300-missile-defense-system/2016/05/10/944afa2e-16ae-11e6-971a-dadf9ab18869_story.html?utm_term=.b45845079a29; 'Russia Agrees to Iran's Condition for Purchase of Su-30 Jets: DM', *Tasnim*, 26 November 2016, https://www.tasnimnews.com/en/news/2016/11/26/1250825/russia-agrees-to-iran-s-condition-for-purchase-of-su-30-jets-dm.

100. 'Rogozin: Iran Wants to Buy Satellites from Russia', *Economics Today*, 19 November 2015, https://rueconomics.ru/125188-rogozin-iran-hochet-zakupat-sputniki-u-rossii.

101. For more about Iran's use of its space programme for intelligence, counterintelligence, and counterterrorism, see Ariane Tabatabai, 'The Other Side of the Iranian Coin: Iran's Counter-Terrorism Efforts', *The Journal of Strategic Studies*, 6 February 2017, http://www.tandfonline.com/eprint/FqZXzGddgRjhScreqWFG/full.

102. 'Rogozin: Iran Wants to Buy Satellites from Russia', *Economics Today*, 19 November 2015, https://rueconomics.ru/125188-rogozin-iran-hochet-zakupat-sputniki-u-rossii.

103. Ben Buchanan and Michael Sulmeyer, 'Russia and Cyber Operations: Challenges and Opportunities for the Next US Administration', Carnegie Endowment for International Peace, 13 December 2016, http://carnegieendowment.org/2016/12/13/russia-and-cyber-operations-challenges-and-opportunities-for-next-US-administration-pub-66433.

104. Dmitri Trenin, 'Russia and Iran: Historical Mistrust and Contemporary Partnership', Carnegie Endowment for Peace Moscow Center, 18 August 2016, http://carnegie.ru/2016/08/18/russia-and-iran-historic-mistrust-and-contemporary-partnership-pub-64365.

105. 'Iran, Russia Plan Joint Naval Drills in Caspian Sea', Fars News, 29 June 2013, http://en.farsnews.com/newstext.aspx?nn=13920408001094.

106. Ibid.

107. 'Iran, Russia Stage Joint Naval Wargames', Fars News, 11 August 2015, http://en.farsnews.com/newstext.aspx?nn=13940520000568.

108. 'Iranian Warships Arrive in Russia for Joint Naval Exercises', Sputnik, 21 October 2015, https://sputniknews.com/russia/201510211028887121-iran-russia-caspian-sea-exercises/.

109. Brian Michael Jenkins, Testimony: 'The Dynamics of the Conflicts in Syria and Iraq and the Threat Posed by Homegrown Terrorists and Returning Western Fighters', 2015, https://www.rand.org/content/dam/rand/pubs/testimonies/CT400/CT443/RAND_CT443.pdf.

110. Dmitri Trenin, 'Russia and Iran: Historical Mistrust and Contemporary Partnership', Carnegie Endowment for Peace Moscow Center, 18 August 2016, http://carnegie.ru/2016/08/18/russia-and-iran-historic-mistrust-and-contemporary-partnership-pub-64365.

111. 'IRIAF Air Bases', The Arkenstone, 22 July 2014, http://thearkenstone.blogspot.co.uk/2014_07_01_archive.html.

112. 'Russian Tu-22M3 "Backfire" Long-Range Bombers Strike ISIS from Iran's Hamadan Airfield (VIDEO)', *Russia Today*, 16 August 2016, https://www.rt.com/news/356098-russian-bombers-iran-hamadan/.

113. Ellie Geranmayeh and Kadri Liik, 'The New Power Couple: Russia and Iran in the Middle East.' *European Council on Foreign Relations*, 13

September 2016, http://www.ecfr.eu/publications/summary/iran_and_russia_middle_east_power_couple_7113.

114. Iran (Islamic Republic of)'s Constitution of 1979 with Amendments through 1989, Article 146, Chapter 9, http://www.iranonline.com/iran/iran-info/government/constitution.html.

115. 'Russian Use of Airbase Not Halted: Larijani,' *Kayhan*, 23 August 2016, http://kayhan.ir/en/news/30399/russian-use-of-airbase-not-halted-larijani.

116. 'Presence of Russian Jets in Iran Not in Violation of Constitution: MP', *Tasnim News*, 21 August 2016, https://www.tasnimnews.com/en/news/2016/08/21/1163671/presence-of-russian-jets-in-iran-not-in-violation-of-constitution-mp.

117. 'Iran, Russia, Forge "Strategic" Cooperation', *Kayhan*, 16 August 2016, http://kayhan.ir/en/news/30108.

118. Author interviews with senior European military officials, Brussels, August 2016.

119. Nasser Karimi, 'Iran: Russia has Stopped using Iran Base for Syria Strikes', AP, 22 August 2016, http://bigstory.ap.org/article/0b7e2ae30c704f12ac167dbe43f87411/iran-chastises-russia-publicizing-use-iranian-bases?utm_campaign=SocialFlow&utm_source=Twitter&utm_medium=AP.

120. 'Sardar Dehqan dar nameh-ee be Larijani: Sha'n o jaygah-e Majles baraye mellat-e ma shenakhte shodeh ast', Fars News, 23 August 2016, http://www.farsnews.com/newstext.php?nn=13950602001072.

121. Anne Barnard and Andrew E. Kramer, 'Iran revokes Russia's use of air base, saying Moscow "betrayed trust"', *New York Times*, 22 August 2016, https://www.nytimes.com/2016/08/23/world/middleeast/iran-russia-syria.html.

122. Ibid.

123. 'Iran Says Russia Can Use Its Military Bases "On Case by Case Basis"', Reuters, 28 March 2017, http://www.reuters.com/article/us-russia-iran-rouhani-base-idUSKBN16Z0NU.

124. Ibid.; Thomas Erdbrink, 'Iran Joins Russia in Denouncing US Strike on Syria, but Stops There,' *New York Times*, 10 April 2017, https://www.nytimes.com/2017/04/10/world/middleeast/iran-syria-missile-strike.html.

125. Dmitri Trenin, 'Russia and Iran: Historical Mistrust and Contemporary Partnership', Carnegie Endowment for Peace Moscow Center, 18 August 2016, http://carnegie.ru/2016/08/18/russia-and-iran-historic-mistrust-and-contemporary-partnership-pub-64365.

126. Collin Clarke and Phillip Smyth, 'The Implications of Iran's Expanding Sh'a Foreign Fighter Network', 27 November 2017, https://ctc.usma.edu/posts/the-implications-of-irans-expanding-shia-foreign-fighter-network.

127. Andrei Akulov, 'China Joins Russia in Syria: Shaping New Anti-Terrorist Alliance', Strategic Culture Online Journal, 22 September 2016, http://www.strategic-culture.org/news/2016/09/22/china-joins-russia-in-syria-shaping-new-anti-terrorist-alliance.html.

128. Robert D. Crews, 'A Patriotic Islam? Russia's Muslims under Putin', World Politics Review, 8 March 2016, http://www.worldpoliticsreview.com/articles/18150/a-patriotic-islam-russia-s-muslims-under-putin.

129. Ilan Berman, 'Terrorism in Russia,' Foreign Affairs, 5 April 2017, https://www.foreignaffairs.com/articles/russian-federation/2017-04-05/terrorism-russia?cid=int-lea&pgtype=hpg.

130. 'Islamic State Declares Foothold in Russia's North Caucasus', Moscow Times, 24 June 2015, https://themoscowtimes.com/news/islamic-state-declares-foothold-in-russias-north-caucasus-47666.

131. Andrew Roth and David Filipov, 'Bomb in St. Petersburg Subway, Killing 11, Sets a City on Edge', Washington Post, 3 April 2017, https://www.washingtonpost.com/world/europe/major-blast-rocks-metro-station-in-st-petersburg/2017/04/03/7ff73ef2-1865-11e7-8003-f55b4c1cfae2_story.html?utm_term=.6dffb19c0c91.

132. Marc Walker, 'New ISIS Video Vowing Revenge on Putin Promises Terror Attacks on Russian Soil', Mirror, 28 December 2016, http://www.mirror.co.uk/news/world-news/new-isis-video-vows-revenge-9526752.

133. Author interview with Sam Charap, Senior Political Scientist, RAND, Washington, DC, 10 April 2017.

134. Ibid.

135. For detailed explanations of Iran's views of ISIS and its counter-ISIS strategy, see Dina Esfandiary and Ariane Tabatabai, 'Iran's ISIS Policy', International Affairs, January 2015, Vol. 91, N. 1, pp. 1–15, https://www.chathamhouse.org/publication/iran%E2%80%99s-isis-policy; and Dina Esfandiary and Ariane Tabatabai, 'A Comparative Study of US and Iranian Counter-ISIS Strategies', Studies in Conflict and Terrorism, Vol. 40, Issue 6, 2017, pp. 455–69, http://dx.doi.org/10.1080/1057610X.2016.1221265.

136. 'Iraq Says it Shared Information that France, US, Iran were Targets', Reuters, 15 November 2015, http://www.reuters.com/article/us-france-shooting-iraq-idUSKCN0T40EF20151115.

137. 'Jozeeyat-e jadid aza kashf-e amaliat-e Daesh dar 50 noghte-ye Tehran', IRIB, 4 July 2016, http://www.iribnews.ir/fa/news/1199020/%D8%AC%D8%B2%D8%A6%DB%8C%D8%A7%D8%AA-%D8%AC%D8%AF%DB%8C%D8%AF-%D8%A7%D8%B2-%DA%A9%D8%B4%D9%81-%D8%B9%D9%85%D9%84%DB%8C%D8%A7%D8%AA-%D8%AF%D8%A7%D8%B9%D8%B4-%D8%AF%D8%B1-%DB%B5%

229

DB%B0-%D9%86%D9%82%D8%B7%D9%87-%D8%AA%D9%
87%D8%B1%D8%A7%D9%86.

138. Thomas Erdbrink and Mujib Mashal, 'At Least 12 Killed in Pair of Terrorist Attacks in Iran', *New York Times*, 7 June 2017, https://www.nytimes.com/2017/06/07/world/middleeast/iran-parliament-attack-khomeini-mausoleum.html?_r=0.

139. 'Russia: Iran–Russia Anti-terror Campaign not Violating Resolution 2231, IRNA, 17 August 2016, http://www8.irna.ir/en/News/82192436/.

140. Jian Zhou, 'PLA Delegation Visits Syria, Pledges Assistance and Training for Syrian Army' (in Chinese), Zhonghua Wang XinWen (Chinese internet news), 17 August 2016, http://military.china.com/important/11132797/20160817/23310078.html.

141. Leith Fadel, 'Aleppo Governor Thanks Russia, China, Iran for Helping Syria's Fight Against Terror', Al-Masdar, 22 March 2017, https://www.almasdarnews.com/article/aleppo-governor-thanks-russia-china-iran-helping-syrias-fight-terror/.

142. Author interviews with senior Iranian officials, Tehran and New York, 2014.

143. Joshua Yaffa, 'Chechnya's ISIS Problem', *New Yorker*, 12 February 2016, http://www.newyorker.com/news/news-desk/chechnyas-isis-problem.

144. Nate Rosenbaltt, *All Jihad Is Local* (Washington, DC: New America, July 2016), https://na-production.s3.amazonaws.com/documents/ISIS-Files. pdf 26; Justine Drennan, 'Is China Making Its Own Terrorism Problem Worse?' *Foreign Policy*, 9 February 2015, http://foreignpolicy.com/2015/02/09/is-china-making-its-own-terrorism-problem-worse-uighurs-islamic-state/.

145. Rosenbaltt (2016).

146. Lucy Hornby, 'Isis Uighurs Threaten "Rivers of Blood" in China', *Financial Times*, 2 March 2017, https://www.ft.com/content/ddeb5872-ff1f-11e6-96f8-3700c5664d30.

147. Ariane M. Tabatabai, 'Saudi Arabia and Iran face off in Afghanistan', *Foreign Affairs*, 5 October 2016, https://www.foreignaffairs.com/articles/afghanistan/2016-10-05/saudi-arabia-and-iran-face-afghanistan.

148. Erin Cunningham, 'While the US Wasn't Looking, Russia and Iran Began Carving Out A Bigger Role in Afghanistan', *Washington Post*, 13 April 2017, https://www.washingtonpost.com/world/asia_pacific/with-us-policy-in-flux-russia-and-iran-challenge-american-power-in-afghanistan/2017/04/12/f8c768bc-1eb8-11e7-bb59-a74ccaf1d02f_story.html?utm_term=.b69c8681741e.

149. Charles Clover, 'Mystery Deepens Over Chinese Forces in Afghanistan', *Financial Times*, 26 February 2017, https://www.ft.com/content/0c8a5a2a-f9b7-11e6-9516-2d969e0d3b65.

150. Erin Cunningham, 'While the US Wasn't Looking, Russia and Iran Began Carving Out A Bigger Role in Afghanistan', *Washington Post*, 13 April 2017, https://www.washingtonpost.com/world/asia_pacific/with-us-policy-in-flux-russia-and-iran-challenge-american-power-in-afghanistan/2017/04/12/f8c768bc-1eb8-11e7-bb59-a74ccaf1d02f_story.html?utm_term=.b69c8681741e.

151. Author interviews with US former military members and officials, Washington, DC, 2013–17.

152. 'Leader Names New Year "Year of Economy of Resistance: Production and employment"', Khamenei.ir, 20 March 2017, http://english.khamenei.ir/news/4727/Leader-names-New-Year-Year-of-Economy-of-Resistance-Production.

Chapter 5   Post-JCPOA: Future Prospects

1. Samia Nakhoul and Richard Mably, 'In Iran, Dividends of Nuclear Deal are Slow to Appear', Reuters, 24 May 2016, http://www.reuters.com/article/us-iran-sanctions-insight-idUSKCN0YF0Z4.

2. 'Major European Banks Avoiding Iran', *Kayhan*, 14 September 2016, http://kayhan.ir/en/news/31226/major-european-banks-avoiding-iran.

3. '22 Iranian Banks Link up with Oberbank', *Financial Tribune*, 13 June, 2017, https://financialtribune.com/articles/economy-business-and-markets/66330/22-iranian-banks-link-up-with-oberbank/; https://www.bloomberg.com/news/articles/2017-12-08/halkbank-s-atilla-reassured-treasury-as-plot-went-on-u-s-says.

4. Ben Riley-Smith and Rob Crilly, 'Trump Refuses to Certify Iran Nuclear Deal', *Telegraph*, 13 October 2017, http://www.telegraph.co.uk/news/2017/10/13/donald-trump-expected-promise-tough-action-iran-landmark-speech/.

5. Mathew Lee, 'Trump Hands Nuke Deal "last chance", Waives Iran Sanctions', Associated Press, 12 January 2018, https://www.washingtonpost.com/world/national-security/officials-iran-deal-survives-trump-will-waive-sanctions/2018/01/12/02677228-f7b1-11e7-9af7-a50bc3300042_story.html?utm_term=.b4fcfa939949.

6. Statistical Center of Iran, 'Selected Findings of the 2011 National Population and Housing Census', 2011, https://www.amar.org.ir/Portals/1/Iran/census-2.pdf.

7. 'Iran's Parliament Passes Bill to Boost Defence Budget', *Tasnim News*, 2 May 2016, https://www.tasnimnews.com/en/news/2016/05/02/1064569/iran-s-parliament-passes-bill-to-boost-defense-budget.

8. 'Russia has 25% of Global Arms Sales, Second Only to US – study', *Russia Today*, 22 February 2016, https://www.rt.com/business/333223-russia-global-arms-market/.

9. 'Iran Seeks Constructive Marine Interaction with Russia: Commander', PressTV, 11 March 2017, http://www.presstv.ir/Detail/2017/03/11/513946/Iran-Russia-Pakistan-Makhachkala-Damavand-Derafsh-Alvand-Bushehr-Tippu-Sultan-PNS-Jurrat.

10. Neil MacFarquhar, 'Russia's Greatest Problem in Syria: Its ally, President Assad', *New York Times* (8 March 2018), https://www.nytimes.com/2018/03/08/world/europe/russia-syria-assad.html

11. 'Russian Use of Airbase Not Halted: Larijani,' *Kayhan*, 23 August 2016, http://kayhan.ir/en/news/30399/russian-use-of-airbase-not-halted-larijani.

12. 'Iranian Newspaper Cites Brawl with Russia over Cuts in Syria', *Asharq-al Awsat*, 19 January 2018, https://aawsat.com/english/home/article/1148491/iranian-newspaper-cites-brawl-russia-over-cuts-syria.

13. Tuvan Gumrukcu, 'Turkey Urges Russia, Iran to Stop Syrian Army Offensive in Idlib', Reuters, 10 January 2018, https://www.reuters.com/article/us-mideast-crisis-syria-turkey/turkey-urges-russia-iran-to-stop-syrian-army-offensive-in-idlib-idUSKBN1EZ0JG.

14. Robin Wright, 'Russia and Iran deepend ties to challenge Trump and the United States', The New Yorker (2 March 2018), https://www.newyorker.com/news/news-desk/russia-and-iran-deepen-ties-to-challenge-trump-and-the-united-states.

15. Richard Roth, 'Russia, US Spar on Iran, North Korea, Syria', CNN, 18 January 2018, http://www.cnn.com/2018/01/18/us/un-security-council-russia-united-states-spar/index.html.

16. 'Iran, Russian Diplomats Discuss Regional Issues in Moscow', Iran Front Page News, 19 January 2018, http://ifpnews.com/exclusive/iranian-russian-diplomats-discuss-regional-issues-moscow/#.WmIho2xc-lk.twitter.

17. Rick Gladstone, 'Russia vetoes UN Resolution to Pressure Iran Over Yemen Missiles', *New York Times* (26 February 2018), https://www.nytimes.com/2018/02/26/world/middleeast/iran-yemen-security-council.html.

18. 'President: Iran Ready for Counter-Terrorism Cooperation with Russia', *Tasnim News*, 4 April 2017, https://www.tasnimnews.com/en/news/2017/04/04/1370326/president-iran-ready-for-counter-terrorism-cooperation-with-russia.

19. 'Putin-Rouhani Meeting Round-up', TASS, 28 March 2017, http://tass.com/world/938043.

20. 'Russia may Produce Sukhoi Superjets in Iran', Press TV, 19 November 2015, http://www.presstv.com/Detail/2015/11/19/438316/Russia-may-locally-produce-Sukhoi-Superjets-in-Iran.

21. Author interviews with Iranian officials, New York, Geneva, Lausanne, Vienna, 2014–16.

22. Tim Hepher, 'Boeing defers Iran deliveries, eases output concerns', Reuters (25 April 2018), https://www.reuters.com/article/us-boeing-results-777/boeing-defers-iran-deliveries-eases-output-concerns-idUSKBN1HW2A3

23. Ali Dadpay, 'A Review of the Iranian Aviation Industry: Victim of Sanctions or Creation of Mismanagement', http://iraneconomy.csames.illinois.edu/full%20papers/Dadpay%20-%20IranAviation.pdf.

24. 'Russian SSJ-100 airliners to dominate Iranian skies as Moscow strikes new aviation deal', *Russia Today* (26 April 2018), https://www.rt.com/business/425185-sukhoi-airplanes-iran-purchase/.

25. 'Russia Wins First Large Contract in Post-Sanctions Iran – Kommersant', Reuters, 1 August, 2016, https://www.reuters.com/article/idUSL8-N1AI1VW.

26. Technopromexport press statement, 23 November 2015.

27. 'Russia to Loan Iran 2.2 Billion Euros', *Kayhan*, 30 July 2016, http://kayhan.ir/en/news/29394/russia-to-loan-iran-22-billion-euros.

28. 'NIOC Inks 3 MOUs with Giant Russian Firms', Fars News, 18, November 2016, http://en.farsnews.com/newstext.aspx?nn=13950828000356.

29. 'Water in Crisis in Iran: A Desperate Call for Action', *Tehran Times*, 7 May 2016, http://www.tehrantimes.com/news/301198/Water-crisis-in-Iran-A-desperate-call-for-action.

30. http://www.rosgeo.com/ru/content/rosgeologiya-zaymetsya-poiskom-vody-v-irane.

31. 'Rouhani to Visit Russia on Monday, Details Announced', *Tehran Times*, 25 March 2017, http://www.tehrantimes.com/news/412165/Rouhani-to-visit-Russia-on-Monday-details-announced.

32. 'Iran, Russia Closely Cooperating on Fighting Terrorism: Rouhani', PressTV, 28 March 2017, http://www.presstv.com/Detail/2017/03/28/515905/Iran-Russia-Hassan-Rouhani-Vladimir-Putin-Kremlin-Moscow-terrorism.

33. 'Putin-Rouhani Meeting Round-Up', TASS, 18 March 2017, http://tass.com/world/938043.

34. Anatoly Medetsky, 'Russia gets another market for its wheat after deal with Iran', Bloomberg (7 March 2018).

35. Ibid.

36. 'Russians to Build, Rehabilitate Power Plants in Iran.' Mehr News, 18 January 2017, https://en.mehrnews.com/news/122810/Russians-to-build-rehabilitate-power-plants-in-Iran.

37. Ibid.
38. 'Iran-Russia Trade Surges 70% in 2016', *Iran Daily*, 21 February 2017, http://www.iran-daily.com/News/188123.html?catid=3&title=Iran-Russia-trade-surges-70–in-2016.
39. For more on US–Russia relations and US perceptions of Russia, see 'Russia: Background and US interests', Congressional Research Service, 1 March 2017, https://fas.org/sgp/crs/row/R44775.pdf.
40. For more on the allegations, see ibid.
41. Readout of the President's Call with Russian President Vladimir Putin, the White House, 28 January 2017, https://www.whitehouse.gov/the-press-office/2017/01/28/readout-presidents-call-russian-president-vladimir-putin.
42. See for example, Remarks by Rex W. Tillerson, Secretary of State, World Conference Center, Bonn, Germany, 16 February 2017, https://www.state.gov/secretary/remarks/2017/02/267671.htm.
43. 'Trump White House says its Putting Iran "On Notice"', AP, 1 February 2017, http://www.cnbc.com/2017/02/01/trump-white-house-says-its-putting-iran-on-notice.html; 'Iran Continues to Sponsor Terrorism', Press Statement, Rex W. Tillerson, Secretary of State, Washington, DC, 18 April 2017, https://www.state.gov/secretary/remarks/2017/04/270315.htm.
44. The White House must certify to Congress every three months that Iran is compliant with the JCPOA. 'Trump says Would be Surprised if Iran Compliant with Nuclear Deal: WSJ', Reuters, 25 July 2017, https://www.reuters.com/article/us-iran-nuclear-trump-certification-idUSKBN1AB03R.
45. Ben Riley-Smith and Rob Crilly, 'Trump Refuses to Certify Iran Nuclear Deal', *Telegraph*, 13 October 2017, http://www.telegraph.co.uk/news/2017/10/13/donald-trump-expected-promise-tough-action-iran-landmark-speech/.
46. Mathew Lee, 'Trump Hands Nuke Deal "last chance", Waives Iran Sanctions', Associated Press, 12 January 2018, https://www.washingtonpost.com/world/national-security/officials-iran-deal-survives-trump-will-waive-sanctions/2018/01/12/02677228-f7b1-11e7-9af7-a50bc3300042_story.html?utm_term=.b4fcfa939949.
47. Dina Esfandiary, 'Trump Uses Uncertainty Against Iran', Lobelog, 16 January 2018, https://lobelog.com/trumps-uses-uncertainty-against-iran/.
48. Author interviews with Iranian officials and Russian experts, Moscow, February 7, 2017.
49. 'ENI CEO Says Iran Needs $150 Billion of Energy Investment', Reuters, 17 January 2016, http://www.reuters.com/article/us-eni-iran-idUSKCN0UV0NC.

50. Author phone interview with Iranian oil and gas expert, 31 March 2017.

51. Marc Champion, 'Iran is Stuck with China to Finance its Oil Dreams', *Bloomberg*, October 12, 2016, https://www.bloomberg.com/news/articles/2016-10-12/tired-of-china-s-grip-iran-confronts-a-harsh-oil-market-reality.

52. Najmeh Bozorgmehr, 'China Ties Lose Lustre as Iran Refocuses on Trade with West', *Financial Times*, 23 September 2015, https://www.ft.com/content/9d1564bc-603f-11e5-a28b-50226830d644.

53. Ibid.

54. Ibid.

55. Brenda Goh, John Ruwitch, 'Pressure On as Xi's "Belt and Road" Enshrined in Chinese Party Charter', Reuters, 24 October 2017, https://www.cnbc.com/2017/10/24/reuters-america-pressure-on-as-xis-belt-and-road-enshrined-in-chinese-party-charter.html.

56. Thomas Erdbrink, 'For China's Global Ambitions, "Iran is at the Center of Everything"', *New York Times*, 25 July 2017, https://www.nytimes.com/2017/07/25/world/middleeast/iran-china-business-ties.html.

57. Marc Champion, 'Iran is Stuck with China to Finance its Oil Dreams', Bloomberg, 12 October 2016, https://www.bloomberg.com/news/articles/2016-10-12/tired-of-china-s-grip-iran-confronts-a-harsh-oil-market-reality.

58. Scobell and Nader (2016), p. 64.

59. Xi Jinping, Full Text of Xi's Signed Article in Iranian Newspaper, Xi Jinping, 'Work Together For A Bright Future Of China-Iran Relations', Full text in English in China Daily, 21 January 2016, http://www.chinadaily.com.cn/world/2016xivisitmiddleeast/2016-01-21/content_23189585.htm.

60. 'China, Iran Agree to Expand Trade to $600 Billion in a Decade', *Bloomberg*, 23 January 2016, https://www.bloomberg.com/news/articles/2016-01-23/china-iran-agree-to-expand-trade-to-600-billion-in-a-decade.

61. Henning Gloystein, 'China Set to Top Japan as World's Biggest Natural Gas Importer', Reuters, 3 January 2018, https://www.reuters.com/article/us-china-natural-gas-imports/china-set-to-top-japan-as-worlds-biggest-natural-gas-importer-idUSKBN1ES099.

62. 'Iran Oil Industry Needs $150 Billion Investment', *Kayhan*, 23 December 2015, http://kayhan.ir/en/news/21905/iran-oil-industry-needs-$150b-investment.

63. 'China Agrees to Invest $3.6bln in Development of Iran's Oil Refinery', Fars News, 15 February 2017, http://en.farsnews.com/newstext.aspx?nn=13951127000885.

64. For more on the new IPC, see 'IPC Woos International Firms', Tender Committee for Upstream Oil and Gas Contract Secretariat, NIOC, 29 November 2015, http://ipc.nioc.ir/Portal/Home/ShowPage.aspx?Object= NEWS&ID=0c2d3620-9063-4aa8-9cd3-1914c4a88e2a&LayoutID= 218a9172-c49d-4564-8819-20b14267c753&CategoryID=4d72e300-3ba4-4c7f-92af-0c6c00a4d3f8.

65. 'Iran New Oil Contract Comes Under Criticism', Press TV, 29 November 2015, http://www.presstv.com/Detail/2015/11/29/439606/Iran-oil-gas-contract-IPC-investment. For more on the internal political dynamics and how they related to Iran's energy sector, as well as a comprehensive overview of Iran's IPC, see David Ramin Jalilvand, 'Iranian Energy: A Comeback with Hurdles', Oxford Energy Comment, the Oxford Institute for Energy Studies, January 2017, https://www.oxfordenergy.org/wpcms/wp-content/uploads/2017/01/Iranian-Energy-a-comeback-with-hurdles.pdf.

66. 'Iran's Rouhani Submits Conservative 2018 Budget as US Tensions Overshadow Economy', Reuters. 10 December 2017. https://uk.reuters.com/article/us-iran-budget/irans-rouhani-submits-conservative-2018-budget-as-u-s-tensions-overshadow-economy-idUKKBN1E40I3.

67. Dina Esfandiary, 'Iran After the Protests: What Comes Next?', Washington Post, 19 January 2018, https://www.washingtonpost.com/news/democracy-post/wp/2018/01/18/iran-after-the-protests-what-comes-next/?utm_term= .a2192e5b3377.

68. Karen Gilchrist, 'What Total's $4.8 Billion Investment Means for Iran', CNBC, 3 July 2017, https://www.cnbc.com/2017/07/03/iran-to-sign-new-ipc-gas-deal-with-total-for-south-pars.html.

69. Zahraa Alkhalisi, 'Trump Could Kill Total's Iran Gas Deal', CNN Money, 15 November 2017, http://money.cnn.com/2017/11/13/investing/iran-total-trump-sanctions/index.html.

70. Chen Aizhu, Ron Bousso, 'Exclusive: China's CNPC Weighs Taking over Iran Project if Total Leaves – Sources', Reuters, 15 December 2017, https://uk.reuters.com/article/uk-iran-oil-exclusive/exclusive-chinas-cnpc-weighs-taking-over-iran-project-if-total-leaves-sources-idUKKB-N1E90LH.

71. Georgi Kantchev, 'China to Shake up Global Market with Yuan-based Oil Futures Contract', Wall Street Journal, 20 December 2017, https://www.wsj.com/articles/china-will-launch-yuan-based-oil-futures-contract-set-to-shake-up-global-market-1513759822.

72. Liu Caiyu, 'Iran's Oil Sector Opens Up to Chinese', Global Times, 17 August 2015, http://www.globaltimes.cn/content/1001105.shtml.

73. For more on the resistance economy, see Bijan Khajehpour, 'Decoding Iran's Resistance Economy', *Al-Monitor*, 24 February 2014, http://www.al-monitor.com/pulse/originals/2014/02/decoding-resistance-economy-iran.html.

74. 'Iran Boosts Iron Imports to China, India', Iran – China Chamber of Commerce and Industries, 25 August 2013, http://en.iran-chinachamber.ir/index.php?option=com_content&view=article&id=462:iran-boosts-iron-exports-to-china-india&catid = 48:september–2013&Itemid=66.

75. 'Iran's Non-Oil Trade Exceeds $76b', *Financial Tribune*, 26 February 2017, https://financialtribune.com/articles/economy-domestic-economy/60379/iran-s-non-oil-trade-exceeds-76b.

76. Sumeet Chatterjee, Meng Meng, 'Exclusive - China taking first steps to pay for oil in yuan this year - sources', Reuters (29 March 2018), https://uk.reuters.com/article/uk-china-oil-yuan/exclusive-china-taking-first-steps-to-pay-for-oil-in-yuan-this-year-sources-idUKKBN1H51M5.

77. 'Iran Air secures Chinese funding for aircraft, Aviator' (14 March 2018), https://newsroom.aviator.aero/iran-air-secures-chinese-funding-for-aircraft/

78. Zheng Yanpeng, 'New Rail Route Proposed from Urumqi to Iran', *China Daily*, 21 November 2016, http://www.chinadaily.com.cn/china/2015-11/21/content_22506412.htm.

79. Chen Aizhu and Bozorgmehr Sharafedin, 'China Firms Push for Multi-billion Dollar Iran Rail and Ship Deals', Reuters, 10 March 2016, http://www.reuters.com/article/us-iran-china-transportation-idUSKCN0WC1OC.

80. 'China Plans to Invest in Tram Projects in Northern Iran', Fars News, 25 August 2014, http://en.farsnews.com/newstext.aspx?nn=13930603000822.

81. 'China Made Subway Trains Run in Iranian city Mashad', *China Daily*, 23 February 2017, http://www.chinadaily.com.cn/world/2017-02/23/content_28319908.htm.

82. 'Iran Plans Massive Railway Expansion', Press TV, 18 March 2015, http://www.presstv.com/Detail/2015/05/18/411638/Iran-transport-rail-metro.

83. 'Gernot Heller, 'Siemens Signs Iran Rail Contract as Germany Drums Up Business', Reuters, 3 October 2016, http://www.reuters.com/article/us-germany-iran-idUSKCN1230DB.

84. Chen Aizhu and Bozorgmehr Sharafedin, 'China Firms Push for Multi-billion Dollar Iran Rail and Ship Deals', Reuters, 10 March 2016, http://www.reuters.com/article/us-iran-china-transportation-idUSKCN0WC1OC.

85. 'China to Build 2 New Nuclear Power Plants in Iran: AEOI chief', *Tasnim News*, 19 January 2016, https://www.tasnimnews.com/en/

news/2016/01/19/975906/china-to-build-2-nuclear-power-plants-in-iran-aeoi-chief.

86. 'China May Build Iran's 4th Nuclear Power Plant', Press TV, 13 September 2016, http://www.presstv.com/Detail/2016/09/13/484486/Iran-nuclear-power-plants-Europe-China-Japan.

87. Ali Kushki, 'Iran Forges Deal with China to Redesign Arak Reactor', *Tehran Times*, 16 April 2017, http://www.tehrantimes.com/news/412661/Iran-forges-deal-with-China-to-redesign-Arak-reactor.

88. Bozorgmehr Sharafedin, 'World Powers to Help Iran Redesign Reactor as Part of Nuclear Deal', Reuters, 21 November 2015, http://www.reuters.com/article/us-iran-nuclear-arak-idUSKCN0TA0IK20151121.

89. 'Nuclear Power in China' fact sheet, World Nuclear Association, updated July 2017, http://www.world-nuclear.org/information-library/country-profiles/countries-a-f/china-nuclear-power.aspx.

90. Meia Nouwens, 'China's 19th Party Congress: Streamlined Top Military Tier to Push Xi's Reforms Further', IISS Military Defence Blog, 20 November 2017, http://www.iiss.org/en/militarybalanceblog/blogsections/2017-edcc/november-f876/chinese-military-reform-0900.

91. 'Iran, China Sign Defence Cooperation Deal', *Tehran Times*, 14 November 2016, http://www.tehrantimes.com/news/408324/Iran-China-sign-defense-cooperation-deal.

92. 'Iran, China Sign Agreement to Boost Defense-Military Cooperation', PressTV. 14 November 2016, http://www.presstv.com/Detail/2016/11/14/493549/Iran-China-Hossein-Dehqan-Chang-Wanquan-military-defense.

93. Ben Blanchard, 'China Passes Controversial Counter-Terrorism Law', Reuters, 27 December 2015, http://uk.reuters.com/article/us-china-security-idUKKBN0UA07220151228.

94. On more on how to ensure the effectiveness of sanctions, see Dina Esfandiary, 'Assessing the European Union's Sanctions Policy: Iran as a Case Study', EU Non-Proliferation Consortium, *Non-Proliferation Papers*, No. 34, December 2015, https://www.nonproliferation.eu/web/documents/nonproliferationpapers/dinaesfandiary52b41ff5cbaf6.pdf (and footnotes in it).

95. 'Iran, China to expand nuclear cooperation: Ambassador', Press TV (11 April 2018), http://www.presstv.com/Detail/2018/04/11/558137/Iran-China-nuclear-US-Trump.

96. 'China reiterates call to continue upholding Iran nuclear deal', Reuters (2 May 2018), https://www.reuters.com/article/us-israel-iran-china/china-reiterates-call-to-continue-upholding-iran-nuclear-deal-idUSKB-N1I30ZX.

Conclusion and Recommendation

1. 'US Defense Chief Mattis, "Wherever there's Trouble in the Middle East, You Find Iran"', *Haaretz*, 19 April 2017, http://www.haaretz.com/middle-east-news/iran/1.784394.
2. 'Fiscal Year 2018 State Department Budget,' C-SPAN, 14 June 2017, https://www.c-span.org/video/?429946-1/secretary-tillerson-testifies-fy-2018-state-department-budget.
3. Rudi Giuliani, now cybersecurity advisor to Trump, attended and spoke at the rally. Guy Taylor, 'Trump's Sober View of Iranian Theocracy Lends Energy to Dissident Rally in France', *Washington Times*, 1 July 2017, https://www.washingtontimes.com/news/2017/jul/1/iranian-dissidents-rally-france-overthrow-irans-th/.
4. In June 2017, Saudi Arabia, the UAE, Egypt and Bahrain issued statements announcing diplomatic breaks with their ally, Qatar. For more on the Gulf Crisis, see Ishaan Tharoor, 'The Persian Gulf Crisis Over Qatar, Explained', *Washington Post*, 6 June 2017, https://www.washingtonpost.com/news/worldviews/wp/2017/06/06/the-persian-gulf-crisis-over-qatar-explained/?utm_term=.85310737a35a.
5. Tariq Tahir, 'French President Emmanuel Macron Accuses Trump of Putting America on a "Path to War" with Iran with His Inflammatory Comments.' *Daily Mail*, 3 January 2018, http://www.dailymail.co.uk/news/article-5233109/Macron-says-Trump-putting-U-S-path-war-Iran.html.
6. James Dobbins, 'How to Talk to Iran', *Washington Post*, 22 July 2007, http://www.washingtonpost.com/wp-dyn/content/article/2007/07/20/AR2007072002056.html.
7. Author interview with French member of parliament, La Republique en Marche party, Paris, 21 November 2017.
8. 'BPI to Fund French Projects in Iran', *Financial Tribune*, 25 September 2017, https://financialtribune.com/articles/economy-business-and-markets/73046/bpi-to-fund-french-projects-in-iran.
9. Angela Charlton, 'Europe isn't US 'vassal', wants to uphold Iran nuclear deal', Associated Press, 12 May 2018.
10. Author interviews with Iranian officials, Berlin, 26 June 2017.
11. Author interviews with Iranian officials, Berlin, 26 June 2017.
12. 'Iran foreign minister sets off on tour to save nuclear deal', Reuters, 12 May 2018, https://www.reuters.com/article/us-iran-nuclear-zarif/iran-foreign-minister-sets-off-on-tour-to-save-nuclear-deal-idUSKCN1ID0F0.
13. Author interviews with Iranian officials, Berlin, 26 June 2017.

14. Arthur Beesley, 'Trump Chastises NATO for Not Contributing "Their Fair Share"', *Financial Times*, 25 May 2017, https://www.ft.com/content/73a5090c-8be8-39ee-91d2-9ecc7a0cdc39?mhq5j=e1.
15. Author interviews with Iranian officials, Berlin, 26 June 2017.
16. Thomas Erdbrink, 'For China's Global Ambitions, "Iran is at the Center of Everything"', *New York Times*, 25 July 2017, https://www.nytimes.com/2017/07/25/world/middleeast/iran-china-business-ties.html?rref=collection%2Ftimestopic%2FChina&action=click&contentCollection=world&region=stream&module=stream_unit&version=latest&contentPlacement=4&pgtype=collection&_r=0.
17. For more on the EU's post JCPOA strategy regarding Iran, see 'An EU strategy for relations with Iran after the nuclear deal', European Parliament, June 2016, http://www.europarl.europa.eu/RegData/etudes/IDAN/2016/578005/EXPO_IDA(2016)578005_EN.pdf.
18. 'Iran's eastern shift shows patience running out with the West', AFP (26 February 2018), https://www.japantimes.co.jp/news/2018/02/26/world/politics-diplomacy-world/irans-eastern-shift-shows-patience-running-west/#.Wunc_NPwau4.
19. Thomas Erdbrink, 'For China's Global Ambitions, "Iran is at the Center of Everything"', *New York Times*, 25 July 2017, https://www.nytimes.com/2017/07/25/world/middleeast/iran-china-business-ties.html?rref=collection%2Ftimestopic%2FChina&action=click&contentCollection=world&region=stream&module=stream_unit&version=latest&contentPlacement=4&pgtype=collection&_r=0.
20. Steven Erlanger and Julie Hirschfield Davis, 'Once Dominant, the United States Finds Itself Isolated at G-20', *New York Times*, 7 July 2017, https://www.nytimes.com/2017/07/07/world/europe/trump-g-20-trade-climate.html?smid=tw-share.

SELECT BIBLIOGRAPHY

Abrahamian, Ervand, *Iran Between Two Revolutions* (Princeton, NJ: Princeton University Press, 1982).
———— *A History of Modern Iran* (Cambridge: Cambridge University Press, 2008).
Aghaie, Kamran and Afshin Marashi, eds, *Rethinking Iranian Nationalism and Modernity* (Austin: University of Texas Press, 2014).
Amanat, Abbas, *Pivot of the Universe: Nasir al-Din Shah and the Iranian Monarchy* (London: I.B.Tauris, 2008).
Arjomand, Said Amir, *The Turban for the Crown: The Islamic Revolution in Iran* (Oxford: Oxford University Press, 1988).
Bakhash, Shaul, *The Reign of the Ayatollahs* (New York: Basic Books, 1984).
Bowen, Wyn, Matthew Moran and Dina Esfandiary, *Living on the Edge: Iran and the Practice of Nuclear Hedging* (London: Palgrave Macmillan, 2016).
Burman, Edward, *China and Iran: Parallel History, Future Threat?* (Stroud: The History Press, 2009).
Butler, Richard and Wantanee Suntikul, *Tourism and Political* Change (Oxford: Goodfellow Publishers, 2017).
Cooper, Andrew Scott, *The Oil Kings* (New York: Simon and Schuster, 2011).
Cronin, Stephanie, *The Army and the Creation of the Pahlavi State in Iran, 1910–1926* (London: I.B.Tauris, 1997).
———— *Soldiers, Shahs and Subalterns in Iran: Opposition, Protest and Revolt, 1921–1941* (London: Palgrave MacMillan, 2010).
———— *Iranian–Russian Encounters: Empires and Revolutions Since 1800* (Oxon: Routledge, 2013).
Garver, John W., *China and Iran: Ancient Partners in a Post-Imperial World* (Seattle: University of Washington Press, 2006).
———— *China's Quest: The History of the Foreign Relations of the People's Republic of China* (Oxford: Oxford University Press, 2016).

Hewlett, Richard G. and Jack M. Holl, *Atoms for Peace and War, 1953–1961: Eisenhower and the Atomic Energy Commission* (Berkeley, CA: University of California Press, 1989).

Hughes, Christopher, *Taiwan and Chinese Nationalism* (London: Routledge, 1997).

Huwaidin, Mohamed Bin, *China's Relations with Arabia and the Gulf: 1949–1999* (London: RoutledgeCurzon, 2002).

Juneau, Thomas and Sam Razavi, *Iranian Foreign Policy Since 2001: Alone in the World* (London: Routledge, 2013).

Kostø, Pål and Helge Blakkisrud, *The New Russian Nationalism: Imperialism, Ethnicity and Authoritarianism 2000–15* (Edinburgh: Edinburgh University Press, 2016).

Mankoff, Jeffrey, *Russian Foreign Policy: The Return of Great Power Politics* (New York: Rowman & Littlefield Publishers, Inc, 2012).

McGlinchey, Stephen, *US Arms Policies Towards the Shah's Iran* (New York: Routledge, 2014).

Mohaddes, Kamiar and M. Hashem Pesaran, *One Hundred Years of Oil Income and the Iranian Economy: A Curse or a Blessing?* (Cambridge: Cambridge University Press, 2012).

Mousavian, Seyed Hossein, *The Iranian Nuclear Crisis: a Memoir* (Washington DC: Brookings Institution Press, July 2012).

Murray, Williamson and Kevin M. Woods, *The Iran–Iraq War: A Military and Strategic History* (Cambridge: Cambridge University Press, 2014).

Nikolayevna Zabortseva, Yelena, *Russia's Relations with Kazakhstan: Rethinking Ex-Soviet Transitions in the Emerging World System.*

Ning, Lu, *The Dynamics of Foreign-Policy Decision-making in China* (Boulder, CO: Westview Press, 2000).

Parvizi Amineh, Mehd, *Towards the Control of Oil Resources in the Caspian Region* (New York: St. Martin's Press, 1999).

Pelletiere, Stephen C., *The Iran–Iraq War: Chaos in a Vacuum* (Westport, CT: Praeger, 1992).

Rouhani, Hassan, *National Security and Nuclear Diplomacy* (Tehran: Center for Strategic Research, 2011).

Rozman, Gilbert, *Misunderstanding Asia* (New York: Palgrave Macmillan, 2015).

Sick, Gary, *All Fall Down* (London: I.B.Tauris, 1985).

Spence, Jonathan D., *The Search for Modern China* (New York: Norton Paperback, 1991).

White, Hugh, *The China Choice: Why America Should Share Power* (Oxford: Oxford University Press, 2013).

Zheng, Yongnian, *Discovering Chinese Nationalism in China* (Cambridge: Cambridge University Press, 1999).

INDEX